PLAYING THE

PLAYING THE GREY MAN

ROBERT MOON

All characters within this work are fictitious.
Any resemblance to real people, living or dead, is purely coincidental.

YOUCAXTON PUBLICATIONS
OXFORD & SHREWSBURY

ISBN 978-191117-540-7
Printed and bound in Great Britain.
Published by YouCaxton Publications 2016

My thanks to every down trodden, shat upon, bullied, harassed and overworked cop: thanks for keeping me going. I genuinely don't know how you keep doing the job I couldn't do any longer.

and to G. C. and J.
and H. and L.

'Dogs are our link to paradise. They don't know evil or jealousy or discontent. To sit with a dog on a hillside on a glorious afternoon is to be back in Eden, where doing nothing was not boring—it was peace.'

Milan Kundera

CHAPTER 1

I love the snow at night.

I love the peace and the way the snow muffles sound and makes everything appear clean and fresh.

I love the way the sky seems heavy, tinged with purple snow-laden clouds and the distant sodium-glow of the village lights, illuminating the whole glen with a dull, orange, reflected glow.

I love hearing the quiet creaking of ice-laden branches in the dark forest around me, the sharp scent of snow and pine in my nostrils.

I love the snow at night.

I sat on the grass verge by the road, eating fish and chips before they got cold, from a warm wrap of vinegar-scented paper in the soft falling snow, with my tin of coke propped next to the measuring staff and data unit from the 'crash kit', which lay on the road in front of me. I watched in tranquillity as the gentle delicate snowflakes landed and melted on top of the crash kit.

Life was pretty good away from work; I loved my job and felt needed and I had no comprehension that inside I was falling to pieces.

Lying beside me next to the grass verge was the body of a young boy. The congealing blood had saturated his 'Bob the Builder' sleepy suit and seeped slowly away into the ground and tarmac, now covered by a layer of pure white snow, snow which was also now starting to cover the cooling body of his young mother. He was still in his car seat after the crash; it was a shame it wasn't properly fixed to the back seat of the car. His mother lay on her back in the roadway twenty metres or so downhill from the left bend, near the mangled wreckage of the car and the tree that had killed them both. She still had the resuscitation pads attached to her chest from futile attempts to bring her back, wires trailing away where they had been disconnected from a defibrillator machine that coldly announced life or death instructions in its clinical metallic voice.

She was gone long before then. I could see from the way she was lying that her spine was the wrong shape, the abandoned sterile paper bags and rubber gloves from the paramedics fluttering around on the roadway when I had first arrived like playful children in the new snow. I suspected the sister would shortly be joining mum and brother, although she'd left in the ambulance before I arrived.

The family car had no roof, having already fallen victim to the fire service and the 'jaws of life' to remove the sister, but although the roof had gone, the windows and frames were still intact on the rear passenger doors, including the bright yellow face of 'Winnie the Poo' smiling back at me from the sun blind. I really hate that sun blind when I see it in a passing car now.

But then I loved dealing with death, the more the merrier. It was just so wrong; I was so flawed.

I wish I could go back in time and give myself of those days a shake, have a look at myself in the mirror with the benefit of the hindsight I now possess and make myself realise what I had become. I joined the police as a young, enthusiastic and principled man. I would become the most deployed family liaison officer (FLO) in Clydeside Police for two years running and would travel internationally as a FLO and crash investigator, but underneath I was slowly and almost imperceptibly collapsing into an emotionally screwed-up mess.

I sacrificed my health and well-being, my personal and family life and, for that, got little or no support when I needed it. I was surrounded by the new police machine, working on a process of nepotism, corruption, incompetence, sexism and racism, concealed under a veneer of politically correct spin-doctoring. The public was a cash cow to be milked and the 'right thing' was to produce the statistics the politicians wanted. I would see what I considered to be a suspicious death hidden by senior bureaucrats who had never even visited the scene or read the report. I would see one of the best cops I had ever met hounded out the job for refusing to lie in court to protect a manager who had screwed up. I would see a rape covered up while the force pretended to protect women's rights. I was disillusioned and emotionally exhausted by years of death. And then, out of nowhere, when I thought I had found someone who was strong enough to save me, I lost it all through my own stupidity.

This is my story; I suggest you go get a beer and I'll get one too.

Walking into 'D' squadron for the last time I had a strangely sad 'end of an era' feeling. I signed in, having parked my trusty old white Citroen in the car park, and made my way to the empty locker room. As I walked past the large wooden plaque with the regimental cap badge on it that had been a familiar sight for two years of my life, since my transfer of squadron, I had a lot of memories and regrets running through my mind. I had walked into 'A' squadron almost four years before and had begun a journey that would see me become a much quieter person, content to lead a strange grey life, a life that I hid from all except my closest relatives.

A nice quiet lie.

'Lassen House', was 'D' squadron 23rd Special Air Service Regiment's Scottish base. A subdued office and training centre on the outskirts of a Scottish city, easily mistaken for a council depot if it hadn't been for the occasional army truck or Land Rover parked in the yard. At the time, 23 SAS had two active units in Scotland. Not many, even within the armed forces, knew they existed, most people assuming that everything was in Hereford at Stirling Lines. In fact, the reserve units, 21 and 23, were spread all over the country. 'A' squadron was located in Highholm St. in Port Glasgow, a small side street in a rough area, cunningly hidden behind Mecca bingo, sandwiched between the railway line and opposite old grey-stone tenements, where the IRA would never suspect that the elite would often stagger back pissed on a Friday night, from the British Legion just down the street. That's not to say that we weren't cautious and every one of us would discretely search with a mirror under our cars before leaving just in case, a sort of odd ritual at a time when terrorism came from nearer to home. Years later the building became a cadet centre and finally it was demolished for flats.

I had received a letter with my start date in the police which spelled the end of my time with the squadron. I walked into the musty sweaty smell of the locker room and collected the last few things I had to dispose of, to keep or return from my standard army-green locker, cunningly designed by someone to be exactly an inch too narrow to get a Bergen rucksack in or out without damaging your knuckles. On the top shelf my epaulettes, sand coloured beret and deep blue stable belt were all I wanted to keep. I would have loved to go into the armoury and to hold my assault rifle one last time. Strange how something inert could be comforting after the many times I'd had to carry it for weeks on end. I loved my personal weapon, but that was also because I had no girlfriend and I was, frankly, a bit weird.

But that was true of a lot of people in the regiment. They had to have huge drive to get in against all the odds and usually there was some story behind it that you discovered when you knew them well enough. I returned the rest of my kit to stores and made a final trip to the Adjutant down the corridor.

'Boss?'

'Fuck a duck, look what the cat dragged in. I see you got that map the RSM sent to all the tossers telling them how to find the Squadron again.'

'Cheers, boss. I don't care what everyone says about you — you're OK'

'I heard you've called it a day?'

'Yeah, joining the police, boss'

'Quite right, good job. You'll do fine, try and stop wetting the bed though, mate'

We had a good chat then I had a last walk into the squadron bar. The toy Airfix Hercules aircraft still hung in its rightful place from the ceiling, rear door open as if tiny Airfix troopers were waiting on a green light from within. In the corridor across from the bar a sea of pictures adorned the walls, mostly of a recent counter-terrorism exercise we'd done, and a big exercise with the Danish home guard where, as usual, the regiment were the bad guys, skirmishing with, and annoying the crap out of any UK troops.

The counter-terrorism exercise had been in Scotland, at an old disused airfield — and really good fun.

The distraction and fire-support team I was in had been taken ashore by rigid raider, a sort of big, metal, open speed-boat, with a huge outboard motor on the back. The Royal Marines driving them were borrowed from Condor, near Arbroath, and very professional. They seemed to like working with us as we often did, although it was handy to have a translator who spoke 'Bootneck'. The job in the counter-terrorism exercise had been to sneak into the perimeter area of an airfield while a four-man snatch team went to rescue the hostage; the hostage was known to be in a metal shipping container near the perimeter at the end of one of the old runway.

We had spent most of the day before practicing in the sun at a local training area. The RAF had supplied two aging Wessex Helicopters, and in the afternoon we had practiced fast-roping into increasingly small target areas. Fast-roping is falling slowly with a degree of style and not a lot of control. A thick thirty-metre rope is coiled in the open side-doorway of the helicopter as it comes into a low hover. At one end the rope is connected to the winch point so, when it's thrown out, it hangs down below the helicopter, just about touching the ground. Inside the helo, the guys all wear thick gloves designed to absorb the heat and provide a bit of grip. The trick is to throw yourself out the door and grab the rope, sliding gracefully down it to the ground and hopefully landing ready to fight. It's a very quick way of getting a patrol to the ground. More so, if you forget to grab the rope, although clearly, in that case, you have to balance the speed advantage against the disadvantage of being slightly dead or having two broken legs. We all had a good go because it was fun, but only the four in the snatch squad would actually do it that night.

I was in the larger eight-man ambush team. We would be the distraction and fire power to let the snatch squad do their job. Two of us had big General Purpose Machine Guns, or GPMGs. I had picked the short straw and swapped my assault rifle for one of them. It's a big heavy cumbersome beast of a thing, belt-fed with heavy 7.62 mm rounds and hard to carry long distances — but capable of laying down a lot of firepower.

The rest had the usual automatic 5.56 rifles, with optical sights.

That night we were taken by our new Royal Marine friends up an estuary and to within a mile or two of the disused airfield. Sound travels well over water so, at a certain point, the engine was cut and the Rigid Raider was rowed the last part of the journey, finally getting into long grass and what appeared to be shallows. I was first out the front of the raider and immediately sank up to my chest in deep, muddy, cold, river water, the big GPMG weighing me down as I struggled ashore and up a muddy grass bank.

Over the next few hours we made our way towards and around the old airfield, skirting farms and small roads, climbing fences and generally being sneaky until we were lying in the grass next to the perimeter fence. It had been very slow work, stopping frequently just to wait and listen for signs of movement or a waiting ambush, but at least we hadn't been watching the target for days or weeks beforehand as was often normal.

On exercise I would often look at people's houses and wonder what was going on inside, watch cars driving along roads and think about who was in them, how strange it was to be the man hiding in the shadows, wondering about their lives and dreams. We waited for ages in the cold damp grass, watching the routine of the target, the single steel container sitting away from all the other buildings and tantalisingly close.

In the distance I could hear the noise of the distant motorway and thought about how it would soon start getting busy with morning traffic as dawn approached. We were lying side by side, just near enough to communicate with a quick tap on the shoulder. The GPMG felt clumsy and cold, and I'd rather have had my normal weapon with an optical sight to scan the target, but the ambush group needed firepower. Our job was to distract and harass the bad people in the target area when the snatch squad went in. I was still cold and wet from my earlier dunking in the river and would have loved to get some dry clothes on. Fuck being cold and wet, although the public probably think the SAS are full of tough people who thrive on that sort of stuff, in reality being smart enough to stay warm, dry and alert in the field is far more important. Any idiot can be cold, wet or hungry and a good soldier avoids all three if he can.

I could just hear the distant thumping of the helos approaching above the distant quiet drone of the motorway. Our 'terrorists', didn't seem to hear them though; they were just talking and joking. It seemed to take forever; the Wessex helicopter was old and slow, but even at that the hostiles were not paying attention. Maybe there was too much background noise where they were, perhaps just the noise of conversation echoing in the container was enough in itself to stop them hearing what I thought was impossible not to hear.

The seconds ticked past and I couldn't believe they hadn't heard, then suddenly the world erupted in light and noise; either side of me the 5.56's had opened up, taking the lead from our patrol commander, and taking carefully aimed crackling bursts while the grass and fence was illuminated by orange and blue flashes from their muzzles. I pulled the GPMG into my shoulder and squeezed: a loud bang, followed by a dull clack and the weapon jolted in a way that just felt wrong. It was jammed after one round. I cleared the blockage, placing the belt of ammunition back into the feed tray and slamming the top cover back down and cocking the weapon. Inside I was raging, maybe weeds or grass from the earlier trip in the river had got into the space between the bolt head and the breach, and hopefully it was gone now. To my right the other GPMG was hammering out 4- and 5-round busts, bright flashes of light and deafening noise as the smaller weapons sharply spat out controlled bursts. I saw movement off to the left and squeezed again holding the butt of the weapon tight. Angry at what felt like lost minutes, although in reality I had cleared the jam in a couple of seconds.

This time the GPMG exploded into life shuddering as I let half the first 50-round belt go in one sustained burst. It always amuses me in war films when people talk to each other in a fire fight. As I released the pressure on the trigger and reassessed the target my ears were screaming, my eyes were already stinging, and the strong stench of burnt ammunition filled my nostrils, I love that smell. We had switched fire to the left and right of the container, leaving a large cone in the middle of the killing zone for the snatch team. By now the first Wessex was in a hover over the container and I could just make out the shadows of the snatch team crouching on the roof then quickly disappearing, a bright flash illuminating the orange smoke kicked away in big curving swirls by the rotor wash below the helo, which banked off sideways and set down on the grass beside the target.

A double tap on the shoulder and then up and running, 'pepper-potting' each other which means that only half of us moved whilst the other half fired, quickly throwing Hessian sacking over the barbed-wire fence and scrambling over into the airfield as the second helo set down. The first helo lifted and nosed down, engine howling as it lumbered away, door gunner letting rip towards the buildings and the occasional rattle of returned fire. I scrambled into the second Wessex and almost immediately we were up and away.

Relative calm.

Just the roar of the wind through the open door and the engine's high-pitched howl. I could make out the shape of the other helo and see the flashing nav lights in the distance against the city lights as we banked down the coast and home.

Splendid. Home in time for tea, cake and medals.

I didn't know the Adjutant playing the hostage was kicking up hell in the other Wessex because his thumbs were cable-tied together and no one could undo them. The problem with being a hostage is you can't expect to be treated as one until you've proven you are not a terrorist pretending to be hostage. And the snatch team had been a little too good at that. It was all discussed a few hours later in the bar; every fucker in the Squadron seemed to revel in sidling up to me: '*Sooooo*, sounded like the GPMG jammed, care to explain yourself?'. I was embarrassed; I should have cleared and checked the weapon after I dunked it underwater in the long grass, but I hadn't.

It was a good exercise though and I enjoyed it. And now on the main corridor wall opposite the bar was a picture taken during the daylight practice runs. I was mid-jump into the surf as the Rigid Raider hit the beach, faithful black woollen tammy hat on my head and that stupid big GPMG in my hands. 'War-e-as-fuck' as they say.

It made me sad to think I'd never do it again.

Some reminiscing, a few insults and a handshake later I was out the door and watching the security gates close behind me for the last time. Despite the sadness I felt at leaving, the world was a good place and I was young and ready to start a new career, full of hope and enthusiasm. By the standards of the regiment I'd been an underachiever and I'm sure a disappointment and yet they treated me as an equal.

Twenty-one years later, when I resigned from the police, I would look back on those years in the Squadron as some of the most amazing hopeful and fulfilling of my life, and those in the Police as the most frustrating sad and strangest of my life.

The way the police changed from a thing I believed in, to a corrupt and morally bankrupt organisation left me feeling unable to carry on betraying the public. When I left I refused to accept my twenty-year, police-long-service medal in disgust due to one particularly corrupt incident. No one cared that I refused to accept it and it's probably languishing in a drawer somewhere. I asked for an exit interview and then ticked the box on the resignation form saying I wanted an interview.

I didn't get one; they refused. Eventually the Superintendent responded to a phone call and said he would see me but, when he found out I was leaving because of 'an issue' that he clearly didn't want to hear about, he did everything he could to avoid me. Even when he arranged an appointment and I messaged the day before to check it was still on, I got a response: 'I'm sorry I'm in the USA'.

Seriously? Obviously he didn't know he was going to be in the USA until after sometime after breakfast.

Just before I left the Police a female probationer was sexually assaulted at the Police college. 4 cops were detained. The entire course were assembled and were told that if it leaked out they would be sacked. After weeks of lecturing these young cops about the honesty of the Police, they were bullied into lying before they ever hit the street. If it had happened in a park, hospital or almost anywhere else the Police would have been shouting their success from the rooftops, but instead it had to be hidden from the Public.

The Police hate to hear anything bad about themselves and they will go to any lengths to cover it up. You can get away with most things — bullying, racism and sexism are all fine — but make them look bad and you're in a world of hatred. Civilian staff can complain to some extent because they are governed by different legislation, but they are also far easier to get rid of. Cops simply can't raise issues, well not unless they want to be the subject of a witch hunt.

In contrast to leaving the Regiment and although I had given years of my life to the police, there was no one to say good luck and no hand shake when I left; I put my kit in a black plastic bag and walked out the door. I'd saved lives, been injured, watched people die, and done my best to uphold the law for twenty-one years of my life and no one cared or wanted to say goodbye, not even an inspector. It was never a surprise. I didn't really expect the Chief Constable to hand me a card made out of sticky-back plastic, Crayola crayons and glitter, but a handshake and someone to say 'thanks and good luck' might have been nice.

But twenty-one years earlier, as I drove back from the squadron to my parents' house, I had no idea then that I had just made the second-worst decision of my life.

CHAPTER 2

THE INTERVIEW

I had applied to join the police off the back of an army exercise in Denmark. I hated parachuting, absolutely detested it, and this particular plummet from the sky had really not gone well at all.

For a start it had been pitch black. Well, that was normal, it was very rare to jump in daylight, but the C130 Hercules that was due to drop us off into 'enemy' Denmark had broken down at RAF Lyneham. Nice, although better than breaking down in the air. Presumably some little RAF chap had gone and hit things with a big hammer and now it worked again. It does make me happy that these things don't break down in the sky. The Wessex helicopter I mentioned earlier has a big nut on top nicknamed the 'Jesus nut' that holds the rotor-head on. They tighten it on the ground, quite frequently apparently; it does make you wonder why it's loose on the ground but its ok to fly. I mean, at what point does it get loose?

The 'Herc' break down at Lyneham gave the opportunity for many of the upstanding members of my patrol to engage in a light carbonated refreshment courtesy of the RAF bar. Relaxing was the order of the day and the jokers in my patrol were in high spirits. 23 Delta 24 was a new patrol to me and we were all off to work with the Danish home guard for two weeks. I was still the new keen guy, newly 'Sabre' only a few years before, and fit as fuck after continuation training and selection. Hence, I had a lot of heavy kit to parachute with. A PRC 319 Clansman backpack radio, which weighed about the same as a large heavy thing and had the capabilities of a broken useless large heavy thing. It had proven its use as a large paper weight some years earlier during the Gulf war, during what has now become an infamous patrol and book. The regiment were a bit miffed about that book. They may not want to hug me at reunions either now, after this book, although I've really only selection to talk about because I was a bit of a wimp and, anyway, I've made a point of only mentioning what's already known.

Getting onto the 'Herc' and smelling the lovely burnt aviation fuel being blasted by warm air from the big turbo props and seeing the dark outline of the aircraft on the taxi way was the usual prelude to a jump. No one was allowed to have a drink beforehand — or at least get caught. Most of 'D' squadron were still miffed they'd been forced to make a long road journey because the Reluctant Air Force couldn't be bothered bringing their broken big plane to us; not as if it didn't have both wings and engines, and presumably a man at the pointy end who could drive and park it somewhere near us, RAF Leuchars for example, or even Edinburgh which had a duty-free, and then the Pilot could have filled up and maybe had enough Shell Tiger Tokens for a decanter. But no, RAF Lyneham it was.

The regiment is full of dry humour and as usual before a big exercise the atmosphere for practical jokes was crackling. I should probably have had the word 'victim' written on my helmet. Parachuting was the only time we wore helmets.

In the field there are: no berets, no markings, no rank, no insignia; just a card to hand to any hunter force that has the misfortune to capture and search anyone who had not washed for two weeks.

Just play the grey man.

On a low-altitude jump the parachute is opened by a big canvas strip called a 'static line', because if the parachute relied on the average squaddie following an instruction, there would be a lot of squaddie shaped holes in the ground across training areas all over Europe. Its only seven seconds from plane to ground for a low altitude night jump without opening a parachute, although that tends to result in a prolonged case of being dead; it's thirty-seven seconds or so if it opens correctly, depending on your weight, in other words on how many PRC319 batteries the rest of your patrol have hidden in your kit when you weren't looking.

To make sure the parachute opens, the static line effectively drags the parachute out the bag just after you leave the door of the plane. Of course, it has to be attached to the plane for this to happen but that's ok, because there's a big hook on the end of the static line for exactly that purpose. You hook up to a cable that runs the length of the plane before the jump, you check it, your mate behind checks it, and the nice air load master checks it. Nice. I wouldn't have cared if God himself had checked it; I still kept looking at it.

So when the light goes green, the nice RAF man smiles, thanks you for your choice of airline and shouts 'GREEN ON — GO!'. You step on the last bit of plane and are fractions of a second from plummeting out the dark night-time windy door of death that awaits. And the last thing you want to see is your patrol signaller, standing behind you holding the hook end of a static line, clearly not attached to any bit of aeroplane, and grinning.

I went 'rivet counting' as they called it. A poor exit, too close to the plane, spinning in the turbulent air. It was a joke using a spare training static line but fuck me did my mind race for the next two seconds whizzing groundwards. Competing thoughts in my head fought for attention, during those long two seconds. On one hand, I was clearly going to pull my reserve or die, but either way I intended to haunt someone for unclipping me, but on the other hand I could feel the rapid pulsing through my parachute harness as my PX4 parachute and static line snapped each tie and pulled the canopy away from the bag and into its rightful position above me. Swinging under my parachute in the dark night and hearing hysterical laughter in the sky around me as the sound of the big C130 Hercules faded into the night sky and as the patch of missing stars it blotted out grew smaller, was a moment to remember.

Utter Fuds.

So I hated parachuting which is a pretty big part of the Special Air Service regiment. The clue is in the name.

My mother had suggested the police because my grandmother lived next door to a cop and he went to the same church. Presumably he said, 'young Rob should join the Police' although I can't imagine in what context this conversation happened; I certainly hadn't been shaking and crying in a corner when I'd been home to raise any of my mother's concerns. But on the other hand she did seem fairly certain my staying in the regiment would result in my untimely death and that would be inconvenient because she was a very busy person, what with the sewing bee and golf and all. And joining the police would get me away from home which seemed better than slow death by a thousand cutting comments at my parents' house, about what I was going to do with my degree and why wasn't I seeing that nice English girl, Catherine, whom they had liked a lot and I shouldn't have split up with.

I did point out that I'd been dumped. It happened in a Blue Ford on the way to see that awful film 'Ghost' with the whole pottery-scene thing. We saw the film despite the dumping, it's just I was watching the pottery bit thinking about sex and she was thinking about strangling me — although somehow we stayed good friends.

I've only had one ex who couldn't stay friends with me and that's lots of chapters away.

Application forms arrived for three local forces: Deeside where I lived, Forthside where the posh people of the world live, and Clydeside, where, as far as I was concerned, the whole criminal underworld of Scotland lived.

Clydeside seemed the most exciting but I filled in all three forms anyway and sent them off, completely failing to read any of them as to the 'only apply for one force at a time' bit; I didn't get where I am today by reading instructions. It's just not a manly thing to do, as every man who's bought any electrical gadget ever will agree. A man reading instructions shows signs of weakness and possibly hints at wearing ladies' underwear and singing 'ABBA' songs in the shower.

After a while I was summoned to do an exam at Rudolfield, Forthside Scotland's HQ.

I turned up in a suit and sat in a room full of people who, frankly, all looked like they wanted to be in the police. I didn't want to pass and genuinely did my best to fail but, honestly, a retarded drunk monkey with a partial lobotomy could have passed the exam back then. In the years to follow I'm pretty sure I worked with some of them. To be fair most of them joined elite, paperwork-filing, office units because they played golf with the right senior retarded drunk monkeys.

A month or so passed and a second letter arrived asking me to go to the big city for another exciting police-entry exam. Well, it's not often God looks down on you from his shiny big gold chair and gives you another chance to royally fuck up an exam so off I went. I knew the score so no suit this time. I wandered into Clydeside's Headquarters at Prat St in a set of tight red and white motorcycle leathers, having parked my trusty rusty Kawasaki GPZ600 right opposite. That Kawasaki wouldn't start without a bump start because it was, frankly, fucked. My entire life riding it was spent looking for opportunities to park or fill up with fuel as long as they were at the top of hills so I could get going again. Stalling was never an option so the throttle really only had an on and off position.

I was shown into a long waiting room in the personnel department. Lots of very smart young people were looking at each other in nervous silence; all were holding an invitation letter just like the one I'd lost and were wearing that suit last worn for granny's funeral, with either a tie borrowed from Dad or a sensible handbag borrowed from Mum. All looked terrified. You just knew that as they left the house their mum had taken a hanky, spat on it and wiped their face saying something nice like, 'don't slouch and remember and make a good impression, dear'.

A slightly older, pretty, blonde-haired girl gave me what can best be described as a long Paddington-Bear stare. I hated her straight away. She clearly was a stuck up nurse type who liked hurting people with needles.

'Hi, I'm Rob, I don't really want to join the Police at all; what do you do?'

Everyone looked stunned at this reprobate in leather, who had the audacity to speak,

'Ermmm, I'm Jackie. I'm a Nurse'.

It was very tempting to ask if she'd killed any patients today, but at this point really I felt conversation would be very awkward and strained. It didn't help that every time I moved I made squeaky farty noises between the leather of my lovely motorcycle leathers and the plastic seats.

After an awkward eternity, an important looking Sgt came along and ushered everyone into a second room with desks and seats. Typical exam-type hall really; they have that nice atmosphere where anyone a bit OCD like me feels the urge to line up all the pencils and rubbers symmetrically, before you 'may now turn the exam paper over'.

But there was no seat for me.

Everyone quietly sat down and the usual opening stuff about how to behave in an exam didn't happen.

'Are you Mr Robert Moon?'

Not really a difficult start.

'Hello! That's me.'

I was led out the room and into a separate interview room. Now, having been through SAS selection I was pretty much ready for a Hessian sack over my head and a burly man to start questioning my parenthood, but this was more disconcerting. The Sgt looked at me like I'd violated his favourite Labrador and asked if I'd applied to any other forces. I told him that I had, and this was met with a look that suggested that applying for something other than Clydeside Police had made him vomit just a tiny bit.

'Forthside police have told us you have already done this exam and passed, and you are going to have to choose who you want to apply for. Obviously we are the best'. He smiled because this was presumably funny. He also suggested next time I should wear a suit.

So next time I wore a suit.

Again, I made my way down to Clydeside Police HQ, full of the certain knowledge that I didn't want in. I had already phoned Deeside and Forthside and let them down gently. It's always hard to break up after a relationship. The intermediate interview was with a Sgt who, presumably, was there to vet out the insane and criminally bad. I was led into the same room as before and asked lots of searching questions then eventually:

'So, have you been in trouble with the police?'

Well technically no, but there were a few issues as to this point. I'd been taken home by the police before when I was fifteen for issues to do with mixing vodka and cider, and that's before we mention running away from an army short-wheel-base land rover on exercise after the Officer Cadet Unit driver crashed it whilst pissed on the way back to camp from the pub.

'Well, not really.'

'What do you mean "not really"?'

'Well, I've spoken to the police a few times, they seemed nice… people'

I felt I'd covered all the bases, but apparently not so.

'That's not what I asked.'

'Eh, well I've maybe been told off for mucking around a bit'

'It's like pulling teeth with you; just answer the question'

'No, nothing bad.' A blatant lie, surely I would be able to go home now.

'Do you know anyone in the police?'

'No.' Ha! No problem with that question

'You sure?'

'Yup'

'Sure?'

'Yup.'

'Sure?'

'Well, actually, maybe my grandmother's next-door neighbour, but I don't know where he works'

'I do,' the Sgt replied looking serious. 'What's your grandmother's neighbour's name?'

'Ermmm — Paul'

'Really? Just Paul?'

'I think he might be a supervisor.'

'Ah yes, Indeed. He phoned earlier to see how you were doing — you should maybe find out who all the assistant chief constables are before your next interview...'

Well, at least I knew who Granny's next-door friend from church was now.

The second interview was much more formal. A table of three serious-looking officers asked me lots of searching questions, and commented on one of my referees. To be fair, having the commanding officer of the SAS saying you are a great guy is a good reference. Knowing that, in private, he probably thought I was incapable of covertly fighting my way into a packet of crisps without air support made it much sweeter.

After the interview two other potential recruits and I were taken to Cambridge Street, the force training and recruitment centre, for a fitness test. The pretty blonde-haired killer nurse seemed very surprised to see me again. A tall lanky guy was there too and seemed awfully keen. I guessed all the others at the exam had proven to have an IQ below that of a drunk retarded monkey.

'Weren't you the guy who turned up to the exam in motorcycle leathers?'

'Yes, I kind'a misjudged that one.'

'God, we all thought you would be gone for that.'

'I wish…' I'm sure I sighed deeply.

Killer nurse seemed happy though.

At Cambridge Street we were all asked to do a bleep test in the force training-centre gym. It was the first time I'd done such a thing which basically consisted of running back and forward between two lines in time to increasingly fast beeps, and keeps going until you get fed up or see your breakfast again. I gave up, but the tall, lanky recruit kept going for ages. He was awfully keen and clearly wanted to impress. Killer nurse gave up quite early, presumably because her patients couldn't run that fast and she wasn't used to it.

A few weeks later I received a letter giving me my start date. Bollocks.

CAMBRIDGE ST, CLYDESIDE POLICE TRAINING AND RECRUITMENT CENTRE.

Being a non-city-dweller, I arranged to drive down to the force recruitment and training centre the evening before I started. Cambridge Street training centre was a large Victorian building on the south side of the city next to the modern Sheriff court. I parked in a small rough area of ground opposite and made my way through the double doors. On the right, a small concierge office contained a man who gave me a set of keys to a tiny cupboard-sized bedroom a short walk away through a courtyard.

The next morning I joined the nineteen fellow recruits including Lanky and Nursie. We were transported in mini buses to Prat Street, Force Headquarters, better known as

'Coward's Castle' or 'the Crystal Maze' and entered the main hall downstairs, for swearing-in, coffee and cake. It was a bit like a school assembly hall only without an upright, out-of-tune piano at the side of the stage and a list of head boys and girls on a wooden plaque at the side. It quickly became apparent that my fellow inmates were actually proud to be there and, furthermore, wanted to mingle and shake hands with the senior officers wandering around.

I hated them all a tiny bit more.

A senior officer wandered over to me. I assumed this was because I'd taken the last custard crème, but it turned out he felt I should have got a haircut before I arrived. I was fairly quick to point out that I had, less than forty-eight hours before, however that didn't seem to make him happy at all.

Soon stores were visited and were a welcoming sight to me. They appeared and smelt just like every clothing store everywhere ever, in the whole world, and probably other planets too. A small man guarded a broad wooden counter with a metal ruler glued along one edge and wielded huge power over all who dared to enter his domain, a sort of tiny, angry, dungeon-master type, grudgingly handing over his treasured precious stores, in exchange for 'chitties', signed forms worth more than mere money. Behind, on row after row of grey metal shelves, were assorted treasures in plain brown boxes or wrapped in clear plastic packaging.

Stores are of course called 'stores', because they are for storing things. 'If you were meant to get stuff they'd be called "issues",' the stock retort of every store man, ever.

In the years to come I would perfect the ability to get free shiny stuff from stores. A single triplicate carbonated chitty signed by an inspector was all that was required, and the trick was to get the inspector to sign a form for a non-descript item that he or she believed you actually needed, or even better he or she needed, then add all sorts of fun things to the form on the drive to stores. I never met an inspector smart enough to score through the blank lines on the form; it was almost like they thought I was honest and trustworthy.

Some years later in 'Juliet Bravo', myself and my regular 'neebs' would regularly be sent to stores for others as we drove the divisional response van. (Neebs is a Clydeside term for your regular crewmate, not used by other lesser forces who refer to two cops working together as a 'set', a bit like matching his and hers toilet roll holders, and to the 'shift' as the 'team'. That one really annoyed me; we were most certainly never a team.) For almost a year we added a chrome whistle onto every single stores form we took there, also countless big yellow floating torches, hats and, for some bizarre reason, white parade gloves. I have no idea why; it just became a tradition.

I long suspected that somewhere in the meditation room in the Tibetan monastery of all 'stores people', high in the snowy mountains at the foot of Everest, where all the chitties were carefully audited and indexed and all stores were symmetrically ordered in shelves for all eternity, and audited every morning at sunrise in some sacred ceremony involving a gong, that a tiny angry monk was suddenly shocked out of a meditative trance by the sudden realisation that somewhere in the universe one of his miniature brethren had been cheated out of another three whistles, chrome, police and chain; two sets of gloves, parade-white, size-large and another big, yellow, floating waterproof torch.

The stores man in Coward's Castle seemed to get smaller and angrier every year and became increasingly exasperated at his diminishing whistle stocks, all apparently going to the office where the whistle-eating monster lived in the locker room. When I left 'Juliet Bravo' the bottom of my locker was infested with shiny chrome whistles, while hats and white parade-gloves were littered all over radiators and chairs the length of the office. I felt I had won a rare victory against all store-goblins the world over.

Back at Cambridge Street the local barber had been requisitioned along with his electric razor and all the male recruits were told they were a disgrace to humanity, and that they were clearly long-haired, drug-smoking hippies, and were lined up for a haircut that was allowed to be short or shorter. None of the young ladies received haircuts. They were however all taken away and presumably told how bad the boys were in a separate room because when they came back they all stood and sniggered at the row of baldy bastards.

The next week consisted of runs around the city park, and lots of forms to sign which meant nothing. We were taught how to use an iron. (One of our number, Neil from Elgin could master the ironing bit but not so much the turning the iron on bit.) Then, after a few talks by impressive people. The wonders of the fantastic pension were explained to me:

How good it was. (It was.)

Retire in thirty years. (Liars.)

It wouldn't change. (Liars.)

We would always pay just 11% into it. (Liars)

And finally how great the Federation were at looking after us all. (Liar, liar pants on fire.)

They completely neglected to tell anyone that paying into the Federation was voluntary and that they were actually a statutory organisation who had to support you anyway. In twenty-one years my only dealing with the Federation was when the local fed rep, whose partner was the local Chief Inspector, told one of my colleagues, while they were at a road crash together, that I was getting into bother for something. I had no idea and my whole office knew before me.

They did tell us all about the internal police lottery, which is a strange thing. No one ever seems to win it unless you phone up, ask what your numbers are and say that you are thinking of leaving. I used that trick twice and it worked within a month both times.

What was good was the chance to subscribe to the police recuperation home in Harrogate. It became one of the few things that I felt genuinely helped me in the years to come. Also, I got really really drunk with some RUC (Royal Ulster Constabulary) boys there. Later a second recuperation home would open in Auchterarder.

A couple of things did stick with me during that week though. We were told the police was the biggest gang in the world and we would always win because there were lots of us and we never slept. Obviously this was before the cuts and reorganisation to come. The other thing we were told was to beware, because women would find us irresistible in uniform…. uh huh! Well, I'm still waiting on that one. And lastly we were told not to lose our friends from outwith the job, and this was said with real feeling. I think one of the things that made the police in Britain special was that we still had that bond with the public, both on a personal and organisational level—but it was rapidly being eroded.

The week flew by quickly and soon we were off to the Police College at Tulliallan Castle, near Alloa for an initial ten weeks' training before being allocated to our divisions.

CHAPTER 3

THE COLLEGE, OR 'CASTLE GREYSKULL'

Every police officer in Scotland attends basic training at the Scottish Police College. It's situated just outside Kincardine, near Alloa and it would be our home for the next ten weeks. It's situated within a large, grassy estate with many miles of the Devilla Forest, lurking on the hill behind. At its core is a large old house in the style of a castle bought from a private landowner after World War II. It's impressive, but in reality the students on probationer courses didn't ever get into there, except to use the college tuck shop.

As an aside it has two snooker tables down in the basement that nobody seems to know about and a tiny 'Alice in Wonderland' style door into a creepy underground basement that really needs to be haunted; it would be wrong if it weren't. I went in there once, because that's where they store the exam papers for every student ever, and found a room with a single lightbulb hanging from the low, stone vaulted ceiling and a single chair in the middle facing a wall with the word 'Help' written on it. It was presumably at one time a wine cellar. How very odd.

A more modern large dining hall and assembly hall had been built near to the Castle and next to that a large oval parade square with a daïs area on one side for formal passing-out parades. On the other side from the daïs a large glass corridor looks onto the parade square, with adjacent corridors running off into various blocks built in the 60's to accommodate the expansion of the college. The main dormitories for the males were four large, twelve-person dormitories on the ground floor of Culzean block. The female accommodation was in Glamis block, and, as you may have guessed, these accommodation blocks all had names that came from real Scottish Castles. It's all changed now though and a new curved accommodation and training block has been built.

We all turned up at lunch time on the first day, parking our cars on the large oval parade square, and made our way towards the double glass doors at the head of the square, which lead into an entrance hallway and 'Crush Hall', the main assembly hall. On the parade square in front of the doors a Drill Sgt resplendent in full parade uniform with highly polished boots and a red sash shouted at every infringement or thing that annoyed him.

I seemed very much to be one of those things. Maybe even all of them.

We were lined up, nineteen of us from Clydeside and another eighteen or so from other forces in Scotland, then we were walked through the double doors and into the large assembly hall where we listened to a senior officer telling us what wonderful lovely people we were; as soon as he'd gone, the drill Sgt explained how incredibly horrible we all were and told us all the college standards and rules. We were ordered, sorted and familiarised with the college in a whirlwind of a first day, and finally, that evening, were shown how to make our beds to the required standards. Dark grey woolly blankets white sheets and 'hospital corners', in the twelve-bed dormitories overlooking the 'Italian gardens', just gravel and a statue of a naked lady—when I returned years later it was full of 'porta cabin' classrooms.

Our normal uniform in class was a smart white shirt, epaulettes and tie, with pressed woollen trousers and highly polished shoes. For inspections though we would wear our tunics and white gloves, whistle and chain between the second and third tunic buttons, removing dust beforehand with a ritual of patting down each other using the reverse side of packing tape.

The weeks passed. We were taught legislation, the power of arrest, something never to be misused, although one of my main reasons for leaving twenty-one years later was that I had seen it misused.

We were taught all the crimes first, then GPD (general police duties), legislation on found property, poaching and so forth, before finally two weeks of traffic legislation and powers. Knowledge of these subjects was central to doing the job and would form an essential part of the promotion process as well.

We were taken out regularly for runs in the forest behind the College and up 'Rice Crispy Hill', so named because of the frequent reappearance of breakfast. Health and safety was not a big issue and we would also be taken deep into the reservoir in the woods to search the mud for something that clearly wasn't there, and then run around carrying benches from the gym. The swimming pool was another place of pain. Swimming was something I loved and I liked the physical training sessions in that old, deep, cold pool. There were lessons in life-saving skills, dragging each other in and out the deep end and jumping from one of the three diving boards fully clothed to rescue 'casualties'. Years later, the diving boards and the use of the pool for training was ended. Health and Safety meant it was not the police's job to save people anymore. After one particular drowning we would be issued throw lines in the vehicles, but the days of actually getting in the water were, probably rightly, over.

The college bar became a nightly ritual. The 'Copper Lounge' was the only place we could go because leaving the grounds was forbidden — and enforced; each night a group of students on a rota would patrol the grounds in tunics and long rain coats. The 'duty team' was a short straw, and involved patrolling from 6pm until 11.30pm when the swimming pool was shut, the copper lounge cleared and the dormitories checked one last time.

Officer safety training was a couple of one hour sessions with the PTI, and consisted of how to hand-cuff someone. Back then the cuffs were just linked by a chain, so it was quite normal to handcuff a prisoner to yourself, or two to each other. Even years later I would always keep a set of old cuffs in my kit bag in case I arrested more than one person and I was a couple of hours from the office. Those cuffs mostly disappeared from general issue in the mid-1990s when the new solid bar-cuffs appeared. Only in single crewed vehicles in remote areas did the chain cuffs stay in official use.

The baton was a wooden stick. It was a rite of passage to get it drilled out and filled with a metal bar, and every shift had someone with a lathe who knew how to do it. Without a metal bar, the wood would shatter on use because the newer ones were pretty much made of Balsa, but the reality was they were completely unsuitable for anything anyway. They had a short leather wrist strap and the issue trousers all had a baton pocket so you could hide your baton away, the emphasis being on appearing smart and not aggressive to the public. What was even crazier was that women in the police were given an even smaller baton, about eight inches long, and a hand bag to carry it in. I'm sure there must be one of these in the police museum, but if not you can get an idea what it was like from any sex shop. I can only assume if it was ever taken out for use the idea was that the angry suspect would dissolve into hysterical laughter.

We were always told that policing in Scotland must be with the consent of the public, but whilst that was maybe true back then it became less and less possible in future years when crimes were 'managed', and the law-abiding public became increasingly a cash cow for the Force for generating numbers and statistics.

During my years in the Force, it always amused me that past crime statistics could be 'managed', by a crime manager when no part of that included trying to stop future crimes. How can you control what's already happened? You might as well try and place a bet after you know the winner of a race. Well, in the modern police service we manage the past better than Dr Who on steroids because we can hide it in a spread sheet. Crimes and offences are ordered and classified; robbery gets changed into assault and theft, but only if it's undetected; vandalism becomes nothing. That last one made me laugh in the late 90's when we were told not to take reports of vandalisms because a broken window, for example, could have been caused by a bird flying into it. According to one crime manager some quite clever birds in my division had even managed to take a set of keys down the side of a car and let the tyres down. Hitchcock, it turns out, was spot on.

The College course flew past with everyone desperate to get onto the street and start the job we were training for. When the ten weeks were over we returned to Cambridge Street and then out to our respective offices, before we could return for a last eight weeks at the college, eighteen weeks in total. The courses were longer and less frequent, presumably because the police at that time did not have the high turnover of staff that would happen in future years. The job was still very much a career. Staff were treated very well and that was returned by a degree of loyalty. If you were needed to do something, it was done because it was appreciated.

CHAPTER 4

1ST DAY AT DIVISION
'THIS SHIT JUST GOT REAL'

Blair, my fellow 'J' or 'Juliet' division recruit and I arrived at 'Juliet Alpha' police office, Shetland St, for our first real day in the job. All the divisions had the names of letters to identify them and the headquarters for each division was always 'Alpha'. My uniform was perfectly pressed, tunic sleeves ironed perfectly, new 'J' shoulder numbers proudly adorning my shoulders, lovely new notebook in my upper left tunic pocket all ready to note details of the first murderer I would catch, hopefully before lunch, and baton ready to defend some beautiful young virgin maiden from attack by neds.

Of course, finding a beautiful young virgin in that area of the city would have required a magic wand from 'Olivanders' never mind a baton from stores. 'Ned' is a lovely term in Scotland descending from the term 'Ner do well' apparently. More frequently nowadays it means Non-educated-delinquent.

Shetland street police office was yet another old Victorian building with what can best be described at rustic charm, if rustic is taken to mean 'fuck awful', and charm is taken to mean 'dead rats'. The cell block just needed a warden yelling 'Fletcher!' in a Scottish accent and Ronnie Barker to pop his head out from a vacant cell to be complete. The metal walkways on the three-floor cell block, heavy cell doors and white tiles everywhere made it more cold and miserable than I would have thought possible.

The muster room was a small room about the size of normal living room with desk space around three sides, and a lectern at one end. Outside, a larger locker room featured a worn-out pool table and another few rows of lockers and the opposite corner featured a fabulous Victorian wrought-iron spiral staircase up to the CID and admin floor. Not everything was awful.

The CID office had been the local court back in the day when presumably nefarious people were taken outside and dunked in the Clyde to see if they were possessed by witchcraft. The admin office housed four officers who covered all paper work and administrative stuff for the division, with the help of a civilian employee to file the warrants and a Sgt. When I left the police 'J' division admin staff had grown to fill the entire office car park, and this was normal everywhere. So much so that when the fire alarm went off at one divisional HQ office in 2008, allegedly forty people left the building while two cops were out covering the street. But all that was unforeseen back in the nineties, when the first personal computer had only just arrived in the muster room and when we had been told we would soon going to be working in a paperless office and everything would be much more efficient, we didn't believe it – and we were right.

After a guided tour of the office Blair and I were taken to outside the divisional commander's office. Our guide knocked on the door and Blair and I marched proudly in, myself in front. The divisional commander's desk was on our left and as I marched in I saw him look up and stare, presumably astounded by the fine pair of officers sent to him by the college. I called 'parade halt' and smartly came to a halt, stamping my foot on the floor; Blair marched straight into my back having set off on the wrong foot. I heard sniggering from outside the office as the door shut behind us and I called 'Leeeeeeeft turn' and, as we saluted, I realised that my new divisional commander did not look entirely happy.

I learned in years to come that senior officers set up their room depending on purpose. If you walked in and there was a chair for you to sit on that was good, for an appraisal, or even better a good appraisal; if he was sitting at the coffee table in the corner and smiling, then something had gone wrong and it needed fixed or forgotten about; if you walked in and were clearly expected to stand in front of the big desk then you had been naughty and you were about to be sent to the naughty step to think about what you'd done until you were very very sorry, and said you wouldn't ever do it again. Under no circumstances should you sit cross legged on the floor peering over the edge of the desk in this eventuality.

On this occasion we were interrogated in a manner that was famous for our divisional commander,

He always asked everyone who came to the division the same question.

'How many 'O' grades do you think I have?'

Now, this kind of threw me because clearly it was a trick question. Should I guess very high or very low? I went high. That was surely a complement.

'All of them, Sir?'

He frowned and stared intensely at us both. He had piercing cold blue eyes, a gaunt serious face, and as it turned out precisely zero 'O' grades. Yup, the man was a complete fuckwit at school it seemed but had done amazingly well in the police. Actually he was a very smart and intuitive man and someone whom I was sad to see go when he got the inevitable job at a local football club years later. Nepotism worked as well then as it does now.

(This does not directly involve my story, but I think you should know. While I was doing my best to un-impress everyone in 'J' division, good old Neil from Elgin was off to his new office for his first day—a backshift starting at 2pm. Sadly, he couldn't find the office. He could have asked anyone in 'The Port' as most of them have been offered the hospitality of the splendidly appointed ensuite facilities there at one time or another, but he started to panic as it approached 2pm and, in what I still feel was a moment of utter genius to put Clarke Kent to shame, he started to get changed in a telephone box. *Really*.

A member of the public contacted the 999 control room and his new shift colleagues were actioned to the telephone box where they found their new probationer only partially ready for duty. What a nice way to meet your new shift supervisor! His gaffer ended up in the traffic as my gaffer years later and he often recounted stories about Neil—but they alone would require a bigger book than this.)

The rest of the day was spent with the community involvement branch or CIB. A very nice police lady showed us lots of interesting things and gave us a tour of the division. The thing I liked best was Penguin Pete. Penguin Pete was a huge penguin costume in the CIB room, except this penguin was wearing a police uniform. It was a PR thing of course, some poor probationer would wear it if they could find one who would fit, or it was just left sitting with one of the personal radios inside it on a 'back to back' channel. Someone would be just outside the room with another radio to make Penguin Pete talk. Penguin Pete was in disgrace though. On a trip to a primary school, he was made to talk to the kiddies using the radio technique. It worked for a while until two traffic bikers parked up and decided to use the same channel:

'Oi! Jimmy, stop that cunt in the blue Ford; fucker's doin' 51'

Which was not really what all the little boys and girls or their teacher wanted to hear Penguin Pete tell them about strangers.

The Shift.

First muster was a back shift, I arrived early and got changed into my best tunic and pressed shirt.

Walking into the muster room I was met by fifteen or sixteen grinning cops standing around a single chair in the middle of the room. Hanging from the ceiling was a large set of learner driver 'L' plates and, to the sound of laughing, I realised I was expected to sit in the chair. At Cambridge Street we had been warned that at muster the old cops expected to have their own seats and woe betide the probationer who dared to sit in a chair until they had achieved the required 1.5 million years' service. But this chair was just for me; it was terribly lonely sitting there. Steve, the previous probationer, introduced himself and looked delighted not to be the new boy any more.

The first question I was asked by the older cops was, 'what school did you go to son?'

I hadn't gone to school in the city so that kind of threw them because they couldn't tell if I was a Tim or Proddie, city slang for Catholic or Protestant. Miffed, they asked outright

37

which team I supported so they could find out which half of the shift would decide to not like me. I was no help because I don't like football and have never been to a game in my life.

The shift could be quite a clique and I tried, as always, to play the grey man and get on with everyone. I knew Steve pretty well within a few months but he'd made the mistake of actually being himself and I think, as a result of this, some of the more insular members of the shift had taken a dislike to him. It happens on most shifts and anyone new is seen as a threat, especially if it's perceived that they are any good, more so, if they have the character to change the shift dynamic.

Muster began and I wrote everything I could down in my notebook although I understood none of it.

'19, 23, 7 and 8 and 2nd'

'25, 47, 14, 15 and 1st'

'11, 27, 2, 3 and 2nd'

… and so on and so forth, like an American football team chanting random numbers.

I had no idea what they meant.

It turned out that they were shoulder numbers, beat numbers and break times. I was neighboured with 423 and would apparently be out walking somewhere (7 and 8 beats wherever they were) and taking second break.

423 was Pedro, or 'Pedro the Perv' as he was better known. He'd been moved to 'Juliet Alpha' police office from another division for looking up ladies' skirts in a local twenty-four-hour garage and had finally gone too far by groping a police woman. He was awaiting a trial at the sheriff court although you could tell just looking at him that he was guilty both of sexual assault and of being a dick. A female supervisor told me months later that she had tried to counsel him regarding his behaviour but he

just spent the entire time staring at her tits. He was subsequently found 'not proven' at court although I have absolutely no idea how. Some of the police witnesses failed to show up at court resulting in its being thrown out so I suspect there was a degree of interference to avoid the public shame of a conviction. I took an instant dislike to Pedro even though I was unaware at this stage of his pending cases and police database record. What upset me was his referring to me as 'the boy' and generally being a fud.

We were issued radios and immediately given a call to Brimstone Court, a block of flats a mile or so away. I had my nice new tunic on, shiny buttons and long black outer coat and felt very uncomfortable being out on patrol for the first time. The walk, because, yes, police officers used to walk everywhere back then, gave me lots of time to get to know my new neebs properly. I really hated him; he spent ages telling me how to walk at the correct speed. Seriously, I'd been walking since I was, well, a toddler and I thought I was pretty good at it.

As an aside he would later run off aged forty-eight with the twenty-four-year-old daughter of his niece. Honestly, I couldn't make this shit up if I tried.

When we arrived at the concierge's office at Brimstone Court, a very angry drunk man in a wheel chair was throwing his excrement at anyone he could. He was an old housebreaker called James who had fallen off a drain pipe for the last time and would housebreak no more. I would end up seeing him around a lot and he always remembered me as the one who was 'nice' to him. All relative of course, but years later I would tell my students at the Police College to always be nice to prisoners because they'll always remember you whereas, with the exception of your very first arrest, you may not remember them. You may arrest others that day and you have no reason to recall things; for them, it may be the only time they will ever deal with the police and they will recall every tiny detail and every word you say, so always be professional and polite. It costs absolutely nothing.

On this occasion though, throwing poop and shouting is a good 'breach of the peace' and I should have taken careful notes and huge and detailed statements just like the nice college people had told me to; what actually happened was the divisional Sherpa van turned up, we deposited our angry man in the back of the Sherpa van, and went for a nice cup of tea. Policing was not going to be the exciting roller-coaster of adrenaline I had expected.

Sgt MacDougall

'Son, you're going sick next back shift, it's your turn; I've put it through the book'

That I had sick leave I could pre-book was a fantastic thing; I usually used mine to go to watch the North West 200 motorcycle race in Northern Ireland. The downside was that actually being sick was seriously frowned upon, because if you went sick then, then someone who was on sick leave might have to come back and not be sick. Getting time off was rarely the problem it would become in years to come.

Wee Tam aka Herr Flick, took Adolph Hitler's birthday off every year to go to Munich, but he had a picture in his locker of Hedrick Reinhart grand protector of Czechoslovakia during the occupation so that was understandable. He loved walking around in an overly long, black, police issue coat like a cloak flowing behind him in the wind, his hat tipped backwards like bat man. Herr Flick was a genuinely very nice guy and it was all just show. Although he once went to wake up a Jewish shop keeper in the middle of the night because their shop alarm had gone off, and when she came to the door looking shocked and tired, said to her:

'You lot should be used to people in long dark coats coming to get you in the middle of the night.' It was all just dark humour. I came to trust him a lot before he quit a few years later and moved abroad.

The shift was huge but the admin departments were tiny and all the funny little teams that don't seem to do anything hadn't been thought of back then. We normally had enough out walking to have a minimum of every three beat areas assigned to each pair of cops. For Juliet Alpha subdivision that meant about twelve cops out walking each shift, plus the Mike One response car which had an 'AS' or 'all stations' radio to talk to HQ in Coward's Castle direct. Mike 10 was the divisional van which, in addition to Mike 3, and Alpha 11 would cover the same area, and usually a couple of cops out in plain clothes. I have no idea where everyone went over the next twenty years as shifts shrank again and again. It was inconceivable to me that divisional administration could ever need more than five people. We even did all the court citations back then in admin for the whole division—before they decided to just post them to save money.

There were some days off that were harder to get than others, but if you had a good reason then time off was always there. Minimum manning levels existed but over years in the police they would be eroded away to nothing. Back in the 90's even at minimum levels there were always plenty of people on. As the Force grew to the 17,234 cops where it stood when I finally called it a day, I often wondered what people actually did. I genuinely have no idea, but there are a lot of computer workstations in most offices now. Maybe they all play solitaire like we did on the crime-management system. They tried to uninstall it but anyone with any knowledge at all just opened a 'DOS' prompt and typed in 'sol.exe'. Ah! Many hours I spent playing solitaire. Quality nightshift fun although, most of the time, being in the office at all was frowned upon unless there was whisky involved. Paperwork was never urgent enough that it couldn't be left for a quiet day on the early shift, because if anything was that urgent it simply got dealt with and the paperwork could be completed days or weeks later.

By the time I left the 17,234 number for staff became sacred and we would have new probationers join just to sit doing nothing, as long as they were on the books for the magical 1st day of the financial quarter.

CHAPTER 5

JASPER

Pedro the Perv had been relegated to bar duties where he could not interact or sexually assault members of the public. Well, not unless they came to the public counter anyway, which I suppose is exactly where they would go if they came to the station. Oh well, the alternative was to gaffer tape him up and lock him in a cupboard but I suspect he would enjoy it and it would be even more disturbing for the rest of us to know he was in there. At least in the bar area the duty officer could keep an eye on him although it creeped the two female civilians who controlled the radios out.

One backshift I was working with big Two Worlds, an absolute gentleman. Two Worlds was a quiet, refined and frankly hilarious cop who was very well respected on the shift. He was walking a lot after having taken the divisional response car, Juliet Mike One, and wrapped it around a lamppost, a wall, a bus shelter and a metal fence on the previous night shift. The orange stripe from the car's markings would be seen on the wall for months to come.

He was called 'Two Worlds' because he clearly lived on another planet, and the reason he lived on another planet was that he had blown up a 'doss'. It took good local knowledge on where to go during any shift to get a nice cup of tea and a biscuit and a doss is somewhere every good beat cop should know. Two Worlds however had lit up a cigar in the back of the shop when he was making a visit while making a cup of tea for himself and the shop keeper. When he came round he could see a bus stopped with the passengers all staring at him, because the resultant explosion from the gas leak wiped out the entire front of the shop.

He was badly burned but fortunate. Nothing seemed to get him even slightly ruffled, which I suppose was understandable. His party trick was to put the van in first gear and climb out the window then get back in the passenger side while it was idling along, usually towards a tree in the local park.

That night Two Worlds and I were asked to check out a smell from the flat of a neighbour who hadn't been seen for a while. Now, as any cop knows this is generally not going to be a good call, but I was young, naive and hopeful. We arrived at the flat on the top floor of a tenement block near to the motorway. Knocking on the door produced a quiet whimpering sound from within and the sound of someone moving close to the other side of it. Clearly the occupant was incapacitated behind the door and in urgent need of saving; there would be cakes, tea and letters of commendation before break time.

Two World's radio confirmed that we could force entry and he stood back to let me kick in my first door. It turned out to be very difficult, and it took a long time with Two Worlds quietly advising me on my technique before finally the door frame splintered and the door crashed open under repeated kicking from my size-ten boots.

Two things immediately hit me.

The first was a black and white Border Collie, with lovely white teeth and a wet tongue that gratefully leapt into my arms and began proper sloppy dog kisses all over my face; I love dogs and I am a real sucker for a fur baby in need of cuddles.

The second thing to hit me was the smell.

Never ever before had I experienced anything like it nor the dull buzzing of thousands of bluebottles escaping out the door. Two Worlds wandered nonchalantly into the flat before calling out with an amused hint to his voice from the living room on the right.

'Eh, Rob, you might want to come see this.'

The old man had clearly died masturbating in front of an electric fire and TV in the living room some weeks before. Fortunately, Jasper the dog had not been short of food, as the lack of legs and splintered human bones all round the room demonstrated. A dripping tap had kept him alive too.

I slightly regretted using so much tongue during our doggie/human bonding seconds before. The dog was still in my arms panting and looking delighted at finally being rescued.

Jasper the dog looked at me happily, or possibly as dessert? It was hard to tell.

Two Worlds took Jasper the dog back to the office kennels whilst I waited with a bottle of whisky mouthwash on the arrival of the police casualty surgeon to pronounce life extinct. It's a strange legal requirement that has to be done unless the victim is very obviously dead. I felt we, or at least Jasper the dog, had this evidential point covered actually, but the control room wanted the doctor to come and check anyway. I spent the time looking through the mail to try and work out how long poor doggie had been on his Atkins human diet. The first envelope contained a lovely letter from presumably a young female relative instructing the reader to 'give Jasper a big smacky kiss from me'.

Consider it done my dear.

Having ascertained when the oldest letter was posted and having found some details for next of kin, I decided to rewind the video player and find out what the old gent had been watching. Just as I pressed play and a naughty naked lady began doing something indecent on the screen in front of myself and Jasper's dinner, the most stunningly attractive doctor in the world walked into the flat.

Awkward.

We gave Jasper to the family later on that night. I was glad we didn't tell them what had happened; Jasper needed a few happy years. A curious aside to this story is that while searching the flat and securing it, it became apparent that Jasper's owner was a lonely but not poor man. Sad to die and be there so long. Money does not buy happiness.

I had been strangely cautious about dealing with the first of my sudden deaths. Over the next twenty-one years I would find death was a companion, a constant source of entertainment, horror, and ultimately it became something I came to see as so integral to my way of life that it fundamentally changed who I was.

Many years later I would find myself having a fish supper sitting on a roadside verge next to a dead child and I would feel nothing whatsoever. Even as a father of two children I had been drained of the capacity to see death as anything other than the thing I enjoyed most. The Police College had prepared us all for death with legislation and some photographs. I remember the pictures well because the instructor told my class that the dead naked man lying in the depression in the woods was an SAS man and they like to do that sort of thing. I don't think I could have sold it to 'D' Squadron as a night out. The last one I remembered had fewer pine needles and more beer, women, fighting and nightclubs.

'Juliet Alpha' office bar.

Shetland St had not been designed with modern policing in mind. It was a very old divisional HQ, the front public bar was straight off a doorway from the ground-floor control room. The entire city division was controlled from a room slightly larger than a large tenement living room. A set of three workstations with some of the first computers I had seen in the police faced into the room. A radio that looked like it had made the first transatlantic radio call allowed access to the channel used by just that division. Two 'command and control' terminals with aging green screen cathode-ray tube monitors, and plain grey keyboards sat either side of an even older Police National Computer (PNC) terminal directly connected to the Scottish Criminal Records Office machine and PNC at Hendon. All three would stop working with staggering regularity, usually prompting one of the two female operators on my shift to broadcast on the 'J' division channel the words 'stand by; the computer has gone down on me'.

That one never got old.

The duty officer and the bar officer also had simple desks and phones, and through the second access to the bar was the charge bar area where prisoners were processed. Beyond this, in the cell corridor, was a security door restricting access to the back yard. Bizarrely you needed to buzz in to the corridor from the back yard but could just open the door to get out. I always felt that was sort of the wrong way round. It didn't matter much because the security door could be opened with a good kick, a shove or a prisoner's head if the need arose. There was a CCTV camera on the office wall facing the door, but it did not record anything. It was purely to let the staff in the bar see who wanted buzzed in.

Once inside the bar area, prisoners stood on one side of the wide charge-bar, facing into the area off the control room. The duty officer, usually an Inspector, would stand behind this big desk while one of the civilian 'turnkeys' or the bar officer would search and process the prisoner's property. The turnkeys would then look after the prisoner's every need in the cells during their luxury stay in our fantastic ensuite single rooms. The civilian turnkeys also had to check the prisoners every hour and make them food. The regular guests could always be identified by strange jail-house etiquette and there was often be retribution between prisoners if these informal rules were broken.

One of our most regular customers kept getting arrested for being called Ronald McDonald. Cops all over the country used to think he was taking the piss and then, this in a time before fingerprint recognition and photographs on the PNC, we would get the phone call to verify who he was. The time in the cells was for most prisoners an opportunity for a rest, a hazard of the job as it were. If one prisoner were overly noisy and shouting for the turnkey repeatedly, there would be threats and abuse yelled from other adjoining cells.

When the prisoner came in they were always taken to the charge bar first, where the prisoner's details were recorded using an archaic old computer program called the 'prisoner management system' that, incredibly, was still in use when I left the police twenty-one years later. In theory this system meant that anything that happened to a prisoner was recorded and timed exactly so that the prisoner's care was auditable throughout. However, the police are very slow to adapt to new things and managers always know best. As a consequence, for many years before they were networked if the computer was booted up into the BIOS (Look this up if you don't like computers) the internal clock could be set to a different time and then anything whatsoever could be written into the prisoner's record. A large book behind the bar provided a back-up and was also, in the hands of the right duty officer, a fearsome weapon that could be brought down on the hands of any prisoner who dared to nonchalantly reach across the bar.

Prisoners were held at all times at the bar, or the duty officer would be quick to have words with the unfortunate cop afterwards. Any prisoner who was excessively aggressive or cheeky could expect to have an interesting time at the charge bar, being held in a gooseneck hold to cause pain or worse.

The strange thing was the guests or 'neds' respected this. It was an odd time when things began to change. I always believed in treating prisoners well and treating them the way you would want to be treated; many years afterwards at the Police College I would tell students about how I regretted it when it became a matter of fact.

I think a lot of cops forget this. It's strange that many jobs in the police have a 'tenure', meaning that you can't do it for more than a set period of time, three years or so usually. I always felt there should be tenure for being a response uniform-shift cop, just so it didn't become too matter of fact to be at the sharp end all the time. Poor Jimmy did nothing else his entire career, thirty years of being on uniform shifts and getting shafted at the sharp end; he went quite quite mad of course.

But being a response cop is, within the police, regarded by many as the lowest of the low. I have no idea why, because it's the best, most important public-facing part of the job — and I loved it.

Shift Induction

At some point in every new probationer's journey comes the first practical joke to be played upon them. To be fair I really didn't see this one coming. I suspect so many people in the office were in on it and it just seemed so unlikely. I came in on an early shift as usual. A second probationer had joined the shift by now, following five weeks behind me. He'd been neighboured with my regular nebs, Brian the Brain, and as a result I was a little miffed to see the cop I trusted and who had guided me for a whole five weeks heading off with someone else. My gaffer asked me to go and see the CID upstairs and off I trotted up the big wrought-iron spiral staircase.

I was met by the ladies of the Female and Child Unit, or FACU, who dealt with rapes and sexual offences. A more inappropriate acronym has probably never existed. I was offered a nice cup of tea by Jen from the FACU and shown into a small room containing six video recorders and six screens. Several large clear plastic bags lay around, each containing hundreds of VHS videos.

The Detective Chief Inspector and a Detective Sgt told me how my day was going to go. It seemed that the bags contained many videos seized in a house raid that were suspected to be videos of an illegal pornographic nature. Some gay, some straight, some just plain old normal run-of-the-mill dwarf-donkey sex. I was quite innocent really; nowadays all this is one search away in Google. The idea was that a court and a jury would not sit and watch them all to prove a case. If need be the court would show one only in order to prove the charge — but all would be documented. I was to watch two at a time until the content was known, fill out a form documenting what sexual acts were on each tape and then return them numbered and cross-referenced to another set of bags for return to the production store.

I began to watch and it soon became quite obvious that some degree of sorting had already been done by the previous owner. One particular bag contained what can best be described as entertaining horizontal gymnastics performed mainly by attractive ladies with some assisting men.

I've had tougher days. The Detective Chief inspector however was taking videos from the other bag which appeared to consist mainly of gay sex and rape-themed gay videos.

The Chief inspector kept leaving the room and my second new CID friend was quick to tell me that this was because he was that way 'motivated' he'd been gay for some time and found watching the videos required a break from time to time as it were. And each time, when he returned, he edged up close to me and started talking about where my flat was and what I did on nights off. I was polite and still quite happy in my little world of not being out walking around Alpha, but, as the conversation progressed, the DCI offered to let me take a video away. At that point, I reasoned this was a test and refused but then, to counter my refusal, he said he was happy to come round that night and watch it with me. I said I was going out to ride my motorbike that night but then he said he would like to see me in leather, asking if it restricted my movement.

Finally, he stroked my leg. I jumped up and the room exploded in laughter, both FACU ladies bursting into the room in hysterics. Of course, neither of my new friends was either in the CID management, divisional managers or anything other than straight, twisted practical jokers. I was sent back out on patrol and the next probationer was brought in for the same wind up.

Crimes and offences were recorded on a triplicate carbonated form called a 3:24:1 or CR.

It was elegantly simple. There was a big box of blank CR's in pretty much every room in the office. After noting details of a crime out on the street, all that was required was to fill out a few boxes on the form. The date, time, details of the reporter, the crime and a little box to be filled out with some details of suspects and the enquiry carried out. The form had three parts,

The first white copy would get sent up to HQ to be filed.

The pink copy was put onto the computer system in the bar so it could be searched force-wide, by the night-shift bar officer and then indexed and filed in the bar, or with CID for more serious things. This meant that they could be found easily.

The green copy stayed with the reporting officer until it had been investigated. 'Always eat your greens', as we used to say.

Joking aside it was a brilliant system and three or four CR's from the day before could be done in minutes while listening to muster. There were no crime managers, no extraneous people involved at all. You could see what had happened in the division in seconds by flicking through the 'pinks', and it was easy to find any CR by virtue of an index sheet at the front of the folder. Clearly it wasn't expensive or complicated enough, and no senior managers with hundreds of staff were required to do a day shift in an office somewhere to make it work. The best bit was that as the crime was recorded on the Command and Control computer and the paper CR was really just the detail needed for the police report. There was no urgency behind it, so they could be done the next day, or even the next week, preferably when things were quiet. In effect when things were busy there was absolutely no reason for cops to be in the office unless they had just arrested someone. It was efficient; cops stayed on the street, relatively incorruptible because crimes couldn't be changed after the white copy was completed.

It had to go. Managers didn't like it — clearly.

Things were a lot simpler back then. Take domestic disputes for instance. Domestic disputes were dealt with like any other call. In Scotland the basic level of evidence that needs to be presented before a court is that of two independent sources both leading the court to prove that piece of evidence or corroboration. Corroboration is an essential part of Scottish law and has formed the cornerstone of one of the finest legal systems in the world for hundreds of years. It does however cause a problem because domestic disputes and domestic assaults are very rarely corroborated.

So when a call was received what would usually would happen is this:

The man of the house was told to 'Get tae fuck', go to his maws, friends or anywhere. If he came back, he would get the jail for a Breach of the Peace; the woman was told to go and see a solicitor the next day and make sure she got an interdict with a power of arrest. Important about the power of arrest, we always stressed that bit or the police had no real power. Then, if the man hadn't already left, we took his money, gave it to the missus, and drove him at least five miles away, ideally in the pissing rain with no jacket. By the time he got back, he was knackered and cold and she would take him back because the police were now the common enemy; either that or she would have left.

There were few repeat calls. In fact, the local beat man would be very aware of what had gone wrong and in the event of a repeat offence it was usually dealt with by the man of the household having a frank and interesting discussion with the local cop and the cop from the neighbouring beat.

This informal way of proceeding had to change, and rightly so, but what happened next, instead of actually dealing with the problem, was a staggering amount of bureaucracy. It started with a form held at the bar so that if a call came in it would be easy to see if this was a repeat call. Then the form was held at the bar and faxed to divisional HQ. Then twenty-six questions needed to be asked of the victim and a Vulnerable Persons Database form (VPD) to be completed too. Then a computerised VPD was created and that involved phoning an operator and waiting in a queue, and a referral to Victim Support. Then the same went for every person or child in the household.

Then the VDP and a CR and you had to detain the man for six hours, even if there was no evidence, as a 'cooling-off period', despite the fact this was clearly illegal. And then an intelligence report and get a supervisor to put a lengthy update on the CR as to why everything that had happened had happened and in what order. Then you had to do all the above and do a special dance in the back yard and click your heels together three times before singing the national anthem backwards. Actually I made that last one up, but I wanted to make sure you were still paying attention.

It wasn't that there was any problem dealing with the call or detaining and dealing with the bad person; the duplicated or triplicate bureaucracy involved became simply staggering and resulted in situation where domestics became things to avoid. And that's a shame because domestics deserve to be dealt with properly and with compassion for the victim, not with politically-correct rules and huge piles of paperwork. Throughout this time, I often heard the older cops utter the phrase 'the job's fucked'. They kinda meant it but as the years progressed and it became a stock phrase it was abbreviated to TJF or Tango Juliet Foxtrot. Eventually the job had been fucked so often it had kids and settled down.

First Interview

My first proper interview of a suspect was for a very minor theft. I had been working with 'The Hack'. He was best described as a bit old school. He had been sent to Juliet Alpha from Juliet Bravo. It was certainly easy to see the locals held him in high esteem when I had occasion to travel to Bravo office due to the number of local walls adorned with the words 'Hack's a bastard'.

Nice. I have to assume the locals had a whip round and got him a nice present when he left.

He told me to note everything down in my notebook and gave me some tactics to use during the interview. Our suspect had been detained in terms of Section 2 of the Criminal Justice Scotland act 1982.

Basically, I had six hours to talk to him after which he must be released, charged or arrested. I got the cell keys and asked the civilian 'turnkey' to sign him out of his detention room for interview.

The hack and I then went and collected him from his cell and led him to an interview room in the CID corridor.

Unlike interviews in 'The Bill', interviews in Scotland are usually carried out simply by noting the replies down on a sheet of paper or within a police notebook—not all officers are tape trained because police officers are, generally, not trusted by police supervisors and certainly not with anything as complicated as a tape recorder. Guns, knives, people's lives and that sort of thing, yes, but not a tape recorder, or, strangely, changing a car light bulb. I really never understood that one. Changing a light bulb involved putting the car off the road or taking a trip to the twenty-four-hour garage at Helen St, which is odd because I can do it in my own car.

I sat opposite the suspect with the Hack with his many years of CID experience on my left. I had prepared five questions, each of which I assumed would result in a lengthy confession.

I meticulously and nervously took all the suspect's details and wrote them down, even though I'd asked them already when he came into the office.

At last I started my interrogation. It was going to be merciless.

'So,... did you do it?'

'No'

That sort of threw me; I was really counting on him saying, yes.

'Ermmmmm—well, I think you did.'

'I really didn't.'

'There's been an allegation made to me regarding a theft.'

'Well I wanna know who the alligator is.'

At this point Hack was visibly shaking trying not to laugh.

'Oh! Ok well, sorry, we'll get you your stuff back and let you go'

I was beginning to suspect the CID was just going to have to manage without my amazing interview skills for a while. Hack meanwhile was laughing his head off and spent the rest of the shift re-enacting my interview to everyone. To be fair, interviewing, surprisingly, hadn't really been taught as such at the college, taking statements was practiced but not really any practice interviews. Many years later there would be limited instruction for basic recruits in the Price model and interview techniques.

First Appraisal.

Skids was a chief inspector who can best be described at eccentric. He was very intelligent and apparently a member of MENSA the organisation for intelligent types. He spent most of his time, as highly intelligent people do in the job, being under-appreciated and getting the piss ripped out of him. One of the first times I met him he had just come into work and had only one epaulette on and a huge bung of cotton wool sticking out one ear. I had no idea why no one said anything. It just seemed so matter of fact.

His office was a 'porta cabin' in the back yard. There were a few of them there including the old typists' ones, which were mainly used for filing and getting pissed up off the Sunday-night shift. It was quite common off the night shift to sit and have a bevy in the 'porta cabin', and usually a few of the gaffers would start long before 7am when the shift ended. Of course drink and the job went together a lot better back them, and I just caught the end of the days where a pub owner would offer you a pint for standing by his pub after the alarm went off. This sounds awful now but you can't judge it by the standards of today.

I had already gone through my appraisal with my Sgt and the Inspector so I was looking forward to seeing the Chief Inspector. After all my report was good and I thought I was doing well. Not so it seemed. I got a horrific appraisal, mainly because it wasn't me. I could just make out that the upside-down name on top of the form wasn't mine and was presumably that of another probationer on a different shift. I pointed this out and was told that I would need to work on it. I wasn't sure how to do that so I just ate humble pie and said I was very sorry and I'd try harder. I then signed the other cop's appraisal and felt I should probably try and sign their name. The problem was, I didn't know it; I was in the bizarre position of having to ask to see the front page to find out who I was so I could sign. This didn't seem to faze the Chief Inspector at all. Odd.

Years later he would write an article for the newspapers criticising our new Chief Constable and what he was doing to policing. He was on the ball when he wrote that article. I like to think whoever got my appraisal was happy; presumably he had to sign my name.

Chapter 6

First Suicide
Gordon the Big Express

It's hard to understand if you've never been there, the thoughts behind someone who feels the world has nothing left to offer. If you've been there and felt the despair, and the overloading sense of grief you might understand. It's a different state of mind and for anyone in that position the potential for the pain to be gone makes it seem worthwhile. Tempting, and a way out. When you're there, suicide isn't something you fear or dread; it's the cure. It can make you happy and make the loneliness go away.

The first suicide I saw was a man hit by a train. He had a family, a job and a wife. He'd stood in the path of the train, turned his back on it and waited. He didn't wait long and it's fair to say the train won. He was impaled on the front of the train, head smashed open by the impact and torso mashed around a large metal bit of Gordon, the big express train from the magical island of Sodor. The fat controller would not have been happy because Gordon got a bit messy. The man's legs had clearly been dragged over the track for the mile or so that the train took to stop, as a result of which there wasn't much left from about ten inches below his knees. Blood ran down the front of the train and swirled in pretty curves down one side of the engine in the streaks and curves caused by the airflow as the train slowed. The passengers on the train were stuck on board while the photographer and British Transport Police were summoned.

I wondered about what went through the man's mind before impact, apart from the front of a train that is. In years to come I wondered a lot about death and what someone thinks just before it, when it is inevitable or even welcome. When I've been low I can understand it, but I also imagine the consequences and this is something I don't think many suicide victims do. In my head when I've been there, I imagine that the world ending for me is the same as the world that's left. I imagine most people are the same. The farmer who puts his shotgun in his mouth and blows the top of his head all over the ceiling, probably doesn't imagine that's the scene that people will find. He'll write a nice letter and imagine his grandchildren reading it. He won't picture it splattered with blood in a police production bag in a dark dusty production storage room for years with no one giving a fuck.

The next train death that I saw, a woman had carefully written a note, taken off her glasses, folded her jacket before stepping out into infinity. She didn't imagine the mess, or the train driver shaking as he gave a statement. The passengers filed out of the stationary train and up an embankment to waiting buses hired by Scotrail in the evening drizzle. No one cared who she was or why, just that they were late home to watch the final of X-factor or Britain's Got Talent.

When I've been there and thought about it, the people I'm angry with, they feel pain after my death and realise I was in pain and maybe they regret things they've done, but I've seen the other side and no one cares. The cops who turn up will have a laugh and a joke then stand with folded arms impatiently complaining about why the identification branch are taking so long; the forensic people won't turn up and cast some amazing insight on anything, which only happens in TV shows. The body will be unceremoniously thrown in a black body-bag and taken away in a black van. No one will care beyond immediate next of kin; life will go on and people will forget.

So if you're there, and wondering if it's worth doing; it isn't. Sort yourself out; go for a walk in the sun; see a doctor; go get pissed. Hell, just go and do *anything*. People don't care — and believe you can get through it, because you can.

And anyway I've never found a good way to go. The best I can think of is hypothermia on a mountain. Strangely people who have gassed themselves in cars look happiest, but that is apparently due to the carbon monoxide in the blood and not because of actually meeting forty virgins or whatever at the gates of heaven, plus it's pretty hard to do nowadays with modern cars.

The first 'jumper' I missed and I was a bit disappointed. My neighbour and I had just left the 'Krazy K', Kilo Divisions HQ office, when we got the call to go to Turdside Oval because of someone on the roof. We started heading up Great West Road at speed when the control room told us, 'Alpha 11 no need to rush, he's on the ground, and he didn't use the lift'.

KENNETHEAD ROAD.

I had become something of a normal cop in Alpha once I could drive police vehicles and I felt confident. It wasn't long before I became increasingly nonchalant. It's a strange gradual thing that happens to all cops, and you don't really notice it happening to yourself. I was working a back shift with Craig who had started six months after me, and Wendy who had started six months before. We were out in a big, long-wheelbase marked LDV Sherpa minivan in Juliet Alpha. It was ok and I was quite enjoying my backshift, having a good laugh, driving around and annoying the local kids. There were the usual calls to the schemes to move on street footballers that could be dealt with by shouting, 'get tae fuck ya wee bastards', out the window of the police car before flooring it and trying to run over the ball.

The usual disturbances. Nothing that wasn't quick and easy to deal with.

Our divisional control room had a cop from Juliet Charlie subdivision working one night, covering for our own controller who was off sick. He was a good calm guy, very capable, and knew the Charlie area really well. I however really didn't know anything but Juliet Alpha. When the control room asked us if we could help out in another area I was happy to help. We were all keen and between us possessed a street map.

The call was a domestic disturbance in Kennethead Road, part of Juliet Bravo sub division apparently. The house number and flat position were given by a screaming female calling 999 before she was cut off. We looked it up on the map and found it pretty easily, a long road running from the south past, old soon-to-be-demolished flats and skirting a rough area of the city and a golf course. So far so good. The road was a couple of miles long and, with the exception of a couple of small houses, all the house numbers on the road clearly related to the south end. We explored, searched and found nothing, no block of flats.

For well over an hour we drove up and down the road and searched side streets it. Only when the nightshift at Juliet Charlie came on and heard us repeatedly asking for directions on the radio did it become clear there was a second Kennethead Road and we had got it all very wrong. When we finally arrived and went into the house, the first thing I noticed was a dog that was cheerfully licking up blood from a full ashtray in the hall and the domestic disturbance was now a serious assault verging on an attempted murder – although, because the lady of the house was uncorroborated, it actually ended up as a 'Complaint Noted' and no further action was taken because that was the way things were back then. The alternative was to close it off as a 'FAGI' (False alarm good intent) or 'LOS' (Lima Oscar Sierra or a Lot of shite).

Of course you could write this 'one off' to human failure, and a controller who normally worked one area, trying to cover calls in another area, combined with three new cops who were uncertain outside the familiarity of their usual beats. I should feel bad, but I never let anyone down on purpose; it was the nature of the job in a time before blame when everyone tries to criticise cops for every tiny human mistake.

The strange thing is the police management never learnt from incidents like this. They blame the individuals that they themselves have set up to fail. When the control rooms in remote areas such as the west coast were moved centrally to the city years later we would lose years' worth of human knowledge worth its weight in gold during a high-pressure incident. Local controllers knew the areas they worked and often the individuals involved, and usually had their own experiences from previous similar incidents; they knew where the roads were dangerous, the regulars who were wanted on warrants and the people out on bail; even which farmer to phone to get sheep from the road and back into a field; or how to get an alarm bell silenced. But when the control rooms for the West Coast first moved to the city, many control staff didn't even know that they were trying to send cops to an island at 3am and that the ferry would not be on until after 8am. It was a complete farce, covered up by the Police in the only way they knew how, by hiding it and denying there was a problem.

Years later I would hear from friends still in the job how the police failed two crash victims on the motorway only a few hundred yards from a service area and, as usual, the gaffers made those arrogant public statements that the police do so well and hoped it would go away. People fuck up from time to time, but the difference now is that the police are so over-stretched and mismanaged that failure is inevitable.

As a little aside, it really annoys me that in movies when the hero or heroine cops gets on the radio to the control room urgently they never get told to 'stand by, we're all on the phone' or there's a long silence 'cos they are all on their break and no one is logged into PNC to do a check anyway.

Just sayin'.

PRISONER ESCORTS

In the days before a well-known security company became closely involved, the police in Scotland managed all the movement of prisoners outside of the Scottish Prison Service themselves. It seems odd now, but it was quite normal for the big bus to arrive at Juliet Alpha Police office every morning and pick up all the bad people to go to court. The courts branch was large and an easy pre-retirement job for older cops in the days when the job still cared about them. If, however, someone needed to be fetched more urgently, then two cops from the shift would be sent to get them. Sometimes this involved a quick flight but what was more fun was if someone who refused to fly was arrested on a Scottish warrant either at the other end of the country or better still in furthest Englandshire, then two cops would drive or go by train and, usually, get a night on the drink. It was great.

The first time this happened, I was sent home to get out of uniform and into a suit. When I returned, myself and Andy, one of the more senior cops on the shift, were given a talking to by the Duty Officer. We were off to Cardiff to get a prisoner arrested on a Scottish apprehension warrant. Woohoo! We would be taken to central station, pick up our tickets and arrive late that day in Cardiff. Our hotel was booked by 'Farce' control in Prat St, and the next day we would be picked up by the local cops, taken to get our prisoner, then would swiftly return home.

Splendid.

There was a catch however. Under no circumstances were we to get completely pissed like the last two cops had on the train on the way north; they rather embarrassingly had to be woken up by their prisoner when they got into central station. He was nice though and had gone to get them both a coffee from the restaurant car before he gave them a shake to wake them up. Warnings heeded and ground rules laid down, we headed off.

On arrival at Cardiff, a really nice, clean, unmarked, traffic car was waiting for us and the cops driving it were quite surprised when they found out who we were.

'I thought it would be your chief constable or something.' They told us that they'd been sent in the nice car because they assumed it was someone high up, due to the choice of hotel.

The hotel was awesome: swimming pool, mint on the pillow, fluffy dressing gown and slippers, and for dinner that night a lovely wine and lobster. I'd never had lobster before but it was nice. Later I went to my room and watched some pay movies on the on-demand TV. Let's not discuss what the movies were, but I would happily pay for the wine and movie when we checked out in the morning.

The next morning, we arrived at reception to find that everything had already been paid for by HQ at Coward's Castle. We sheepishly went to get our prisoner and made our way back to Scotland on the train. After some discussion on the train north, during which our prisoner offered his thoughts, I agreed to phone the admin travel people in Coward's Castle. We didn't take our prisoner's advice because the warrant was for fraud, so clearly he wasn't very good at it: we would pay for what we had got in the way of wine and entertainment because it was clearly out with what we were allowed. I was still in my probation and terrified of getting in trouble.

The girl on the phone just laughed and said that they get bills like that in from senior bosses all the time and not to worry about it—the next prisoner escort I did was a monumental piss up.

Maybe I was starting to get to cocky and needed a change; I was starting to make mistakes.

When Polly came up from Greenock I was quite chuffed to get neighboured up with her. She was quite funny with that dry sense of humour that people in the police develop and it was all new to me being the most experienced person in a crew. I'd probably had a year-and-a-half in the job at this time and I was still learning as I went along.

We were out walking in an area of old housing next to the local hospital when we got a call via our radios to go to 'the Circus', an area of flats and council houses near the motorway. This was not a good 'free cake' type of call; this was more the 'Granny might be dead' sort of thing.

When we got there, Mum, Dad and the kids were milling around. They had a key to the house but they couldn't get in because the chain was on the door, a bad sign because that meant that the somebody who locked the door was still inside or had evaporated. So really the choice was death or death.

Or alien abduction.

I could hear the TV blaring away in the house, but try as I might I could not kick the door in. The chain had enough give that it just bounced back each time, and it was too high up on the door to kick near the chain itself. I borrowed a screwdriver from a neighbour and managed to reach in around the slightly open door and, by feeling my way, slowly unscrew the chain inside. A lot later, and I mean a lot later, we finally got in. By that time, I knew what was in the house so I asked the family to wait while I went inside. I didn't see any point in upsetting them.

We explored the house, slowly climbing stairs up to the noisy TV room. I was a bit cautious because I'd once broken into a house via a first-floor window, thinking the occupant was dead, and had scared the crap out myself and the old deaf woman who was making soup in the kitchen. It pays to move slowly and be cautious. In the room upstairs I found the old lady lying in front of the electric fire, slightly toasty and slightly stuck to the floor as dead bodies tend to after a while. Dead bodies look dead, not like dead bodies on TV which look alive. Dead bodies look waxy and grey with a sort of red tide mark,

67

where the blood has settled with gravity after the heart stops pumping. It's called *livor mortis* incidentally and for some reason they never show it in movies or TV detective shows, which is a shame because every cop in the world watches TV and spoils it for the whole family by yelling at the TV, 'that's not a dead body! Look; you can see the actor breathing! This is pish, and why are there three marked traffic cars outside sitting with blue lights on, the traffic would never bother to turn up to help the CID, and if they did they wouldn't get oot the motor, and why is someone pretending to tape things off when everyone is already inside the locus, and why is the photographer already at the scene photographing bugger all, and not five hours late when everyone else is pissed off, and why isn't there a probationer standing in the rain for hours outside?' And so on and so forth until the rest of the family tell them to go make some tea and calm down by counting backwards from one million.

Anyway, I had a quick look around and turned off the TV; no need to check a pulse as the woman was clearly suffering from a really nasty case of being dead.

Half an hour later, in the spare room while waiting on the casualty surgeon, I was going through some of the questions on the Sudden Death form with the family which included a question on the deceased's parents' occupations. The family said all the details would be on the birth certificates which were in the bureau in the same room as dead lady. I wandered through leaving Polly with the family. As I looked through the paperwork, I heard a slight noise behind me and turned. I was sure the dead old lady had moved. I knelt down and thought I could feel a pulse although I was really not too sure.

Best to be safe. I got on the radio for an ambulance forgetting that Polly's radio would transmit what I was saying to the family. They came storming through while I was still deciding what to do and after a few minutes we were getting a bit of a response. It was the longest, most awkward wait I have ever had for an ambulance — and by the time I left we had the old woman sitting on the couch having a cup of tea. Perhaps she decided being dead just wasn't her thing.

Whoops.

You'd think, considering I'd magically fought and brought Granny back from the grim reaper's icy cold clutches, the family would have cheered up. A curious aside to this story was that after it had been passed round the office and Chinese whispers had exaggerated it, one of the other cops from another shift, now paranoid that a body was still alive because it farted, and having been given a long ETA for an ambulance, decided to put it into the passenger seat of the police car and drive it to the hospital. The hospital staff helpfully pointed out that the dead person was indeed dead, was unlikely to get less dead and therefore he could take his new friend and 'get tae fuck'. And off he fucked, to the morgue, with the body still sitting beside him in the passenger seat and two cops in the back seat finding the whole thing hilarious. Dead bodies make funny groaning noises and fart. It's just a thing.

SUICIDE WATCH OR 'CONSTANT OBSERVATIONS'

Was the short straw. Sitting for a whole shift watching a prisoner through a Perspex screen as they sat in a cell, staring back at you sitting watching them bored outside. If you were lucky and the shift was quiet you got regular tea and biscuits, if you were unlucky you might get a toilet break once a shift.

The absolute worst thing was that it was usually long after your shift had gone home that someone on the new shift would finally get out of muster and come and let you away—maybe. The most important thing was not to get a bit of paper and a pen and try and play hangman with the suicidal prisoner. That was frowned upon for some reason.

Chapter 7

Gaffer Top Trumps

*'We trained hard, but it seemed that every time we were beginning
to form up into teams, we would be reorganized. I was to learn later
in life that we tend to meet any new situation by reorganizing;
and a wonderful method it can be for creating the illusion of progress
while producing confusion, inefficiency, and demoralization.'*

Falsely attributed to Gaius Petronius Arbiter. Quote is from
Charlton Ogburn, JC. (1911-1998), in *Harper's Magazine*,
'Merrill's Marauders: The truth about an incredible adventure'
(Jan 1957), but he could have been discussing the police
instead. Especially when someone needs promoted. Every
year in 'J' Division, cops would get swapped around, usually
just after summer.

Cops would usually get told with about a week's notice,
enough time to sort out paperwork and hopefully have a
goodbye piss-up with their shift. Usually reorganisation was
to redistribute troublemakers and to prevent an outbreak of
morale or competence.

I can imagine the staff officer sitting with each sub-
divisional officer playing top trumps with the personnel cards:

'I'll swap you a drunk for a shagger.'

'Hmmm, Ok but you get the dizzy split-arse who's off sick all the time.'

(Split arse is a nice police term for lady police man)

'Ermmm ok, but if I take the shagger, you swap that one who we all know is stealing drugs out the production store for a decent cop.'

'I've not got any... seriously.'

Actually the above conversation is ridiculous because almost every cop is a shagger, nature of the job as discussed elsewhere in this book. At best, shy ugly bastards like me just couldn't get any.

'J' division could be like a penal colony sometimes; you got in bother elsewhere you were sent to Juliet Alpha. We used to joke that more people had criminal records inside the office than outside.

But now, three years in and I was off to Juliet Bravo. Whoop!

I wonder if I was used as a bargaining card in top trumps or if I was a bad card to have. I like to hope I was a good card, but every shift has a complete fuck-wit and if you thought your shift were all ok then that by deduction meant the fuck-wit had to be you. On another note, I was sad to go to Bravo because at Alpha the delivery driver from the bakers would hand over all the left-over stuff from the shop each day in exchange for us not annoying the fuck out of him. Night-shift cakes were good.

Juliet Bravo was a much smaller and more modern office than divisional HQ at Shetland St.

It was located on the corner of Cockburn Crescent and Cockburn Road, opposite the local shopping centre where all the local kids hung around the heating vents smoking drugs. The shifts were about the same size but Bravo was a very different area. Alpha had some resemblance of industry, from the remaining shipyard, and the number of small businesses dotted around industrial estates the length of the sub-division; Bravo had very little going for it in places, just 60's identical housing blocks that were largely empty and shuttered, with graffiti-covered stainless-steel covering the windows. There were numerous streets of old corporation houses built during the 30's, mostly four-in-a-block houses, two-up-two-down, and council houses with a mix of working people and the unemployed. Drugs were rife and in some areas the anti-police feeling was very strong.

Early on at Bravo I made the mistake of leaving my police-issue notebook on the dashboard of a police car to go to a call, not so I could avoid writing I should point out, but because I could take in a paper Crime report form back then and just fill it out at the scene, or, even better, give it to the complainer and ask them to do it themselves. Leaving a notebook anywhere was a rookie mistake, and leaving it in an office unattended would usually result in one of my colleagues drawing a penis on a random page. It's a police thing. It's funny to see someone's face when they're taking a statement from a member of the public and watch as they have to skip two pages. In theory this is a problem when going to court, but I never knew a cop who didn't have a real notebook and a court notebook.

On this day I got a shout over the radio while I was in the house because another Bravo car had arrived to back us up just as our car was being set on fire. No one in Alpha ever tried to set fire to my car. Welcome to Bravo.

At the other end of sub-division Bravo was an area of expensive, huge, sandstone houses and luxury hotels near the centre of the city with good access onto the newly constructed motorway. When the new motorway to the south was first opened it was ahead of schedule and not many knew the speed-limit legislation had not been passed through parliament yet. I used to scream up that road on my Suzuki to early shift like I was on fire. The office had good morale and I had a great shift. I worked most of the time with 'Kendo', a cop of similar service and equal enthusiasm. Both of us would see our jobs change over the next few years from police officers to statistical whipping boys and both of us would leave in disgust. He went long before me and I wish I'd left when he did.

One difference was in the care of prisoners. Bravo had a small number of cells, which were used for holding prisoners who would not go to court. If they were going to go to court they would be transferred to Shetland St by the nightshift around 4am. But the cells in Bravo were used for more than just prisoners; they also became temporary production stores on occasion and also holding areas for the identification parade room, due to the ID parade room being adjacent to the cell block.

I preferred them to the huge Victorian cells at Alpha and we came to know our regular customers pretty well. It was nice being so near to a cell block and a big change from the huge custody stations that would be centralised and used years later. They resulted in hours of wasted time driving and waiting to process a prisoner, miles from your own police office.

I was delighted when, one night-shift, a habitual car-thief tried to get away from us by crashing his stolen car and running off into Bellend Secondary School, and while he cleared the fence and 'Fluffy' the faithful police doggie made it too, the rest of us didn't. The fence was too high and the gate too far away and also locked, and I didn't like to run in any case; it was undignified. For what seemed like minutes we would hear ned boy shouting for help as 'Fluffy' played with his new squeaky toy.

Eventually, and after a great deal of shouting by the human half of the dog-car crew, Fluffy sheepishly trotted back. The car-thieving young ned had obviously got some well-placed kicks in, and Fluffy had a few obvious cuts around his face, although it's fair to say the dog had won. After being put on his leash and waiting patiently however our four-legged friend got his revenge. The car thief was retrieved from the school grounds and handcuffed behind his back and as he leant forward to get into the back seat of a waiting police car. Fluffy, seizing the chance, caught his handler off guard, leapt forward and chomped ned boy right on the arse, causing him to straighten up and hit his head on the door frame of the car.

Anyone who says dogs don't have emotions and can't smile has never seen the look on that dog's face. Incidentally, by then an idea had taken hold: every time that particular 'ned' enjoyed the hospitality of our cell block at Bravo we would sneak down the cell corridor, make whimpering and growling noises and scratch at the door. Maybe he was more a cat person.

Another difference was in the menu. No standard prisoner's meals here. The routine was to get a pie supper from the local chippy and, after nabbing a few chips, give the prisoner what was left.

The first time I was sent for a prisoner's meal I didn't know this so I went to the supermarket and got a lovely salad. The turnkey was less than chuffed because the cell needed washing down after the resultant prisoner's protest.

CHAPTER 8

SEEING SOMEONE
DIE UP CLOSE FOR THE FIRST TIME

Before the police I'd seen people die, but from a distance and quickly, almost clinically.

Seeing someone die right in front of you is a humbling experience, when you're close enough to feel their last breath and see their chest stop moving. The day I became nonchalant about it should really have been the day I left the police, but in fact I became blasé about it without knowing I had.

I saw many people die over twenty-one years and every single one left an impression on me.

A hot summer evening in Bravo.

I was working with Kevin, a jovial guy from the community-policing team with a bit more service than me. He had a father who was high up in the job and had been around the police and its culture for a long time and he was confident as a result. Very good to work with though, because he had a lot of authority and a bit of city patter to help him talk to the 'neds' in a way they seemed to respect. I couldn't manage that easily, and I had to have a very different persona at work than at home.

We had attended a call near to the railway line between Juliet Bravo and Juliet Alpha and it had been a busy back shift;

Bravo was 'jumping' so our car and every other car had been going from call to call, with the controllers stacking more and more outstanding incidents.

When the call first came out it was given as a 'Code 71, two males fighting on the grass near to the shops on Lillyside Road'. A pretty usual hot evening call when the locals would fight over very little as tempers frayed in the summer sun. There's no better police officer than the rain and the cold. Initially there was no one free to attend this call, but it seemed matter of fact and routine in any case but, as the call was repeated over the radio, it became more urgent. This was one of those very rare occasions when I thought I could hear something in the controller's voice that gave away something of what the person phoning the police was really saying to them. Of course, for us, it would simply come over the radio as an assault, the controller having to be concise and accurate to cut down on radio time. This was in the days before digital 'airwave' radios, so when the controller was transmitting it meant no one could talk back urgently. I could never have carried out the job that our controllers did because, even though they heard people screaming, complaining and even dying on the phone, they always tried to stay relatively calm on the radio.

Kevin and I left our call; we were the first car able to respond. This was in the days before body armour and due to the hot weather my stab protection came in the form of a white shirt and tie. It did look very smart though; I would be a really well dressed corpse if it all went wrong. We advised the control room that we could now go and started making our way towards the shops on Lillyside Road. The initial location had been on a grass area next to the river but had since been updated. As we approached we were told over the radio that a male had made off and that the fight had involved a sword. This wasn't too unusual as an update actually. Often members of the public will panic or phone in exaggerated reports but not this time.

As we pulled up outside the shops and I got out of the car I saw a young man lying on his back on the footpath. He was wearing a red and white T-shirt and jeans. There was something very wrong; his T-shirt was lifted up and his head was rolling from side to side and a glazed look filled his eyes as we went to him. As we did so it became obvious he had very serious injuries: he had been attacked with a samurai sword and blood was the reason his top was white and blood-red. His gut was cut open and it was easy to see the weakening of his heart beat as the spurts of blood from his gaping wounds became weaker and less frequent. I remember thinking how odd it was to be able to see the layers of yellow fat on a human body under the skin and the way that the locals watching us couldn't stop looking but wouldn't come close. Dark red blood was seeping across the pavement as I knelt on his right side, real thick congealing blood and not the sort that adorns cheap horror films. I kept glancing up at Kevin facing me as we tried to do CPR. We had a flimsy mouth guard but I couldn't find my gloves. It made no difference anyway. I could feel blood through my trousers at the knees as I knelt. It was all up my arms and soon splattered on my white shirt from the young man's rasping, last death-breaths.

Kevin seemed much calmer than me and he'd shouted in for help but both of us forgot the actual danger in the original call; we were far too busy watching this young man running out of time. I have so much respect for uniform response cops because at that stage in anyone's service you just run into whatever scene everyone else is running away from. The public always idolise the CID or firearms or the special teams but the hardest most adrenaline-filled years of my service were the first few on the street. In reality there is no heroic insightful CID in the drawing room announcing a 'one of you in this room killed Professor Plum' moment, and major enquiries are usually very boring. Uniform cops, the ones who arrive first with no idea what they are facing, are the ones who get the real excitement, and deserve the praise — but they almost never get it.

I was on autopilot, covered in so much warm blood that I could smell it mingled with the fresh smell of grass on that lovely summer evening with its perfect blue skies blending into a blood-orange sunset. I would go home exhausted to wonder why neither of us had thought about where the sword or where the second male was, although it didn't matter because that wasn't our first concern.

Ross, who years later was to be my inspector at the college, was next to arrive, but by this stage I was too busy watching this young man die while Kevin and I tried to save him, to speak much. A sword does a really amazing amount of damage. I hadn't realised it was easier to reach inside his chest and compress the heart by hand rather than do compressions. I wouldn't have anyway but the doctors who tried to bring him back briefly in accident and emergency gave it a try.

When extras die in movies because they are stabbed or shot, it happens quickly; only the good guy survives being wounded. Real life is never like that. Real people often die slowly and in pain.

The Ambulance crew arrived quickly but for me it seemed like an eternity. Afterwards I stood by that patch of blood for hours, with a jacket to keep me warm and to hide the mess I was in, protecting the scene while the murder investigation began. CID officers leisurely turning up in nice suits and shiny shoes carrying folders full of paperwork and an air of authority. At that stage in my career it was always nice to hand over a murder or a fatal road crash to the professionals. It was almost as if an air of calm descended when the CID or traffic turned up to a scene.

I tried to save nine people with no luck during the rest of my time in the job, before finally bringing someone back, giving an end to my 100% CPR kill rate. In truth many were beyond saving but I did what I could anyway, often for the benefit of those who were watching. During one of my initial driving courses an elderly man fell over on the pavement next to our car. We were heading west on Great West Road and although the car was a plain white Rover and we were generally discouraged from getting involved in anything during the driving course, this was clearly something we had to deal with.

The civilian driving instructor tried to get hold of the control room, whilst my fellow student driver and I tried our best to save the old man. A nurse had also seen what was happening and came over to help. After a very short while she gave me a look and whispered to me that it looked like 'he had gone'. We kept going though and the nurse gave me a funny look because I guess maybe she just thought I was wasting my time. I suppose in a hospital she would work under different set of rules, but the things that kept me going until the ambulance arrived were the two tiny crying eyes from the old man's granddaughter, who was watching the whole thing from a few metres away. The nurse must have picked up on this too and on the reason why I kept looking behind her, because when the ambulance crew arrived she spoke in medical terms and they too kept the act up even after the machine clearly said no — at least until he was lifted into the ambulance and door shut behind him. Luckily he was a local man and known to passers-by so the kid was looked after by others until her parents could arrive.

I seemed to know anyway. I always felt there was a time, a spark or a look that told me when someone had died. It's just there and then it's gone. I couldn't see it for a long time but in later years I felt it was there. I'm not religious at all; I just think it's a thing we're all slightly programmed to pick up on. Years later, when my mother died, I'd been with her that day but had left to stay at my sister's. When I was woken at 4am by my mobile phone ringing and drove the mile to the hospital it was already too late.

I walked into the room and knew.

I'd missed my dad dying too, in exactly the same room some years earlier, but when my mother died I was trying to deal with two family-liaison officer deployments at the same time, so I think it hit me harder.

Death became a sort of odd travelling companion and one of whom I was quite proud. It was rewarding to deal with something so important and to be able to help others through it. And the way to deal with that was simply – humour, sickly, dark and offensive to anyone outside the circle of those of us who dealt with it but, for many cops, that was the thing that kept work as work and let you go home and forget about it. Leading that double life of death at work and a lie at home became harder with time, but I always thought I was in control. I don't think the public, and I include myself in this when I've needed the police, really see the struggle that can exist between the job and the emotions of the person behind the uniform, nor the kindness and hurt that can build up there. Dealing with the intimacy of death becomes a burden as well as a buzz, especially when it's close.

Working in Baytown way up on the west coast many years later, I attended a meeting in Lochord with the rest of the traffic unit for the subdivision. It was the pre-Christmas meeting and the inspector was on good form. The meeting was held on the overlap between the early shift, which consisted of just me from my office, and the backshift from several offices. That way as many people as possible could make it. It sticks in my head that 'Inspector Gadget' was asked what he was doing for Christmas and he dryly chirped back, 'ah just the usual: sacrifice some virgins and chickens and stuff'. He lived in the middle of nowhere and I'm pretty sure they still burn witches that far out west and think the Wicker Man is a documentary.

I had to leave early and drive back up the road to Baytown in the Discovery, the unit's four-wheel drive, not an ideal car on fast sweeping but wet roads. I razzed it up the road as fast as I could and as I took a left hander I completely lost the back end. The rear wheels steeped out and I skidded sideways across onto the opposing lane, before catching it and getting back under control. I carried on and finished work. Later that day a woman travelling up the same road lost it on a left-hand bend a few hundred yards after the one I had skidded on. It was always bad for diesel and oil because of a waste tip that was on that section of road and because of all the trucks climbing the hill out of town, all combined with water running off the hill on one side.

This woman did exactly what I did, but met a council van travelling up the hill out of Baytown. Her family estate took the crash well but it was a sideways impact with the corner of the council van impacting the driver's door. She died in the car but her two very young kids were in the back seat and walked away almost unhurt. What made it so tragic was that their father had died earlier that year from cancer. The outpouring of kindness in the office just before Christmas and the way local businesses offered support, help and presents for the two kids while more distant relatives were informed really humbled me. I was strangely and frustratingly angry with myself that I couldn't think of anything kind to do for them that someone hadn't already thought of. I often thought that if I had crashed, the road would have been closed and she wouldn't have died. There was probably less than an hour in it. Life is a big game of chance. I used to dream about how unfair that was. In the days that followed it I would wake in the night having dreamt that I was trying to hide her from her kids, because they couldn't see that she was dead, even though she was walking around talking to everyone.

You throw the dice and see how it lands.

But this and other incidents always showed me that behind every uniform there are people who really care. Politicians don't see this and the public don't often see it. But it's there. The men and women who go to work every day as police officers humble me. Not the glory hunters, not the office people, not the 'anti-whatever thing is fashionable to complain about task force' nine am to five pm people., but the real cops, the ones who go to work, put on a uniform and run towards trouble.

And yet the strangest deaths I saw in my time in the police did not actually take place in front of me at all. I had gone to a noise complaint in Kennethead Road flats after one of the neighbours in an upper floor of the twenty-story high flats had been complaining about the noise to the caretaker for quite a while, but they had not been able to find the resident of the noisy flat in question. The caretaker had no power to force entry so they'd had to call the police.

Kendo and I were shown to the flat and there was the sound of a radio blaring away at full volume inside, distorted and clearly annoying. As usual the control room was updated and permission was given to force the door. I anticipated someone lying dead within, or perhaps an elderly person collapsed on the floor, but the flat was empty, barely furnished and it looked like it had been unoccupied for a few days. A radio alarm had gone off at full volume.

Problem solved — but there was a new problem. In the living room a large amount of audio-visual equipment and more video tapes than I had ever seen were stacked round the room. It was like an unofficial blockbuster. We left the house once it had been secured with a note for the resident to contact us and returned to the office. After mulling it over for a long time and discussing with some of the more specialist departments I believed we had found a counterfeiting operation, with the tapes presumably being sold at 'the barras' of a Saturday, the city's dodgy open air market.

Nothing for it but to be curious and find out. I was just about to get a warrant when the resident of the flat phoned the office and we went back to see him. A young man around nineteen he lived on his own in the flat and had been out for a few days, forgetting about the alarm. We discussed the videos but he was adamant they were all his, so with no option left they were all seized and taken back to the office to be checked.

I spent the next nightshift watching each tape in the office conference room at fast forward. He was one sick puppy.

Each video contained not the latest block buster as I had anticipated, but instead a collection of seemingly random films and short clips. Thousands of them. Initially most seemed ok, but they all had a common sadistic theme. Eventually they would get more and more extreme: people dying, executions, torture, basically 'snuff movies'. Some were clearly real such as a parachute fatality, and some were contrived.

The freefall death by parachute stuck in my head, the way the body bounced a short way after hitting the ground. Another showed a Japanese girl being tortured and hung in a sack from the ceiling between tortures; she was burnt, cut and broken before a needle was inserted in to her eye. The camera zooming in as she screamed.

I spoke to the experts at Prat Street and to my supervisors. The problem was we couldn't actually think what the offence was. It wasn't pornography, and today the content was all things that are probably a few clicks away on the internet, but in the late 90's it seemed to me wrong to return them to the lad. That was what we had to do though; I had no choice. I made him come to the office with his father and sat him in an interview room before describing why I felt his video collection was frankly weird. He seemed pleased, smiling and at one point proudly saying 'yeah, did you see that one? It's great'.

A fucked up cookie. I wonder if he's killed anyone yet?

All I could do was put in intelligence reports and hand back all the bags of tapes.

CHAPTER 9

KIX ON 666

I have no idea when Gordy appeared. He just seemed to always be there, much like his poop-brown car that kind of skulked around the car park, shamefully hiding behind lampposts looking rightfully embarrassed to exist.

Gordy was quite short and going bald, and reminded me of Baldrick from Blackadder. I couldn't help but think he had been disqualified from the human race on a technicality. But Gordy was always there to help anyone and when the dust settled at any fight he could be found proudly holding someone who may have had something vaguely to do with it, or he had walked by during the incident, or maybe looked at it. Certainly, probably, seen someone guilty of something.

If there's a dangerous time to be a police-response driver it's straight after doing a driving course. During my course I was told the first three months were statistically the most dangerous; self -confidence is high but many of the actual skills taught during the driving course have yet to become muscle memory rather than learned behaviour and, as a result of the new found ability to go very fast, it was usually only a matter of time before the first bump. Not long after I had passed my driving I managed to reverse the Juliet Mike Ten Sherpa van into Charlie Police office. To be fair I always felt the office had sneaked up on me.

Gordy was out with 'Laptop', so named because he was the smallest PC in the office. Laptop was very new to the job, and I was pretty sure I had an egg stain on my tie with more police service than him, but he was very keen and enthusiastic. They were heading up Corrigan Road when a man they wanted to have a lovely chat about international politics with, cycled past them in the opposite direction on the pavement. Presumably they really wanted him just for a stop search or maybe just to annoy him, but as he went past Gordy yelled out the open window,

'get off the bike you black bastard or we'll knock you off', before screaming to a halt in the middle of the street.

A tad too enthusiastic.

Cycling man, who was in fact technically of mixed racial origin, but never let that spoil the story, kept cycling and turned down a side street.

I did see some overtly racist things such as on the night shift someone lining up a packet of jelly babies to watch the black ones being hung, but in terms of how the public were treated it was very rare to see racism. I wish the same could be said of police management. Years later I would read about how organisations would have forums for one section of employees and promote people positively to achieve the correct KPI's (Key Performance Indicators) for diversity.

The 'Turbinator' in J division was a good example of this, a cop so cowardly that when anyone needed help he would run away and lock himself in the police car. But he was beyond criticism. For all the police did they caused a 'glass ceiling' for those who were promoted ahead of others and caused disquiet amongst those discriminated against. The job adored being seen to favour minority groups in public, while behind the scenes the reality was very different, and it was inevitably unfair on the many good cops from minority groups who were promoted, because they worked in an environment where they knew there was scepticism as to the promotion process.

Gordy was not one to be deterred by the mere fact that to the best of his knowledge the man on the bike had yet to actually do anything. He reversed at speed, turning in a cloud of tyre smoke and taking off down the residential side street. The man on the bike tenaciously tried to get away, but good old Gordy managed to catch him by the simple method of mounting the pavement and knocking him over. Perhaps as he flew through the garden hedge and imminent incarceration he would be more careful and not cycle in public again.

After Gordy and Laptop had shouted in on the radio asking for assistance, supervisors and JM4 attended and got all the shocked members of the public to go away by telling them to 'fuck off or youse'll get the jail' before noting that there were no witnesses to take statements from. Just as well really. The traffic gaffer would later demand that everyone 'rethink' their statements but nothing changed.

Chapter 10

The Cat and the Super

The nightshift super is a curious animal; it's essentially a senior manager at least a Superintendent, who covers important decisions that need made during the night shift, such as: what sort of cakes are best, which office to eat them in and which office the firearms cars should go to instead of driving to the actual scene so they don't actually ever get the chance to shoot anyone.

I assume there was some sort of rota but basically some poor sod from the traffic would take the shift's shiniest newest car, pretend they were all maintained like that, and go and pick the super up from his home address. I would have to drive one around years later who stayed in Argyll. By the time I'd got there and had driven them to the city, had a cup of tea and a chat with the duty officer at Coward's Castle, it was time to turn round and go back again. The trick to driving the nightshift super was to drive really fast. They got bored in offices and seemed to like that; maybe it made them feel important.

On this occasion the nightshift super was from J division and, as with all of them, they would sneak up on their own to the office to catch the plebs out, just in case we were sleeping, drinking tea or perhaps having unauthorised fun. Fun is frowned upon by police managers in case it raises morale.

We were in the charge-bar area in Juliet Bravo when the 'bat phone' rang from divisional HQ with the news that the nightshift super was coming to visit us. Like a Chicago speakeasy, cards and gambling pots were hidden under important-looking paperwork, personal computers and playstations were thrown in the cells and anyone not supposed to be in the office disappeared like roadrunner in a cloud of dust. A few years before it would have been bottles of whisky and short glasses.

There was a problem though, because earlier that night a dead cat had been brought in. The motorist who brought the cat in was traumatised; Kitty was deceased and they felt that we should do something. I don't know what — maybe call the cat funeral directors or have some sort of accident scene protection team out? But here's the thing — cats, for whatever reason, are not animals. Might be a shock for those of you who possess one, and for feline experts the world over, but I assure you the Road Traffic Act 1988, as amended 1991, is quite specific regarding this.

An animal is one of the following Sheep, horse, ass, mule, pig, ox, goat, dog, fowl, cow.

Every student at the Police College knows this because there used to be a little loch in the grounds there called the Shampog. They used to make recruits wade in there and do press ups, although that was before health and safety so I'm sure it's been replaced with teddy bear time.

Anyway, running over a cat is not a road accident, because it's not an animal, fact. Even if you have to drive onto the pavement to get the little bastard, it still doesn't count.

On this occasion deceased kitty was in the front bar area of the office, propped up against the PNC terminal screen awaiting rigor mortis and the arrival of the early shift who would find it reading the kitty times in the driving seat of Mike 3. I'd made a tiny newspaper for it to read by using the miniaturize function on the photocopier and I was quite chuffed with myself.

But now the countdown clock was ticking and the nightshift super would be there soon. I suspect he wouldn't want to have his chocolate bourbons and tea with milk and one sugar, whilst being watched by Felix the Zombie Cat. So Jimmy, an old dinosaur of a cop, was told to remove kitty from the bar area. Jimmy was usually in the bar to prevent interaction with the public, and shuffled off into the back yard with the cat, his eternal cigarette stuck on his bottom lip and his hat tipped back on his head, mumbling and grumbling about the world in general and the fact it wasn't his fucking cat in particular.

I imagined the cat would go into the dog kennels for a little lie down, maybe to see if it felt better.

But no, with some amateur shot putting Felix the cat took a flying lesson over the back wall of the office onto Cockburn road, followed by a loud thump and screech of tyres. Later a pale faced old woman was calmed down with a cup of consoling tea while a dead cat, that had clearly leapt an infeasible distance off the office wall onto the windscreen of her car, was sympathetically taken away for disposal under the watchful scowl of the duty Sgt. The nightshift super ate his chocolate bourbons unaware of why Jimmy had a face like thunder and why I kept looking at the floor and giggling. Silly cat.

You Know When You've Been Tango'd

Going to the Traffic department was an odd thing for me to want to do. From my early days in the Police I'd always seen surveillance as a natural calling—until I became involved with people who did it and asked for their advice. It was a big shock to be told that seventy percent of surveillance operations were on cops and it had a big effect on my motivation, not because I wouldn't see catching a bad cop as a good thing to do, but because of the hypocrisy behind these surveillance operations. They were for the most part for far more minor things than would be used to justify any other operation. I did unofficially help a cop I knew from the Serious Crime squad, who knew I'd been in the regiment because one of the rural surveillance guys had been in too, and I spent two nights alone watching for a target from the side of a railway line as a favour, but I was miserable and I needed something more fun to do.

So I applied for the traffic. I loved driving fast and I loved motorbikes so it seemed a natural way to go. Another big factor behind this was my background. I had paid for myself to go back to university part time to become a crash investigator. At the time just because it seemed a fun thing to do. I liked maths and physics and it was nice that part of the job would stretch my geeky brain a bit.

Joining the traffic is intense in relation to the courses one has to take, and the driving course in particular was hard work. It consisted of a two-week induction, a two-week intermediate course and then four weeks back at the Police College. As the courses went on, the speeds went up. By week four of the course there were no speed limits and we were driving round Scotland as fast as the plain white unmarked cars could go.

The Home Secretary exempts police cars from speed limits for training for obvious reasons. I loved every second of it.

At the end of the course each student gets a score. Every drive must be above a 75 to get a class 2, which is a pass. Averaging above 85 is a class one, which allows a driver to continue to become a driving instructor, although not many do that. (Class One drivers only made up around 5% of the traffic department at that time.) 82 or above would allow someone to become a security escort driver.

The traffic department was very much poacher turned gamekeeper and I never met a traffic cop who didn't like going fast. The traffic also had a lovely new office, and, mostly, nice fast well-maintained cars — and car chases, which were bloody fantastic. Everyone lived for them. There is no faster way to get traffic cops out the office than a 'Code 44' or vehicle pursuit coming over the radio; it's like cat nip for traffic cops. I enjoyed a lot of good pursuits and it might be surprising that there are not lots in this book, well — the main reason for that is that they ended up becoming very alike, and I don't see the point in lots of apparently self – glorifying tales of speed. At the end of the day no one died and I think myself lucky because I took a lot of risks. When the red mist comes down and it's you versus them, it becomes a bit gladiatorial, but also ultimately pointless. If you caught them, they were usually back out the next night doing it again.

The only one that became very personal and special to me was a stolen Subaru. It had haunted my neebs and I. Stolen during a house break-in, it had been chased and lost repeatedly for a month all over the South West of Scotland. It had been involved in house break-ins, robbery and gun crime. We had been on the edge chasing it in our new Mercedes the previous night shift and it had got away. Harry my neebs was tenacious, like an angry terrier, and he wanted this car.

As we drove back to the office for lunch and duties at that Saturday afternoon's 'old firm' football match a Subaru sat opposite at the lights. We commented on how we wished it was 'our' Subaru, and when the lights went green and it pulled away, right behind it *was* 'our' Subaru. Harry caught them by surprise; we accelerated straight towards them forcing the driver to mount a high kerb and in doing so the ned blew out his front tyre and within half a mile the pursuit was over, the Subaru abandoned in a busy residential street seconds before we found it.

We had everything we needed to catch the driver — the support unit, the helicopter, division, dogs, and traffic cars — because everyone was heading to the football and near at hand, and yet we couldn't find our elusive ghost and after half an hour or so we had to give up, watched by quiet residents and children as we waited on a recovery truck for the stolen car. At least we got the car.

I often think the biggest failing senior officers have is that they forget that they do actually work for the public. They are employed by them and yet when you watch senior police officers on TV they sound so condescending. They can't help but talk slowly and use simple police report terminology, as though they think the public are stupid. The words they use express outrage and emotion and yet they show none themselves, because the reality is they don't care about the public. They care about how they need to look calm and in control. They don't care about the little people; all they care about is the spreadsheet and best way to extract fixed penalty tickets from the public.

As the Subaru was taken away and we got ready to leave, a woman who had been watching us quietly from the pavement summoned the courage to speak to us. Maybe it was the very first time she'd spoken to a police officer, and I guess with the way we had been together, laughing and talking to the dog handler and the divisional cops for the previous ten minutes, she'd felt that what she had to say was not important. It could wait until the last few cops, just Harry, the dog hander with his dog and I, were there and she could approach.

'Excuse me officer, I know you're really busy but have you got a minute for me?'

Of course we did.

My neebs Harry was a fantastic cop and always took time to talk to people. Even if she'd lost her pet cat, needed directions, or just wanted a chat, we would be there because that's what thousands of cops up and down the country do every day and the senior officers never appreciate it. For them it's wasted time; there's no spreadsheet it can be recorded on and no way can they win their next promotion out of it.

'Thanks officer, my little girl has a toy tent in our back garden just up the road and she says she thinks there is a man hiding in it. He might just be a homeless guy but I don't want to speak to him.'

Forty seconds later when the 'My-Little-Pony' tent was unzipped it was found to contain 'My-Little-Car-Thieving, House-Breaking, Robbing ned' instead. Fluffy the police dog introduced himself from outside the tent and explained in his subtle doggy way how fast he could run and how pointy his teeth were and how, if the car-thieving scum bag would like to play too, he would love to play fetch—using him as the stick. It's amazing how a police dog barks once and pulls on its lead, and suddenly the coward who robs decent members of the public at knife point and is probably the hard man of the cell block suddenly offers to come very quietly from the expanding puddle they are standing in. Very funny.

I do like Police dogs—hairy land sharks. The last Chief Constable got rid of lots of them because dogs can't write traffic tickets. They keep losing the pen apparently.

The road-policing complex was a great place to work, an airy new office almost like a huge greenhouse on one side; it had a large three-floor atrium which was perfect for testing paper aeroplanes on the night shift, although whoever was on duty in the crash unit would always win because they had huge A0- sheets of paper. The building had been opened to great fanfare, and the smell of fish after the night shift cooked kippers at 4am the day Princess Ann was coming to open it officially. The smell was exacerbated because a fellow ex-Juliet Alpha cop had microwaved a tin and blown the door off one of the microwaves the same night leaving the smell of burning and fish in the office for days.

There were a couple of walkways over the atrium which were good for practicing abseiling but the main feature that captivated everyone was the large training room on the ground floor which was used on the nightshift for watching porn. It had what at the time was a very fancy projector screen and was like a mini cinema. Now you will not believe this, but when the building was opened the short-of-cash police paid for plants to be rented and watered every day. Seriously, who rents plants? I could have saved them a fortune with a quick trip to Homebase.

I did once see one female officer complain about the porn to a Sgt, whom I liked to call 'Gordon's Alive' because of his big bushy beard, beards being very rare back then because, believe it or not, Clydeside Police wouldn't let cops have one without a medical reason.

'Sgt, I've a problem with porn on the night shift.'

Gordon's Alive stopped his paper work, leaned back in his chair and looked thoughtfully up for a few seconds, hands in a fingers-spread prayer, looking at the ceiling whilst seemingly pondering a mystery of the universe, then he leaned forward and suggested,

'Well normally, you do need to bring your own, but if you speak to Bert, I'm sure he's got some he can lend you.'

It all stopped when Bert was told, as a wind up, that the projector sometimes started up showing the last few frames from whatever was on last and that one of his films has been shown to a class the next day. That wasn't true but the look on his face was priceless.

The shift had a lot of characters. There was Mike who, like myself, was a Class one driver but, unlike me, actually deserved to be one. Mike was also funny and a good crash investigator, and I entertained myself in thinking his crash experience was enhanced by wrapping the newest BMW in our fleet round a lamp post one night.

Grant was in a league of precisely one. I have never ever known a man so perverted in my entire life. We would regularly time how long it would take for him to make some inappropriate comment during muster at the start of each shift. Usually it would be a comment relating to what the shift termed 'Kilmaurs Style', after one of the guys on the shift confessed to Grant that his girlfriend from the village of Kilmaurs had allowed him stick it somewhere ermmm different.

The day our new inspector came to the shift there was a hushed silence as she walked into the room.

A female inspector.

No one saw this coming. This was going to end really badly. I could see Grant shaking like an over-wound Jack-in-the-Box with frustration in the corner of the room as muster started. Like many of the shift I reached down discreetly and started my stopwatch. Gordon's Alive was looking nervously and anxiously at Grant. I glanced across and saw him, eyes darting around and clearly bursting with excitement. Gordon's Alive mouthed words at Grant. 'Don't you say a fucking word' he seemed to be saying.

As the shift left muster ten minutes later and we left to get our car keys and head up the city drag so Grant could look at the prostitutes and calm down for a while, Bert trotted up behind me grinning. Gordon's Alive wasn't saying anything but had shot everyone an 'I'll have words with you lot later' look as we all left muster.

'39 seconds?'

'I got 38.5 but I think that's within the force guidelines for an acceptable error'

One downside to being in the traffic department was that when you arrested a suspect drink driver you had to go to the nearest local police office which was not always your preferred one for playing Pished Poker. The rules seemed subtly different from office to office but generally it went something like this.

When standing at the prisoner bar with the suspect drink-driver, the duty officer or civilian would call out a number which was actually a sum of money, usually a pound, and then another number.

Voices would be heard from all around also calling numbers

ranging between thirty-five and 250, and, if it was well done, a white board was used to note them down. Myself and my neebs would also suggest a number and then off we went down the yellow brick road to the magical intoximeter room. It was, of course, a sweepstake as to what reading would come back from the machine to show how pissed our driver was. Everyone would chip in a pound for whoever was closest. Unfortunately, it was possible in later years to turn the roadside screening device into 'marine mode', as a result of which it would give you a rough reading, kind of spoiling the game.

CHAPTER 11

THE MIDDLE OF NOWHERE

I had been in the traffic a year or so and in the city for eight years and I wanted a change. My wife was pregnant with son number two and I was wanting a change from the city life. I had the chance of a nice old house to do up a few miles outside Baytown, on the remote west coast, so I submitted a subject sheet to the effect that I would like to be considered for any vacancies that might come up in future. Less than a week later I received a phone call telling me to come to Prat St. the next day to speak to the Traffic Chief Superintendent.

I showed up in full tunic and dress uniform, resplendent in a new traffic hat and saluted as I went in. He seemed really shocked but, after sitting down, it became apparent this was no interview. I was already going to traffic Baytown; all that was up for debate was if I was going yesterday, today or tomorrow. It seemed not many people, if any, ever wanted to go there. Later that day I phoned up Baytown Traffic and introduced myself. I spoke for half an hour or so to Sam who sounded really switched on and was a forensic crash investigator too. At the end of the conversation I asked one last question.

'What's the gaffer like, is he a complete twat?'

'Ermmmm, No, ermm, no — I think I'm Ok actually.'

Great start.

I loved working in Baytown because, for me, it was a trip back in time to proper policing. I could start each shift and get out and talk to people like a real cop should — and the way cops would now if they weren't mismanaged, drowning in paperwork and run off their feet. There were no real targets to be achieved and writing anyone a traffic ticket was a real rarity. I also covered a simply staggering geographical area. Four offices had traffic personnel, but usually only one or two were on duty at any given time so we would each cover all four sub-divisional office areas when we were on. This would mean that from the south tip of the Mull of Kinloch up to the north boundary in Glen Ord it was actually likely the C class Mercedes would need refuelled to do a blue light run and return to the office, even starting with a full tank. It could be almost three hours to get to some areas at full speed, and that was without including the islands. We also had times each day when no one was on duty and the same every night. If anything happened, we were simply phoned at home. I loved my work and driving the long distances, simply loved it. And we had a bit more free rein to do what we wanted. There could be whole weeks when there was not a call on the radio, and I did find it disconcerting the way it seemed that everyone in the town waved and soon knew my name.

99,550 miles said the odometer in the Mercedes. Men understand this; it's a man thing. I've stopped driving before to take a picture of the odometer at 100,000 miles.

Stuart, one of the other traffic cops, had the Mercedes as his regular car, which he had looked after and had cherished since it was a baby car straight out the wrapper. He loved it, hoovered it and polished it every single Sunday. Weirdo.

The Volvo T5 was my usual car at that time. I cleaned the Volvo when I had no room left for more sweeties in the door pocket because it was full of wrappers. Stuart was very protective of his car so getting the keys for the Merc was difficult and he was desperate to do the 100,000th mile, and even more keen that I wouldn't leave it a mess. But he finished at 5pm and then the keys would be unguarded and all mine. The precious!

I volunteered for every call I could go to in any area to try and manage it legitimately, but ended up at Gretna Services over 150 miles out my area and at one point crossing two other force boundaries to manage the required 450 miles in one shift.

It's the simple things that made me giggle. Stuart was raging.

I was an amateur however because two traffic cops from down south landed in the poop that same year for taking an unmarked car to Paris on the Eurotunnel one nightshift. Damn, that's impressive.

Another strange thing about working on the west coast was that any help was a long distance away. Working alone involved a steep learning curve. You had to be able to talk your way out of problems. In the city, you can land in the shit with a violent spitting angry person, you know help is five minutes away. Five minutes is still a long time to struggle with a prisoner but on the west coast being alone and an hour or two from the nearest help was very normal. It could take two hours at least to get a police dog or the support unit, maybe a bit less if the helicopter was available.

Shanksy, one of the dog handlers I knew, once took an hour blue-lighting from the city just to get close to the boundary of my area — and forgot to bring his dog, who was presumably sitting at home watching Rough justice

In remote Scotland I found it was best to have a nice chat and maybe a cup of tea, and explain what was happening to anyone I needed to arrest before discussing what music to have on the way to the office. When Bruce and I worked together he liked to get our prisoners to sing along to tracks on his IPod on a long drive. When I heard he'd played 'Firestarter' and 'I fought the law and the law won' after arresting an arson suspect, and had them joining in, I have to say I was deeply impressed.

Being away from the city also made it easier to get to know the locals and learn who they were. The Police intelligence system clearly still covered the area but, in reality, most of what was known was still by word of mouth. 'Rover' for example was a young man who could not hide what he'd done from the small community; he'd been caught shagging the family Labrador and, as a result, none of the cops I knew really spoke to him. We did occasionally growl or bark out the car window as we drove past – and, obviously, when he was in our custody he got his morning cup of tea in a bowl instead of the usual foam cup.

A cop called John Collins helped me to get to know the area. JC was a very likable, funny and dry character and I worked with him quite a lot for over a year. When 'Burglar Bertie' disappeared in his boat in Loch Errie some years before, some gamekeepers said they'd heard shouting, but they were well down the Loch, near Dallyavik, a good seven miles from the main road to the north side. JC was dispatched one night to carry out a sound check to see if it was possible that they could have heard anything. He stopped at a layby on the north shore while the mountain rescue team and Neil Sunderland, better known as the 'Wing Commander' because he spoke like an RAF fighter pilot from 1941, who was the gaffer for the rural cops, were seven miles down the Loch. A quick radio message to JC from the Wing Co requested that he shout something out to see if any faint sound would make it through the night air.

'SERGEANT SUNDERLAND IS A WANKER' he bellowed at full volume

As the words 'wanker, wanker wanker wanker' echoed away down the loch, his radio crackled into life with the calm-as-ever voice of the Wing Commander.

'Roger, Tango Echo thirteen that message was clear and understood, over.'

It turns out the marines from Condor were right; sound travels really well over water. Who knew?

We had to do much of our work alone, even arresting drink drivers and most arrests would be carried out while working alone although elsewhere in Scotland this was often frowned upon. There's nothing in Scottish law that actually says you need corroboration for an arrest, but in the city it was generally seen as a good thing procedurally.

Being in remote Scotland and working alone did have one huge downside, which was that it was impossible to play traffic snooker. This is when two competing crews in the city leave the office to issue tickets according to the rules of snooker. Red car. Colour Car. Red car. Colour car. Red car etc. Clearly black cars and red cars were much sought after, and most people in white cars were let off because catching the 'cue' car meant missing the points from the next car you caught.

By now we had been issued CS spray and body armour as standard equipment. I would usually leave mine in the office and rely on my police shirt and tie. I had tried putting my body armour, along with my baton and handcuffs in the boot of the car but I had a bad habit of forgetting them if I had to swap cars. I always felt that talking to someone was better than using force and prided myself on looking smart and talking sense. That wouldn't work in the city.

In twenty-one years, including seven years in some of the roughest areas in the city I had drawn my baton just once and felt awful afterward. I'd gone to a call in a rough area, next to the main football stadium with my usual nebs at the time, 'The Brain'. We had earlier been given a look out for a woman who had escaped a secure mental hospital. When her estranged husband phoned to say she was at his tenement house we went straight there, expecting a quick pick-up and a run to the hospital. As we were out on foot, the Juliet Alpha Mike 3 van offered to come pick us and our new, crazy friend up.

Brain and I arrived first and climbed the common tenement stairway. When we got to the top, the door to the tenement opened and a small demure man showed us into a large hallway and gestured towards the huge kitchen with a quiet, 'she's in the kitchen', uttered under hushed tones. He had clearly been waiting nervously for our arrival. I strode in and looked around the empty room. In the centre was a large oak kitchen table, set for a meal. Around the side of the room a dish washer and tumble dryer were quietly running and beyond that I really couldn't see anything of note, in particular no escaped mental patients. I turned back towards the doorway to the hall and as I did so caught her out of the corner of my eye, coming out from what I thought was a sort of hanging tapestry type decoration. She turned towards Brain and as she walked past me I saw a huge kitchen knife held behind her back. I had just been issued the new PR24 side-handled baton. I drew it and as she lifted the knife up in a dramatic stabbing motion above Brain I struck her from behind. Brain had already put out a Code 21, an urgent assistance call. As we struggled with this incredibly strong, tiny, crazy lady, Steve and Gary from JM3 were trying to kick the door in because it had shut on the Yale lock behind us. It turned out, when the dust had settled, that city tenements often had a tiny kitchen or kitchenette off the dining room and that had been what was behind the drape.

We stood at the prisoner bar of the office booking her into a cell, and I felt shit. She was tiny beside me and I had batoned her, and on top of that we had needed assistance. As was usual, most of the shift would find an excuse to walk past the bar on the pretext of doing something else but really to see who had needed four cops to be subdued. Of more concern to me as I played it back in my head, and I watched the blood and sweat running down her head, was the realisation that it must have been for show on her part. She could easily have stabbed me in the back, but she chose to attack my neighbour instead, walking right past me. Secondly, she had held the knife above her head way too long, when she could easily have reached and stabbed me many times. It was a cry for help, and what she needed was a sofa, a cup of tea and someone to listen to her instead of a barren police cell.

That was why, in years to come, I ignored most of the officer-safety training and only wore my baton and handcuffs on very rare occasions. Only when we changed from shirts and ties to scruffy T-shirts would I eventually have to wear my equipment, begrudgingly, when I got out the car. I'm not proud of that and I wasn't a good example to younger cops.

I never professed to be though.

The Truck

I hadn't been at Baytown long and I was supposed to be single-crewed and dayshift, which was a 0800am start. Big Sam was unusually dayshift and dealing with paperwork at the same time, but as soon as we came into the office, we were asked to help the territorial division out with a call. This was no problem and the rural cops out-with Baytown often needed help; there was a good team-spirit to the place. It was a traffic-related call in any event, although it restricted my plans for ice cream.

A heavy goods vehicle had left the road on the Inverarity trunk road heading south and, although the truck itself had been removed by a recovery contractor during the night, the contents of the load were still there. Fair enough. We would just be standing by as the rest of the roadway was cleared of whatever had been left at the side of the road. We picked up some rolls with sausage and headed out.

On arrival I was staggered by the comic genius of what I saw. Twenty-two tonnes of salmon is a serious shit load of fish. I mean really—its more fish than you have ever seen in your life. All huge, fully grown salmon, which were on the way for processing having just been harvested from a fish farm and packed in ice that day. So very many fish.

The roadway was almost clear, but a good ten tonnes of fish were scattered over thirty meters or so of roadside verge on the outside circumference of the bend. In places it was five fish deep, or about a foot. Mostly there were just fish lying around. Very few were damaged in any way, and the manager from the fish farm had arrived to supervise the clear up. He was very apologetic.

'I'm really struggling to get skips delivered today guys; we've already filled the ones I've managed to hire.'

I asked out of curiosity what would happen to the dead fish; would they be sold? After all, finding twigs and small rocks in your tinned salmon would be annoying. Apparently not. They would all have to be disposed of as waste and the company would have to pay for the privilege. I looked at Sam and he looked back. What a horrible waste. And while neither of us liked salmon it seemed a real shame. I asked if they could not be given away to homeless shelters or something, as this must be thousands and thousands of pounds' worth of fantastic Scottish salmon, but apparently no, even the homeless don't want twigs and rocks in their salmon. As the manager went to leave, he told us that there would be no way to get more skips before the next morning — but if anyone wanted to help themselves to the fish just to let them.

Well, we couldn't leave the bend because if people started stopping and helping themselves to fish it was a serious safety hazard on a dangerous corner. I waved down the first car I could, and grabbed a fish. It was a lovely big silver salmon you would probably pay a lot of money for in Tesco's.

The window of the car wound down and the driver looked at me like I had gone mad, a grinning traffic cop with a big three-foot-long fish dangling by the tail from an outstretched hand. I'm not sure if he expected me to slap him with it in a comedy-type style or maybe start some sort of comedy dance routine, but I looked him straight in the eye and keeping a straight face said.

'Hello, would you like a fish? Look! We have many fish.'

As the morning went by things just got stranger and stranger, the pile of fish slowly diminishing. I called up the local beat cop, Bruce, with his marked Land Rover so we could load it with fish and then give it away from a safer point just round the corner. By lunch time some of the local hotel owners had been phoned by Bruce and were turning up while we had traffic queued back with locals wanting fish like it was going out of fashion. Soon after that, the fish-farm manager managed to find another couple of skips and turned up with some staff to help load them up. He needn't have bothered — the bend was somewhat fishless.

THE FINGER IN THE FRIDGE

There was a finger in the freezer section of the fridge, the fridge in the medical room admittedly or it would have undoubtedly ended up in a sandwich or the bin.

Seriously.

It was there for years. Really. It was bitten off a man at a domestic and put in a production bag. I don't think anyone felt they could ever get rid of it so it just stayed there. It was handy to go and get it on quiet boring back shifts and prod people who needed prodded.

STOPPING THE WRONG CAR

Always treat people the way you want treated. If that's one thing that got me through twenty-one years with only one proper complaint that's what it was. The complaint, incidentally, was because I wrote a humorous Thomas the Tank Engine story after going to a train derailment and it was circulated round the office. It was actually one of two occasions that humour and morale were almost allowed to break out but they didn't care about the other one. The email investigation was manipulated to target one individual in particular and I was just collateral damage. I thought it was quite funny but one of my colleagues objected to potentially being the Fat Controller, despite the fact he wasn't actually in the story at all. I can't mention the train derailment however without mentioning Smooth talking Terry, one of the probationers who met a probationer from another office whilst at the scene and got her pregnant. I mean, really, how does anyone manage that? Well, obviously I know how, but at a potentially major incident? I was astounded. He left the job shortly after to look after his many children.

Summer in remote Scotland was a wonderful thing, getting out in a big fast car and blasting round the highlands, stopping for ice creams and watching the world go by, sun glasses on, windows down, parked at the side of the road, guarding, watching and not patrolling—well except for in a stationary eating-ice-cream sort of way. I was in the unmarked Green Volvo T5 with Waz which was even cooler. I preferred the Skoda because it didn't look like a police car at all, and the BMW was nicer to drive until we got God-awful diesel ones to save money. They would actually have been ok too, but came with steptronic gearboxes, which, for most petrol-head traffic drivers, is like taking a shit in front of your grandmother and passing it off as pudding; it's just fucked up. If you don't have a manual gear box how can you do a perfect sustained rev gear change before looking at your neebs and both smiling a knowing contented smile, and making 'mmm… good gear change' approving noises?

Waz was a driving god. He was a class two driver which made me theoretically better than him but in reality he was seriously rapid. He was also completely and utterly bonkers. One of the first times I ever met him was on a hot day down in his area. He'd been round the corner stopping traffic and away from the scene of the crash when I turned up. I had cold cans of coke and shouted him up on the radio to come back and get one.

When his BMW dropped out of warp, howling down the road towards me, I thought I had seen all the horrors life had to offer. What I hadn't seen was that Waz had decided to turn his police-issue trousers into shorts whilst round the corner because he was too hot. Outstanding behaviour. Obviously the quality of the tailoring was not quite up to Saville Row standards, having been done with a blunt Leatherman multi-tool scissors attachment. To be fair, for all the quality of the job it could have been done with the thing that removes stones from donkey hooves; one leg was shorter than the other with big strands of black thread hanging down from his newly made daisy dukes. On one side, the side pocket hung below the bottom of the tattered trouser material. With his big full-height boots and orange socks he looked for the entire world like a gay storm trooper on holiday about to kick ass to get his towel on the sun lounger first.

On this day however, we were both looking bloody good frankly. Babe magnets. We were on the Bridge of Ord straight, a two-mile speed test of a straight, a veritable launch pad of a road. It had sunk a bit due to the peat it was laid on and it was easy to see from a distance if cars were speeding from the way they would bounce over the undulations in the road. We parked the car at a jaunty angle, video camera facing down the road as we polished off our '99' cones bought from the tourist stop a few miles south.

It was always a fast blast from the tourist shop up to my favourite little parking space. Full on, foot-to-the-floor, with the aircon on full blast to get there before the ice creams melted. If I didn't get there quickly Waz would threaten to lick my cone to stop it dripping on his crotch, and I had no idea where his tongue had been, dirty boy.

As we stood in the sun in front of the Volvo, watching cars and bikes whizz by, I heard a car horn sounding in that long annoyed and unhappy I-wish-I-could-get-out-the-car-and-kill-you, road-rage type way. Looking back down the road, a Silver Peugeot 406 was out on a crazy overtake. The car heading straight for it was braking hard and squirming. The Peugeot flashed its lights and kept going, pulling back into its own side of the road at the last minute and hurtling towards us.

But we had ice cream.

Waz walked down towards the road's edge and waved at the car to slow as it rocketed past, the passenger staring us straight in the face and gesturing with one middle finger. Outrage!

We looked at each other horrified. Mother of God! I mean — our ice creams!

They were thrown over our shoulders as we legged it back to the car. The camera was quickly adjusted to point forwards again, and not down the road toward the hotel and scene of this horrific road crime that had resulted in the death and sad loss of our lovely ice creams. I was traumatised.

We left the side road in a cloud of tortured tyre smoke and the howling of Volvo's finest 5-cylinder, high-pressure turbo-charged goodness, out for vengeance. My poor ice cream, cut down in its prime.

The big Volvo ate up the road at a frightening rate, 90, 100, 110 miles per hour, as snow poles and verge markers flashed by. In less than a mile we came howling up behind the Peugeot. I imagined how shocked they would be inside, the realisation that the Green Volvo had been a police car. The shock that they had caused the loss of my beautiful, tasty 99 cone. The feeling of guilt and regret. We were on a mission.

We stopped the car below the Black Mountain at the council car park. I open the door and walked with Waz towards the passenger door. The man who had given us the bird, the criminal who murdered our ice creams would pay and then maybe his lady-friend driver. As we escorted him to the back seat of the car, he feigned innocence. He denied criminal knowledge; he offended me with his mere presence. For ten minutes of so we grilled him. Not so much good cop/bad cop as two really angry, hungry ice-creamless cops. Throughout it all he denied everything, finally apologising and saying he must have done it unintentionally.

We showed him the video, we paused it at the exact second that we could see his face staring defiant out the passenger window at us, a look of burning ice-cream hatred in his eyes.

He apologised and we sent him away telling him to make sure his driver drove more safely in future. There was something there, a sixth sense that said that underneath this was a decent guy. A law-abiding citizen and not what I had expected to be faced with at all. A bit of old fashioned policing and a bit of common sense was required.

Always treat people the way you expect to be treated yourself.

Years later I would resign because of a cop from Professional Standards bragging about fitting up one of my colleagues whilst he was drunk in the Police College bar and I knew it was true which made it worse. I handed in my medals and walked out the door. No one even asked why. The job had changed from doing the right thing and helping the public to persecuting the public and making an excel spreadsheet look good. But I always tried to treat people as I found them; it never hurt to give people a chance if you could.

Some months after the demise of my ice cream I got a request for a copy of part of that day's tape. I made the usual court copy, with just the right section of what had happened for the court to see. However, while I was doing that, I had a look back at the start of that day. I could see the car going past from right to left, the passenger clearly looking at us and giving us the finger. I watched as we turned and ran back to our car as other cars passed. That was odd, because I couldn't remember overtaking that many cars before we caught up with the Peugeot. Then a second silver Peugeot went past, the passenger quietly sitting reading motor cycle news in the passenger seat—unaware he was about to get stopped and given the third degree by two cops when he'd done nothing! Nothing wrong at all.

Always be nice to people. Always try and see the good. Treat people the way you would want to be treated yourself. It costs you nothing.

Chapter 12

Dr Doolittle

Dr Doolittle was a motorcycle cop who transferred up from the city to Baytown because his divorce was going badly and he needed away from the city. He was a larger-than-life and a larger-in-waist size character, who was super cheerful and went around the office agreeing with whoever he spoke to; I have no idea why because this often involved disagreeing in principle with someone else he had just agreed with. He was, I guess, an eager to please diplomat. Clearly also a smooth mover, he quickly won the affections of a not-unattractive cop in the office and settled down locally. Punching above his weight I think would be a good way of putting it, but he was certainly a charmer and his vivacious personality was hard to object to. His desire to please all would inevitably lead people to think he was stabbing people in the back in a metaphorical sense, but that's the cost of trying to be everything to everyone.

He was perhaps overly confident of his own abilities and much to everyone's amusement had bought an online university doctorate so that his credit card had Dr Doolittle on it. I hadn't noticed this until we went to buy presents in the city whilst down shopping in the unmarked car before Christmas, but it made me giggle a bit when the cashier called this cop

'Doctor' after she'd noticed it on his card. It was perhaps a real doctorate; I'm maybe being cruel here.

The first time I went for a pint with my new traffic colleagues, the good doctor made a big point of discussing 'Charity Work' in front of me, and everyone else agreed it was good and discussed in a vague and frankly cloaked manner how much work was being done. I was intrigued and wanted in on this. It involved 'handshakes'. Not so much a secret society as a society with secrets, and one of those secrets was not who went there, because everyone knew, but the fact that actually quite a lot of charity work got done between the boozing sessions.

The Doctor was promoted to a uniform shift at division and return to the traffic some years later when Big Sam had transferred to Dumtoon. I didn't mind; I found him quite fun to work with, but it was the start of KPI's, or key performance indicators. All that was coming from the city at the time were demands for numbers and statistics and this was a hard thing to do in a small town in Scotland. For a start, most people were very law abiding, and generally those that broke road traffic law were doing so out of genuine forgetfulness or were exempt from prosecution because they knew how to shake hands the right way.

Fortunately, not all was lost, because divisional pish-like stop searches counted too. As a result, stopping one car for speeding with four occupants counted as four stop searches. I doubted this at first but that was the line we were told to take from HQ in the city, so much so that it was deemed that looking at passengers was enough to qualify as a search. Well, I suppose it was a visual search, of a sort. It was never questioned how two female cops or two male cops could possibly search someone of the opposite gender when our guidelines prohibited this.

All statistics were good, and the online form for reporting stop searches required none of the actual details that hadn't been taken anyway to be entered so it was all a bit of a free-for-all. The figures were also easy to get. One individual stop searched on the street and found to have a minute bit of cannabis, then searched again at the office on a section 23 Misuse of Drugs act search, then processed as a prisoner at the back bar and then handed back their property on release would result in six stop search forms being submitted including two from the duty officer in the police office. Eleven were once generated from one car being stopped with one person in it, but that was slightly taking the piss. I dread to think how many were simply made up, but figures shot through the roof. Interestingly, when 'J' division got PDAs to put stop searches in straight away but also required actual details to be put in, the numbers of stop searches allegedly dropped 75%. Go figure.

My occasional neebs in Baytown at the time was an older cop by the name of Tom. He reminded me a bit of a meercat and had a dry and cynical attitude to every KPI and thing that the job did. We had also started hiding crimes about this time, under the new, Scottish, crime-recording standard. Basically, if two crimes happened at once, one could 'subsume' the other and then the first one could be downgraded. That wasn't how it was supposed to work but in practice it did. Robbery would become a theft and assault, and then the assault would be subsumed into the theft which would be written off. KPI's ruled and the crime managers for each division were merciless in reducing figures to meet targets.

Tom had seen all this in his previous force. He knew how the system worked and was not impressed with Clydeside who he generally felt to be incompetent in leadership. He had a point.

He also was married to Beyoncé; I shit you not. Really. She was called May but she was very attractive and once again a cop was punching above his weight. Why did that not happen to me?

It would actually but that's another bit of the book.

I had neighboured Tom for a while and we got on ok. I missed big Sam and Tom was always complaining, I mean he should have won a medal for complaining in the grumpy-as-fuck Olympics 100 metre, where he could complain about everything and have a tantrum race, but he knew his stuff and didn't stray away from working hard.

One back shift in summer we went out to play in the new ANPR car. ANPR is a fine invention that makes an assortment of funny noises when a car registration number (automatically read by the camera on the roof) matches a database hit. I liked the noises it made, and we had ours set to make a Homer Simpson 'Woohoo' when an uninsured car went past. There was an assortment of other entertaining noises for other sorts of hits. I had earlier made a strategic decision that our trip out had to involve ice cream and we were heading out country to visit a tourist shop, a hundred-mile or so drive. Doctor Doolittle had decided to tag along and was occupying the back seat of the car, having a leisurely supervisory time of it while shooting the breeze.

As we slowed and trundled through the village of Airdsbay good old Homer Simpson gave us the nod — the Nissan that had just passed us had no insurance. Pesky varmints. I turned and engaged the warp drive, catching the Nissan before we left the 40 mph speed limit and in a handy place to safely stop them. As I got out the car the doctor cheerfully offered words of encouragement:

'Get out and get the black bastards.'

Oh dearie me. Here I was with Beyoncé's man and things were very awkward but I was cool, maybe I misheard it, maybe Tom didn't hear it but a quick look at his face confirmed my fears.

We dealt with the car and let the occupants continue the journey. No great dramas there. The drama was back in the waiting police car. After I got back in and we started driving east again the doctor started digging the hole he was in with gusto. His impersonation of a Pakistani man phoning a call centre for insurance left an icy chill in the car and the rest of the journey became more and more awkward. As soon as I could I took the chance to stop and made excuses to speak to Tom alone. Had he heard what I had and was he offended? It turned out the answer to both was a big affirmative.

It didn't stop there; the doctor was now intent on trashing the English. Now I knew him well enough and long enough to realise this was well-intended banter, a jab at someone he considered a friend. In truth it was no worse than pub banter after a rugby match or between mates, but in this car the number of mates he had had recently reduced by the number one. I made excuses that we had to head back and floored it a bit on the way back to shut everyone up before things got worse. We certainly didn't need aircon in the car to make it chilly.

When we got back, Tom had a closed-door chat in the doctor's office. Afterwards the good doctor looked white faced and clearly taken aback. I genuinely don't think he had a bad bone in him. It was just him having a carry on and forgetting his audience.

I spoke to both, but clearly I was in a position. If Tom complained, I had to back him up, not just because it was true, but I knew very well the politically correct rubber-heelers would be out for blood. The doctor knew enough people high up to survive this; I wouldn't. Tom was also my neighbour and there is a loyalty there. I explained this to both separately and phoned Tom before work the next day. He didn't want to make a complaint. I respected that but also knew he would be up shit creek if he did because there were those who were close friends of the doctor who would be out to get him. And they, including the divisional commander, outranked everyone else.

It went away for a while and I tried to forget it. It was occasionally discussed as we worked through the summer and into the autumn but I'd hoped it had been laid to rest. A young boy racer would ironically be the thing that lit the fuse. He was frankly a little horror in the town. He had learnt to drive and spent the next few months picking up kids far younger than him from the local school and driving like a lunatic all round the town. He was arrogant and his parents believed he could do no wrong. He got stopped a lot but they simply didn't realise that the reason for this was that he deserved to get stopped a lot.

He crashed, of course, with three terrified local kids screaming for him to stop as he skidded through a fence on the Baytown to Lochside back road, and he was soon given points that would remove his licence at court. Problem was, he had cleverly not taken his licence to court which on a technicality meant that until he received the letter from the nice Welsh DVLA office he wasn't disqualified. How bizarre.

So he kept driving but there was a catch: in order to be insured he had to disclose his conviction to the insurance company. The only way to find out was to contact the insurance company and ask if this had happened, which Tom did. He wasn't disclosing computer data about a conviction because the source of the information was us in court. It turned out that the insurance company had not been informed and if the boy had been involved in another accident he was uninsured. They immediately cancelled the policy and wrote to the family to let them know. The family complained and Professional Standards took their side, without I suspect any thought whatsoever; they were trying to appease the public I guess, which is mainly what they are all about. Tom was given a formal warning and the fuse was lit.

Tom wanted payback and he knew how to get it. The whole saga came out the woodwork. Statements were taken and the doctor signed himself sick. He was due to retire in just over a year anyway, but I have no doubt it was a nervous time for him. What would happen was never in doubt, as I became aware when the man from Professional Standards came to talk to me for my statement. He told me exactly what the outcome would be. But only after we had shared the same sort of handshake that the Divisional Commander knew. The strange aftermath for me was that because I had told the truth and in doing so had made a manager look bad. The clock started ticking even before someone stuck the long-reaching knife of revenge in my back.

A few months later, when it happened, I was genuinely taken aback. I don't know why because it came from the doctor's best friend forever. (Who as an aside was known as Rat Balls, because one of the girls who slept with him said he had tiny rat balls.) A strange thing in the police, or certainly the bit that was Clydeside, is the perception that a manager can't be seen to get it wrong, because if they do then it's taken as criticism of the decision to promote them. So they do everything they can to protect managers and destroy anyone who tries to highlight a failing or whistle blow. You see, there is almost no limit to what you can get away with if you are well enough protected by the police. After all who is there to complain too? Senior managers control the careers of those in Professional Standards who in turn are the only ones to investigate what goes on. Her Majesty's Inspectorate of Constabulary (HMIC) and PIRC (The review commissioner) exist but ultimately any complaint is investigated or not by Professional Standards who have a conflicting agenda. The police love this state of affairs and, in effect, no one at a grass-roots level can complain about anything without fear of reprisal. There's no independent body to complain to or whistle-blow, as there is in almost any other comparable organisation or company.

The biggest thing though that stops any reporting of incompetence or mismanagement is the Police Scotland regulations themselves. In effect anything a police officer does that brings disrepute on the force, such as highlighting any failing whatsoever, is a disciplinary offence. That's why books like 'Bravo Two Zero' exist but there's no comparable expose of the police. They would hunt down whoever wrote it—because they can, and no one will ever stop it.

Chapter 13

Being the Family Liaison Officer (FLO)

I was inspired by seeing Clare, one of the cops in Baytown, do a FLO deployment for a Tsunami victim's family, collecting DNA to identify remains and staying in touch with the family to help to sort out their problems. It seemed a chance to get involved with work where I would actually get to help people. Clare was very good at it and I suspect I saw another side to policing I just didn't know existed. She was the only FLO I knew at the time.

And I enjoyed working with death. I felt at home there. I think I have always enjoyed being useful and trying to actually help the public. Usually when I'd been a family contact officer or dealt with a sudden death I would leave feeling that I had done a good job; it was fulfilling. I was already trained in disaster-victim identification and it seemed a good progression.

The procedure to apply to be a FLO involved filling out a simple form and a brief interview. I was quite surprised it wasn't more drawn out or perhaps involved more in the way of psychometric testing. Considering the responsibility placed on you as a FLO and the professionalism that was required I was quite pleased to be accepted.

Although it's technically a force post the FLO role is quite clearly split into three. The CID FLO's deal with murder and homicide type investigations. They don't have to do as many but those they do deal with are long and emotionally tough deployments. It's hard not to get to know and empathise with the family I guess; the plus side is that time will be made available as the FLO will probably be part of a dedicated investigation team, and, as it will undoubtedly be a prolonged and more high-profile enquiry, there will be time, money, resources and support lavished upon them.

Divisional FLOs like Clare would do pretty much any deployment they were asked to do but they didn't seem to get used as much. Maybe I'm wrong here, but that was certainly my impression. Tsunami victims, might be missing-person enquiries, but they were generally seen as routine and underappreciated. In ten years or so I would guess I saw Clare do about four deployments.

Traffic FLOs did very large numbers of deployments but to me these were different. Traffic deployments were generally brief and, for the family, harder to reconcile. Most families will go through a stage of blame where they want to find someone to take their frustrations out on for the loss of a loved one. Understandable of course and natural, and at least in the case of a homicide there is the potential for their need to blame someone to be fulfilled once a suspect has been traced.

Traffic FLOs would usually encounter a family who never saw it coming as it were, as was often the case with the missing family member. They would often have no one to blame except the family member who had gone, and soon the blame turned to guilt; they wanted to blame themselves for letting it happen. It's a horrible thing to watch; it's more horrible to know it's coming.

The course lasted a week at the Police College and involved a lot of alcohol. CID courses and in particular the detectives' course, usually did—and all the probationers call you 'sir' as you walk down the college corridors. It got very tiring because I am certainly not a 'sir', but, for most people outside the police, the CID is seen as a promotion. That's a myth the CID like to perpetuate. I did love the opening words of the first instructor to speak on the course concerning our future, traumatic family interaction.

'If you take only one thing from this course—just dinnae shag the widow'.

Fair enough.

There were only eight of us on the course, and of these there was a fair split of experience and background: the policewoman for whom the FLO job was clearly a bit of a destiny or a calling, the court worker who saw only victims' families burning with the need to see revenge more than justice, the CID cops with scepticism and contempt dripping from them since they'd already seen the worst of society and dealt with the consequences. And finally there was the two sceptical one-thousand-yard stare, the emotionally cold-as-fuck traffic cops joking in the corner. Violent death was matter of fact and all around us traffic cops; it was what we did and then laughed about it. And the people we dealt with were not junkies who had fallen foul of their supplier, or out of control street-gang members, high on drugs and stabbed in a fight, they were people like the mother rushing on the way home to get kids from the childminders, the couple on a relaxing day out enjoying the scenery, people jogging along the road thinking of nothing more than the music on their IPod, people like you or me, normal people who didn't see it coming. The police would ban the word 'accident' from their politically-correct new vocabulary, but for many families who lost a loved one when there was no one else to blame, 'accident' was a good word. No one likes to blame the only victim.

For most of the week, one of the instructors talked away quite happily, interacting normally, helping answer our questions and generally she didn't seem to have much experience as a FLO. We did practical exercises, discussed how to deal with different cultures and death, and generally had a fun time. I couldn't really understand why she was there because she didn't have police experience and didn't seem to be qualified to say much. It interested me though to watch the way the other instructors looked to her for a quiet nod of approval or hushed words of advice when one of us raised an interesting issue. On the second last day we would find out why.

Her sister had been brutally murdered waiting for her kids by someone known to them. Stabbed over forty times outside a school. This inoffensive everyday lady sat in front of the class and talked us through what happened, from the details of the murder, in staggering detail: through the court case to the release of the man convicted after serving his sentence to live in a house nearby to hers. For two hours I sat listening in silence to the detail and emotion pouring from her and felt it wash over me. I was so caught up in myself and used death as something to make jokes about, something routine and matter of fact, that I'd forgotten the people behind it. She made a huge impression on me.

I'd had plenty of experience doing the job of a FLO anyway because it was often covered by a family contact officer which was essentially a way of doing the same job but with someone who hadn't done the course. The first time I was a family contact officer was for Angus Mark McTavish. He was a very talented marine mechanic who was renovating an old steam launch with the dream of sailing it around the islands. His night out had gone well, having a few drinks in the hotel on an island south of Baytown connected to the mainland by a bridge and narrow single-track road which lay twenty-five minutes from the main north-south road that ran to the Mull of Kinloch peninsula. At night that road was the only way to the little village on the island. The village had a couple of pubs, but one was within an old granite-and-slate hotel located at the entrance to the village.

As with many places to drink in remote Scotland it was only possible to get there by car. Taxis were pretty much unheard of and expensive and, in any case, a police car trying to get to the island would have to cross the bridge and pass the first pub on the island. It was pointless because even the unmarked car was so well known that any attempt to get there would be spotted by the first few residents and by the time any police car was five minutes on the island everyone would know.

M15 could do with the intelligence-gathering network on some Scottish Islands. They might pick up a trick or two.

I would occasionally try to get to the Isle of Dull when we had a new unmarked car up from the city. One year we had a Skoda Superb. It was amazing; everyone thought it was a taxi; it was a real stealth car. And yet — we hadn't told anyone that we were heading over to the Isle of Dull and by the time we got off the ferry I had a text from a friend in Balamory, the main town on Dull, to say he'd put the kettle on. Apparently the 'Caledonian MacBrayne' ferry would signal the island if a police car was on board, and the whole island would know before we'd finished our breakfast in the ship's café.

But back on the island and in a surprising moment of common sense, young Angus was offered a lift back by the perfectly sober bar maid. He accepted and got into the passenger seat of the small hatchback. He didn't wear a seatbelt and when his head smashed through the sunroof as the car overturned it was, as Atari would say, 'game over player one'. I was in at 8am in the morning to find the backshift just getting into the office having been at the crash scene all night. All they had to help me identify our man with the mushy head in the morgue was a credit card found in his pocket.

As soon as I could fax off the Data Protection Act forms and get bank details sent through I realised I had a problem. Our young dead chap was from a remote area, difficult to get to without the correct tide times, and, according to the local beat cop, hard to find. Once I had the address details confirmed and got the assistance of the local beat man, we were off seventy miles south and into the area covered by Kinloch's office. We took the Land Rover, because the journey to this house involved a drive along a beach. I would guess we were on the road for 9.30.

I found the main pier access to a bay near 'Crab Bay' fairly easily but from there on it became very difficult. I spent a good hour and a half trying to find the house, being forced to reverse back up a steep forest track from the wrong beach and, at one point, arriving in a field a few hundred yards from where I had started twenty minutes or so earlier. Eventually, in the early afternoon, I found a steep road with a few tight hairpins which led me to another narrow concrete pier and access to a pebble beach. I drove along the beach, glad to be in the big four-wheel drive, before ascending a very steep track through woods. I turned round a tight right bend to see a stunning wooden house directly in front of me, like a Scandinavian house, with a balcony and huge glass windows from the driveway letting me see straight into the huge living room with an amazing central fireplace.

What a beautiful house. I got out and walked up to the door, knocking and waiting patiently on the householder. An elderly man answered and I was invited into his living room.

I asked him to sit down but, as with a lot of people on the west coast, he was far too polite, he invited me to sit down and offered me a cup of tea. There was no easy way to do this and, as was often the case, I suspected he knew it wasn't good news. When a cop comes to your house and takes his or her hat off in respect as you answer the door, it's not often a cheery story. I asked him for his name, to confirm I was in the right place. That's a big one — always make sure you know who you are speaking to!

In this case Angus Mark McTavish.

Fuck.

Thinking on my feet. Clearly he wasn't dead or, if he was, someone better tell him to stop walking around and get back in his fridge in the morgue.

Maybe he had a son? I asked if he did. Yes it turned out, by the name of Mark. Ah, well that helped a bit, but not much. Maybe someone else had taken his credit card?

Only one thing to do. I've always believed that if you tell people the truth and explain things they will respect it. Never lie to a family, even if it's a nice lie; there is no such thing. I wish I'd taken that mantra into one of my personal relationships. I explained to the old man where the bank card had come from, about the crash, and what little I knew about the dead young man.

It was indeed his son.

As is often the case on the west coast of Scotland people

like to go by second names and both the dad and his son did so. The old man collapsed in front of me crying. Soon I would find out that his wife was terminally ill in the bedroom and listening to our conversation. I spent the day with him, taking him to the morgue, talking him through what would happen next, and cleaning up his son so he could see him looking like he was asleep, head turned to one side to hide the injury, running him home and wishing him all the best.

And walking away, until another day and another death.

Cops do every day. It's just a thing.

When I returned to Baytown after the FLO course I waited for my first real deployment. It was odd, waiting for the death of another human. In theory we should have a maximum of six a year but that was for proper CID-type deployments and the rules seemed flexible by agreement in the sticks. I generally had around ten a year but my record was twenty-eight in a rolling two-year period. Later, at the Police College, my old FLO co-ordinator would give me a letter confirming I was the most deployed FLO in Clydeside for two years running.

I had no idea — in fact I was slightly surprised — because Cammy in Lochord, another traffic FLO, always seemed slightly busier than me. Myself and Cammy would travel to the FLO conference at Jackoff every year but it just annoyed us. Usually someone from the CID would get up and be all emotional about how hard and traumatic their one or two annual deployments were while no one mentioned the traffic or divisional FLOs because we were the poor relations. One year in particular the murder of a Polish girl was discussed in some depth and the FLO spent ages telling everyone proudly how they'd managed the minefield of sending a body back to another country. Who knew you needed a clear coffin so that customs could see the body? Well' pretty much every traffic FLO in the room, because we sent someone back home in a box most months in summer. The arrogance was infuriating but tolerable because they did the same job and I respected that, and I guess they had their own problems that we would have had to overcome.

Another issue was that most FLOs would have the luxury of a colleague to work with and even from a safety point of view this was a good thing. For me it was almost unheard of. I was almost always single-crewed as a FLO. I didn't mind though, I could listen to good music and chill. Outside of the city we had to do everything ourselves including taking the body to the morgue and stripping it. But I enjoyed being a FLO and it could be hugely rewarding. I didn't always update the city with all my deployments; if it was just a quick favour for division, such as dealing with the family of a drowning victim for a few days until the body popped up, then I didn't feel it counted.

My first deployment was a young man by the name of Ron. He lived with his family in Baytown and died crossing the road to have a pee behind a road sign in the darkness on the main road.

Ron got collected by a taxi as he stepped out from behind the sign. By the time he was identified and a local cop sent round to the house, it was nearly dawn. His mother screamed the house down and collapsed in the doorway.

I started at 8 am and was asked to go and see them which was no problem except that I didn't know where they were. They weren't at home and presumably had decided to stay with relatives near to the crash scene seventy miles away. Everyone from the night shift involved in the incident from the crash scene had gone home, so I had nothing much to go on and it would take me most of the day to locate the family. Finally, that evening, I would knock on a door down in the city and find the family grieving at a relative's house. I spent an hour or two with them explaining how things would work, how post mortems would be arranged and when bodies would be released for funerals. It's all the little things that need to be talked about.

Strangely when something like this had happened to a family, I would find there was a window of opportunity in terms of the family wanting to talk to me. I could be their source of information and be there to reassure them. There was a time between shock and grief when they could give me all I needed to know. It sounds callous and manipulative but I found they wanted to talk, to tell me all about the deceased, their lives, hopes, future, the happy times and the sad memories that now would make them smile. I soon learnt that the ones who would be coping one day would not be coping the next. The family would support each other in a strange dynamic and without saying anything one would always step up to be the strong one when the others couldn't. It was humbling sometimes to see it playing out, and the more I saw it the more I would be able to predict it.

In the case of Ron's family, I asked them if they would like to go to the morgue. Maybe it was too soon afterwards, but I always said that I would arrange it whenever I could. I would find that most families would only go once. The first time they said goodbye to a loved one and it was a good thing. The second time they were seeing a body and it wasn't a good thing. I could never tell them, but I saw it again and again. I would never stop anyone going to the morgue. Regardless of how bad the injuries were, and, as one mother once told me when she wanted to go see her son: she had changed his nappies, held his head when he was sick and looked after him his whole life, she could cope as long as she had an idea what to expect.

The one and only time I had a family who simply couldn't see their next of kin was because of a plane crash, but there were a few who I advised not to go and they would listen to me.

Ron's parents wanted to go see him again and I would go and I would make it so. It didn't matter that it was getting late, it didn't matter that I was alone and there was no one to help, and it didn't matter that I was supposed to be at home with my own family. I went to the local police office to get the keys to the morgue. It was within the local hospital and easy to find. It was now late evening and I had an hour or so to sort things out for the family. I unlocked the morgue, a low building built across two levels behind the more functionary parts of the hospital that the vast majority of hospital visitors don't see. Opening the door and turning on the lights I started to find my way around, wishing I didn't have to work alone as much. From the main door, a corridor sloped down to the right and straight in front of me was a small room with a trolley and the usual comforting pictures around the wall that indicated this was the viewing room. Usually a scenery picture, a cross and a box of tissues on a low table.

I went down the ramp and turned left into the room with all the big fridges. That's a good start, a cold tiled functionary room. Opposite the row of body fridges, three levels high, was an opening with opaque plastic strips hanging from the ceiling in place of a door. A quick peek through this doorway revealed a stark, clinical room smelling of hospital and death.

You can't describe a morgue and its distinctive smell if you've not been there. It's not unpleasant; it's just that once you've been in one you can only associate that smell with death.

This room had a low table, that could be well lit from above by a row of spotlights, and a microphone hanging from the ceiling. The table's polished chrome surface had a natural slope towards a drain point. All around the walls were a collection of sharp things. Horrible nasty stainless-steel cutting things and power tools that clearly only had one purpose. I don't really understand why they looked like that, I mean I can buy knives from Asda and they look ok, nice bright handles and they still work fine. I can get a nice circular saw or electric drill and it's cheerful and yellow, almost happy. I really don't understand why whoever makes this sort of stuff for morgues has to make everything look like it's for some kind of insane gothic horror film. But it does and it used to creep me the fuck out.

On top of everything it was Halloween. I mean seriously, what the fuck.

As I perused this room a noise came from the sloped corridor behind me: 'pssssst.'

'Hello?' Obviously some nice porter from the hospital coming to see why the light was on, except it just wasn't. I looked, and then I listened, and then I wandered round a bit curious. It was ok though so I started getting Ron out the fridge. I opened the door and found him; well, I would have been quite miffed if I hadn't. He was in a body bag lying on a white tray. The fridges all had rollers to let the trays slide in and out easily.

I unzipped the bag just to make sure it was the right person. You can laugh, but seriously these things need to be done. Everybody has two name tags just in case one gets detached. It has happened that two bodies get mixed up and it's a tragedy for the family if it happens. I lined up the trolley with the fridge and began to pull good old Ron out, having a nice chat to him as I did so. He seemed the quiet sort.

Behind me I heard someone: 'psssst.'

Seriously. We're not amused at all. I asked Ron to just stay where he was and went for a quick wander up to the viewing room and had a look outside. Someone was clearly playing a joke so I locked the door. Now I was locked in with the dead bodies but I was ok with that. As I walked back down the ramp the thought ran through my head that when I turned the corner all the fridges would be open and all the people would be standing facing me. Maybe I should write horror stories, but it's not a good thought to have when you've just decided it's maybe not just you that's in the morgue. I turned the corner and...

Nothing had changed.

So I went back to sorting out Ron, having a nice chat as I did so. I used to like talking to dead people, in the way I felt their relatives would like; I was always very respectful and would tell them it wouldn't take long, and their family would be there soon.

Now this was the first time I'd been in this morgue and it had an unusual feature. Basically because the viewing room was higher up than the fridge room the only way to get the body up there was to raise the trolley. Fortunately, it had a hydraulic mechanism for just such a purpose. I pressed the button and soon Ron was up at shoulder height, lined up with a small doorway in the wall. I could wander round and prepare the trolley in the viewing room but, as I did so, I heard my mystery ghost in the fridge room

'Pssst'

This wasn't funny anymore, and I was still locked in. It occurred to me that the key was in the lock. What if I went to the door and it was locked but the key had gone? I carried on sliding Ron through into the viewing room then turned the second trolley into the middle of the room and did my best to make it look like a bed. There was a store room off the autopsy room full of sheets so I took a pillow, wipes and a hospital blanket. By the time I'd finished Ron looked like he was asleep in a comfortable bed. I made sure his eyes were shut and hid any trace of blood. A nice box of tissues on a table beside him and I turned the lights down. As I did so I heard another 'psssst' in the hallway.

I did what any brave man would do.

I left and waited in the car.

And locked the doors.

Once the family showed up I would do my bit, giving them as much time as they wanted and staying just within question range but out of the way for them to grieve. They were a lovely family and I had as much time for them as they needed. When they said they wanted to leave I offered them the chance to come back but I knew they wouldn't want it. Relatives rarely did. I offered my support and they had my number, so we shook hands and I would see them again the next day anyway. I watched them drive away and turned back into the morgue.

It took just a few minutes to remove all the sheets and the pillow and get them in a yellow burn waste disposal bag. Then I moved the trolley back in line with the low hatch and slid the white tray through the hatch. As I did so something went wrong. The trolley on the lower side, which was extended to full height, was too high, which had made sense earlier so that the tray was sliding slightly downhill onto the lower trolley in the upper room, but now it worked against me. What was worse was that I hadn't put the brake on the trolley in the fridge room and it started rolling away, pushed by the edge of the tray.

Bollocks.

I tried to stop it but, as I did so, the edge of the white tray slipped off and tipped down towards the floor in the lower fridge room and Ron starting to slide off it towards the floor. I grabbed him under his shoulders, his head now tight next to mine as I tried to pull him back through the hatch. His cheek felt icy cold against mine as I held him from sliding away.

'Pssssst', from the corridor behind me.

I had to phone the morgue the next day and explain how much fun you can have using trays as slides

I now hate those automatic air fresheners with a passion.

ON A CHEERIER NOTE

Drink drivers were good fun and probably the prisoners I had least sympathy for. One quirk of the legislation is that if the person has had a drink within twenty minutes of being stopped then they must have twenty minutes at the road side before it's possible to do the screening test. It's so that mouth alcohol doesn't contaminate the test. It's a strange twenty minutes, because they aren't really under arrest yet because they haven't done anything, but they aren't free to go either. Some years later Bruce and I stopped a man in a transit who was drinking from a tin of beer because he was parked sitting in the driver's seat of his van near the waterfall at Lochside, a little village just outside Baytown. Clearly he had twenty minutes of our highly intellectual chat to put up with before we could use the road-side breath-test machine. During some friendly banter the man did some thinking and reasoned that if he could speed up his blood flow he could process any alcohol in his system more quickly. So, he asked if it was ok if he did exercise while we waited.

'Crack on mate' said we, as we stood back against the bonnet of the police car, arms folded and watched in delight as he started doing star jumps and press ups. It must have been a bizarre sight for people driving past, but as the count down to twenty minutes went on, it was suggested that the best way to burn calories and get the blood pumping was to use his brain more.

'Maybe if you told us some jokes?'

So for the last five minutes or so we stood laughing as he tried his best to tell us jokes and did a great work out. It should have been a work-out video really, Rob and Bruce's work-out or you get the jail-fitness programme. I was so happy when the sweating, exhausted driver finally blew a negative. I mean, really, can you imagine what a defence lawyer would have said in court?

CHAPTER 14

MISERY

Every time that any FLO was deployed to a family, regardless of the circumstances, a risk assessment had to be carried out. This was really just the police-management machine protecting itself because any family-contact officer turning up for the first time, or any other cop turning up to destroy a family with a death message, would run exactly the same risks as me. Due to the size of the area that I covered and the normality of being single-crewed, I was almost always alone anyway, so the risk assessment realistically made no difference. This was technically breaking the force procedures for family-liaison deployments, but in reality it was a practical and workable solution. I preferred being alone anyway because it meant I didn't have to worry about anyone that I was with making an insensitive comment. There were many cops I trusted, but a lot I didn't. Some I wouldn't have trusted with a loaded stapler.

The public perception is that the family-liaison officer is there to help the family through the trauma of the enquiry and that is partially true, but from the police perspective the FLO is an information gatherer and a big part of the enquiry team. The vast majority of murder victims know who the killer is and therefore it follows that the family often do too. The FLO then provides the enquiry team with a huge advantage, because every piece of information that the family are given by the enquiry team can only have come from the FLO, and every part of that is documented in a FLO log book. It's a fantastic, controlled, two-way flow of information that benefits the enquiry team hugely.

As a consequence, if the family know something more about the death of their loved one, something they shouldn't know, it follows that that they got this information from a connection with the killer. It's amazing the number of times I've seen a family member or member of the public being interviewed on TV and every switched-on cop I know will say straight away, 'how do they know that?', 'Why have they assumed that?' or more often a dry 'I bet they fucking did it'. Invariably, a day or two later, it will transpire that the same person is now 'helping the police with enquiries'.

Over the next few years I would be deployed every couple of months or so, and because I was also a crash investigator I would usually have either a road death to investigate or a family to liaise with.

The first year I only had six or seven families to see and they tended to be fairly straight-forward as much as these things could be. I became very matter of fact about it, from when I knocked on the door and politely asked if I could come in and speak to them, to the last hand shake or hug as I walked away. I documented everything that I told the family and what they had to tell me. In the case of missing persons, this information could be fantastic. I started to listen out for the way that a family's perception of the deceased changed over the week following death, especially for road deaths in cases where the victims were quite obviously responsible for their own deaths. During week two of an early deployment it was the family who would give away the information that their son was phoned just before he crashed, killing a young girl. Only a few days earlier they were happy to tell me what a great, safe driver he had been.

A drowning, a suicide, a road death, multiple road deaths, each one had its own challenges and its own unique highlights. I enjoyed doing something helpful when I could. I loved being trusted and making sure I paid back that trust. I always told every family early on that if they wanted to know something I'd get them the answer and, if they asked a difficult question, I wouldn't lie to make it easier for them. I would do anything I could for a family if it was reasonable.

I was often invited to funerals, usually with one of the enquiry team, but soon learned through the experience of going to them that it was not healthy for the family to have us there. I could see it from the way they looked at us. It was polite of them to invite me but after going to fifteen or so, I learnt to see just how much it was resented by the other people at the funeral. It upset the dynamic once someone realised who you were and it was easy to see that the reporting officer and I were pointed out to more and more extended family members by whispers and quick glances.

It was quite normal for a family to ask for the clothes the person had been wearing to be returned, and I often got them dry cleaned, although it surprised me how many families felt they had to do this themselves or wanted the clothes back unwashed for their dead relative's smell. One of the strangest requests I received involved a French couple who were killed on a Harley Davidson motorcycle. It was a beautiful day and the bike they were on was part of a group of nearly thirty large touring bikes having a scenic cruise up the west coast. The husband made the mistake of following the bike in front through an overtake on an articulated truck into a sweeping left bend and probably panicked when he saw the car opposing him. Maybe he went back to his default of driving on the right; no one will ever know because both he and his wife paid dearly for it.

Bruce was the first cop there and he tried to do CPR to save one of the bikers with no luck, while the other died crushed underneath the front of the car. By this stage I was very used to Bruce as an amazing collector of death. I would never meet another cop who seemed to attract death so much, and what was more staggering was the variation in the types of death. I got to know him very well over the next few years, and he became a confidant and one of the people I knew I could trust.

I started calling his car 'Binky' after Death's horse in the Terry Pratchett Discworld novels. The name stuck and Binky would later be replaced with Binky 2 then Binky 3 but always Bruce's faithful chariot. Good old Binky. I think it helped that we had a similar sick coping sense of humour. And like me, he received no support in years to come. On occasions when we worked together it was cheerful to hear his 'let's go harvest some souls' quip as we headed out to the car.

The problems associated with the family of these bikers being in France were short lived and within a day the dead husband's brother was in my car and on the way back from Glasgow airport. I'd phoned the airline and they'd been fantastic in helping to get a short-notice seat on the usually busy shuttle.

I'd been lucky the day before to have the advantage of a girl from the office who spoke good French, but now I was struggling with my frankly inadequate skills. I was quite angry with the dead couple. I couldn't quite put my finger on why, but I knew that their kids were quite young and it annoyed me that they had chosen a way to die together while their kids were kept safe. Selfish, I felt and, in a warped way, I felt it would be nice if they'd died too; I don't quite know why. As a biker myself I would do exactly the same thing but, like most bikers, I always rationalise that it would never ever happen to me.

When the extended family in France asked me to take a picture of the mother and father so they could show the kids, I was really taken aback. I initially felt this was a horrible thing to do, after all who wants a picture of a dead body? Especially when they have encountered a fairly violent and disfiguring end. I was quite uncomfortable but the more I thought about it, the more I realised it was actually quite an opportunity. I had dealt before with a cot death and been happy to help arrange a tasteful photograph and have hand and foot prints in plaster for the family to keep, so why should it be any different after all, from them going to the morgue to see them?

Well, it shouldn't, but it gave me a chance to help a family a bit more than I normally could. I asked around but no FLO seemed to have ever done anything like this before. So by the time I was on the way to pick up the brother, we had already discussed in my very limited French that he should bring the kid's favourite two teddy bears. We stopped off at a florist in Baytown and I tried to buy some flowers. I say tried to, because I couldn't persuade the shopkeeper to take any money. She'd been through this too; she knew exactly who I was and what I was doing it for and she just wouldn't take the money. Human kindness when it's not expected makes me feel really humble sometimes, and I could see her eyes getting teary as she tried to speak a little French to the kid's uncle. We gratefully took the flowers and left. This might sound bizarre but the police would happily put me on a discipline charge for that if they had ever known. Even though I tried to pay her, taking something for nothing is a huge 'don't do' and they make no exceptions. Complaints and discipline are inflexible and generally sheltered in offices from the real world.

After dropping the uncle's luggage at a local hotel and having a drink with some of the other bikers from the group who were still staying in Baytown, we went to the hospital morgue and together we spent some time taking his brother and sister-in-law through to the viewing room and laying them side by side, each holding a teddy bear, as though sleeping. Then holding flowers on their chests, and finally together holding hands. I took the pictures as carefully as possible, using my own camera so that I could make sure the aperture and lighting would make the pictures less stark and to add warmth. I made sure there was no sign of injury and, as much as possible, made sure that the pictures were something I felt I could show to anyone without telling them what they were, and would hope they would just wonder why I had a picture of someone sleeping.

It was surprising for me that the end result was far more tasteful for the kids to have to say goodbye to than I had originally imagined. I asked the uncle to destroy the pictures once they'd seen them and explained I felt that the kids should have their memories from the living pictures they already had in my opinion, but I would understand if he couldn't do that. I saw the tears welling up in his eyes as we tried our best to communicate, my poor French matching his poor English. A look in someone's eyes can sometimes say far more than any words. Of course, I maybe told him to not to let squirrels eat his nuts whilst dancing in the bath. My French is pretty crap.

When he left, he took the teddy bears back home and I put the flowers in the glass-topped coffins with mum and dad.

SUBJECT SHEETS

Subject sheets are a curious way the police have of communication. They're a sort-of formal memo made unnecessarily difficult. They're very formal and all the points to be made are listed and numbered. I have no idea why.

In order to create one, and as with police reports, the slightly complicated method used was to phone a big answering-machine and dictate to it, so that it could be typed up by the typists at a later date, usually within a few weeks depending on urgency. It would then arrive nicely typed up with spelling mistakes which need amending by the same process before finally being ready to send to whoever it was intended for in the first place, usually the Sgt or Inspector sitting in the next room.

Of course it would have been easier to have walked through and just said whatever needed to be said in the first place but the police love a good subject sheet; it's fantastically inefficient. I realised the typists had a pretty boring job of it. Harry in the traffic used to phone the voice bank and play them nice music for a few minutes before each dictation. I tried this too but felt maybe they didn't find my choice of Iron Maiden as relaxing Harry's usual choice of Classic FM or Radio 2. I also tried putting jokes on the voice bank and hiding ridiculous words in police reports. Waz used to make up funny middle names for all the police witnesses when he did statements, which was a pain when no-one noticed and you had to say in the witness box that you were in fact Constable Rob Howling Moon. As an aside, the ability to write and sign off another cop's statement disappeared, partly because they were all carbon copies of the same statement but mainly because it ended the days when you got to court to speak about something and realised you had actually been on annual leave in another country that day and had sod all in your notebook.

Awkward.

Back in the city, Alex left his wife to shag one of the typists but I felt that was taking entertaining them too far. So I liked to put strange things on the voice bank to see if they were awake. This was one of mine;

SUBJECT SHEET

To PC John Collins T123 312345

From PC Rob Moon T544 291234

Date 05/04/04

Subject : Your impending demise

With reference to above subject I have to report

1) Today is your last day as a crew member in Road Patrol vehicle call sign TE13.

2) This is because I am going to kill you.

3) Be a good sport and wash the car before then.

4) Thanks ever so much, toodle pip.

I respectfully request that this subject sheet be forwarded to PC Collins for his information and attention. Love and kisses.

Signed *Rob*

PC Moon

291234 T544

CHAPTER 15

PLAYING IN THE SNOW.

'Whether you think you can or think you can't, you're absolutely right'
Henry Ford

Working on the west coast of Scotland in a stunningly beautiful, remote area with amazing scenery and lovely islands could be quite humbling from the long perfect beaches at the south end of the Mull of Kintore up to the bleakness of Glen Ord surrounded by lonely snow-capped mountains and glens.

The longest Sam and I would ever take to get to a road crash scene was thirteen hours, which involved an early-morning ferry to get to a road death on the island of Truk. We were the first car to arrive and were stranded for two days before getting extracted by the police helicopter. That's probably inconceivable for any cop working in the city, but for me a response journey could involve a ferry, or the time it could take might even be dictated by the need to cross a tidal causeway.

When I was on my own, which was most of the time, I would often drive up to the ski centre or 'The Gorge' and park up, get out the car and reflect on the snow-capped mountains and loneliness of it all. I loved the dark, gloomy desolation; especially in winter during the full moon, the long lonely nights when the scenery was lit by soft cold light reflected from the snowy mountaintops; it was quite haunting. On cold clear nights I would sometimes drive into a remote glen and lie alone on the warm bonnet of the car watching for shooting stars or, if I was really lucky, catching the distant glow of the northern lights as my breath froze in clouds in the air.

Part of the winter job of the police in remote Scotland was 'Snow Patrol'. Each traffic command area had a 4x4 patrol car and, when the snow came, we would head up to the mountain roads and close the snow gates. If we didn't get there in time, there was potential for hundreds of motorists to get stranded in the Glen. It had happened before at Bridge of Ord with skiers attempting to return from the ski centre and we always knew it was time for the snow gates to shut when the main road at the Black Mountain started to cause us problems. Once the snow gates were locked we would patrol inside the closed area in case anyone left a farm or house and became stuck. It was a great job, especially when we had the big Range Rover. It would go absolutely anywhere and the day we switched to a Shogun was a big let-down for me.

JC and I were in high spirits on New Year's Eve, out playing in the Land Rover Discovery, a chance for me to work with someone for a change because single-crewed snow patrol was frowned upon. The Discovery was a lot more agricultural, but had a similar go-anywhere ability to the big Rangie. Later that year I would skid it in the snow and crash it into the only roadside telegraph pole for twenty-six miles. So annoying, although what made it funny was phoning up the next morning to apologise to big Sam and JC on the early shift, because they'd travelled to get a replacement from the city while it was fixed, only to find out they'd just crashed its replacement in the snow within an hour of getting it.

And to make it even sweeter JC's last words before they crashed were, 'I bet Rob was fucking about in the snow when he crashed'.

We were up north near Black Mountain in the late afternoon as the snow started to get heavy, drifting down in big flakes in the soft fading daylight, the darkening skies leaden with a purple tinge. I loved the way the snow made everything so quiet and peaceful. A call came over the radio: two hill walkers visiting Scotland from Hong Kong had encountered difficulties up one of the less- climbed Munroes on the North side of Glen Ord. One had returned to their bed and breakfast leaving the other hillwalker alone near the summit of the mountain.

Normally we would shout up Bruce the local beat man with his extensive knowledge of what to do, who to call and where the bacon rolls were, and have a snowball fight while those nice mountain rescue people or the big yellow helicopter arrived to save the day from Lossiemouth, but, sadly, none of the above could happen. The big yellow RAF gasoline budgie couldn't come and play; the RAF mountain-rescue team were playing elsewhere; the Police mountain-rescue team were even further elsewhere, and Bruce was probably in Florida probably trying to stop-search Mickey Mouse for drugs. So it was just us in Narnia.

We went to the bed and breakfast and got details of the missing woman. Small, lightly built and under-dressed with no proper mountaineering equipment. Already I was starting to write the sudden-death report in my head, trying to get details and liaise with abroad, all the while being moderately miffed because I wanted home in time to spend New Year with my family.

After finding out that they had accessed the mountain over a bridge to the north side of Glen Ord about six miles up the glen, we started trying to find a nice RV point for the local charity mountain rescue team when they could finally get there. As we waited at our lovely RV point with the snow now getting deeper and deeper on the bonnet of the Discovery, we were updated that the local, charity-run, mountain-rescue team were also elsewhere and would not be attending. The police team were still unavailable presumably because they were busy in the city on New Year's Eve, with many of their number being from the support unit.

The office had contacted Alan Kerr, the local forest commission ranger, to get the gate on the other side of the bridge over the River Ord opened, and Bruce, it turned out, was not in Florida as I had believed and would, in the style of Winston Wolf, be there directly. So we should chill the fuck out and await the arrival of the cavalry. Alan would allow us access to a Land Rover track that would take us a mile or two up the hill.

I made the decision that our missing Hong Kong lady would most likely be heading down the track anyway and, to speed things up, I should just head up. Also it was so Christmassy and perfect, the walk would be lovely. By now the snow was a few inches deep and the sun had set, leaving a sort-of tranquil, night-time, Christmas-card scene, only with slightly fewer wise men and more all-terrain vehicles.

JC agreed to stay at the RV point, and wait on Alan and Bruce while I left my body armour, baton and handcuffs in the back of the disco. I carried a big black Tardis-like kit back with me in the car and, after some rummaging around in the big bumper kit-bag of fun, had my woollen black snow-patrol fluffy hat, gloves, a jumper and T-shirt plus a neck warmer. I would take a personal radio, map, juice and two torches. I always carried an old army ration pack and a little cooker, but I was at this stage guessing I would just be a twenty-minute walk through Santa's magical kingdom up to the forest clearing where the track stopped on the map.

The body armour was something I still rarely wore anyway. If I was going to the city I would wear it but usually it lived in the back of the car. It didn't matter in any event because I had long since taken out the ballistic stab-proof panels and replaced them with cardboard. It had caused much laughter in the office when I made my new panels out of an old cardboard box, but the issue panels were not comfortable and smelt of baby sick for some reason. I had got away with my lovely cardboard ones for a couple of years until I had to really re-qualify instead of just pretending and getting signed off by a friendly Officer safety-training instructor on the second half of the back shift. Even then I had some pictures of my lovely cardboard body armour to entertain students at the college years later. I'd even written 'this side towards body', on them just like the real ones.

For now, what I had was perfect for the walk up the forest track, past the locked gate. Very therapeutic. The personal radio normally would not let me speak to anyone other than JC at the RV, since this was before the introduction of the digital airwave system. But JC could use the car set as a relay so Baytown could listen in on our transmissions. 'Homeless' was in the office, keeping the incident updated and monitoring the channel which was quite handy because he knew the area well and would keep track of where I was on the big office map. 'Homeless' incidentally was Aly, who stayed in a lovely home. He was called 'Homeless Horse' because, as I had been told when I came to Baytown: 'he's nae stable'. This had, allegedly, followed an incident where he humanely dispatched an injured Vietnamese pot-bellied pig in front of a load of school children. It had been run over after escaping a farm park. I have no idea if this is true but it's a fantastic story.

I started off over the bailey bridge and up the track into the forest. The scrunch scrunch of my feet and the feeling of stepping in virgin snow in the winter half-light was wonderful, all the noise of the night muted and dulled by the big snowflakes. It was easy to see the track with the snow reflecting what little light there was and my eyes quickly adjusting to the darkness. Around me, branches on either side were bending under the weight of snow over the track. I started to jog on the flat and to walk up inclines. A few brief downhills had me watching my step as I relished this eerie, night-time, winter wonderland.

I started to daydream about selection for the SAS. I was only nineteen when I had applied for the regiment, just a daft mucked-up boy with a head full of silly ambitious dreams. At the time it was possible to join the regiment straight off the street amazingly, although this was almost unheard of. I have never met anyone who managed it. In practice most would have come from another unit. I had asked to do selection from Glasgow and Strathclyde University OTC, a Reserve army unit attached to the University in Glasgow. All the people in the unit were students like me, and many were hoping for a career in the army after getting their degree. I had already completed an attachment with 'A' company 15th Parachute regiment who were in Yorkhill at the time.

The Adjutant at the OTC was not impressed when I said I wanted to go and try SAS selection.

'Even if you pass, and very few your age do, you'll just get used until you're no use to anyone and thrown away; you could have a good career in a few years in the Army, as an officer.'

I didn't listen and no one wanting into the regiment would, because here is the thing: if you want in that's all that matters. It's your life, your reason for being and all you dream about. I would go out running in Glasgow, breaking the ice to do press-ups in the shallow River Kelvin in winter, and spend every weekend out in the hills behind my mother and father's house. I was wiry and thin, with very little upper-body strength, not the typical stereotype of a hunky Special Forces soldier, but that was perfect for the SAS;

I did selection for the regiment over the summer of 1989, and from the first eight-mile run something odd happened. When I first met all my hopeful fellow candidates I was quite disheartened by their obvious strength and fitness. I remember a PTI (Physical Training Instructor) from 51 Highland Division, storming off ahead during the early beastings, and a Para Captain, confidently and eagerly disappearing into the distance every time we had a timed navigation march. They spoke to the Directing Staff (DS) on the course as though they could be friends one day, while I shuffled quietly around, keeping my head down, worrying about everything and trying not to fuck up.

We were tested in basic map reading and taught with little enthusiasm some mountain survival techniques by 'Young Man', one of the senior recruit team Sgts, and the oldest guy in the squadron. But if you didn't know how to do that you shouldn't be there. Selection was an odd thing; there was little in the way of shouting or being ordered about. If you didn't want to be there, you got up and left; if you didn't meet the grade, you left; if you fucked up, you were noticed; if you were noticed and fucked up, you left. Play the grey man.

No one ever saw it happen, I have no idea why, but when someone was binned, they would simply disappear. The staff would call them aside and then once you had finished doing, whatever you were all doing, they would be gone: photo scored through on the wall in the main corridor, number struck off, rifle back in the armoury, kit back in the store. Gone forever, and this wasn't a TV reality show where they shook hands and had two minutes to wish us all luck, followed by a quick chat to the camera. People just disappeared. RTU'd, better known as 'Returned to Unit'—or just 'binned'.

On the wall of our training room were two poems. I didn't know them but I liked one in particular because it was so apt. I would later find out it was called 'IF' by Rudyard Kipling and to this day I still read it with nostalgia and a smile. One verse in particular stuck with me.

If all men count with you, but none too much;
If you can fill the unforgiving minute
With sixty seconds' worth of distance run,
Yours is the Earth and everything that's in it,
And—which is more—you'll be a Man, my son!

The basic premise of selection would stay the same but each week we were pushed harder and harder. No one shouted or ordered us about but expectations were incredibly high and if you didn't perform, well, you were binned. One warning for missing an RV point was the best you could expect. Even with experienced hardened soldiers, only one in ten would go forward into continuation.

We would get our kit together every time we were tested. No one offered guidance or help and if you got it wrong you learnt and suffered for it. Kit included a large Bergen rucksack with an orange panel on top so we could be seen on the hill easily, webbing belt including a couple of water bottles, ammo pouches, and an old FN FAL rifle. Holding the rifle anyway other than 'ready to aim', or leaving it out of reach when eating was a huge no-no, and, to encourage that, slings were not allowed.

The FN was essentially the same as the standard British Army SLR, L1A1. A 7.62 mm semi-automatic rifle, designed in a different era. It was long, heavy, cumbersome and a joy to use. That sounds like a contradiction but speak to anyone who used it and they loved it. It fired a big heavy mother of a round very fast due to the long barrel and, by God, if you hit something it would go down.

The FN's used in selection were presumably old Argentinean ones nabbed after the Falklands and therefore disposable. The cocking handle was different from the fold-forward UK issue SLR and the fire selector had an automatic position. I liked mine. We would have all our kit checked for weight and then we would be taken somewhere — somewhere with hills. The Brecon Beacons in Wales are famous for their use by the regiment, but in a time of increasing threat from the IRA, we would often use the Pennines, or even Scotland. Everyone would start at a known point and be given a six-figure grid reference, before setting off at minute intervals. The task was simple; find the RV point on the OS Landranger 1:50,000 map and go there. The rules were simple too: don't get caught on a path or road, don't walk in a group, and assume you had to cover the ground at an absolute minimum of 4km per hour, which sounds slow until you realised the terrain was becoming increasingly rough and steep as the walks went on and the basic route distance was as the crow flies. In practice most of the route was covered at a medium jog, walking up hills and running downhill. If anyone quit during a route they were banned from re-applying.

Arriving at the first RV there would normally be a queue because most people were still in sight of each other, the racing snakes having not yet pushed far enough ahead. One at a time we would be called forward to the DS, present the map and tell them: 'Staff, I came from here (point at map) and I am here (point at map)'. Rather than point a big stubby finger at the map (which at 1:50,000 is about 800m wide) we had to use a blade of grass to point out the exact location. Nothing could ever be written down and the map could never be marked. A captured map gives away too much, even from the impressions of a sharp point pressed into the paper.

The DS would then give you a new six-figure grid reference and you would show the DS where it was on your map before trotting off for the next leg of your exciting journey. Sounds fun doesn't it? Well after ten weeks of rain, heat, blisters, aching muscles and progressively longer and longer routes it really wasn't. And then there were the games. The first time I encountered this was early in the morning after walking overnight. We were all held at what we were told was the final RV. A four-tonne truck sat on the road nearby. When the slower ones got into the RV we were told we were heading back to base, 'so get on the truck'—which promptly drove away with us watching. There was no organised battle march and we were already shattered from the night and day before. There was nothing for it but to tighten the shoulder straps on our bergens, pull the FN in tight and start running. It was an infeasible to run the 60 km back, but it was just to see who would try. Eight miles later the truck had stopped and those who made it would clamber in collapsing, in a sweaty exhausted but deeply suspicious heap in the truck.

I enjoyed it on a strange sort of level. Being alone against the clock, just me and the mountains. There was no magic number of recruits that would get through, and they would happily fail everyone or no one. There were ways to cheat too, but being caught was instant RTU. One cheat was to have a set of scales. Each Bergen was weighted at the beginning, randomly during and at the end of the selection routes. By week five we were up to 60lb, but the problem was without hiding a set of scales you didn't know what your Bergen would weigh, so every time I took a drink or ate food I would add some stones.

I cut up a foam ground mat and wrapped it round the shoulder straps of my Bergen to make it more comfortable and also padded the inside of my water bottle and webbing pouches to stop them rubbing and hurting so much as I ran, but there was only so much that could be done. It was normal that my shoulders bled after a route.

During week five that year was an infamous route called 'zig zag.' It started at the bottom of Loch Lomond and, as the name suggested, the route crossed the Lomond range from east to west and back, zig-zagging up the east side of the loch. RV points would mean crossing the summit and shoulders of Ben Lomond four times back and forward as we headed north, finally resting up for four hours after 35km or so.

When the night route started, the first RV was the penultimate one from the day walk. You never knew what the route would be and certainly never when it would end, but it was the fear that the route was the day walk in reverse that made some quit there and then. It was the only long Scottish route and I didn't ever hear of it being used again, but mentally it was a killer. I would see a part of it years later in a reality TV show about the regiment, but they had cut it right down to make it easier for TV.

It was a strange day, when I looked around and realised how un-crowded things had become. We had started that year's selection course with forty-four. We were down to five and I had no idea when this had happened. Of those five, one was coming back to the regiment after a two-year enforced break, but the rest of us were an odd bunch. Gone were the tough PTI, the Para Captain, and all the others I had envied for their confidence on day one. What was left was a small group of quiet, shy and very driven misfits. None of us stood out at all in a crowd or were the life of the party; we didn't shout or boast; we wouldn't be noticed.

The thinking man's soldier. Grey men.

The walks became longer and harder, but I noticed a big change in the way those in the regiment spoke to us. It was now first-name terms and the 'Sabre' troops were clearly sizing us up. 'Sabre' refers to those active troops in the regiment who have been 'badged' and completed continuation training and all the courses and qualifications. Come 'RSM's test', the final two walks before 'Long Drag', we were all confident and desperate to get it over.

I completely fucked up the day walk. I stopped for fifteen minutes and couldn't make up the time. The day walk was only 40km or so but I knew as the night walk started I had some making up to do. I got my head down and, in a more determined way than ever before, ran, scrambled and in almost blind panic at being so close came running into the final RV a couple of hours after dawn. Bergen weighed and handed back, I made my first big mistake, asking the DS if I'd passed.

Behind the DS a short figure with a handlebar moustache would snap round and tell me to fuck off, and that I was cheeky cunt. It was the RSM. I'd been noticed and knew I was close to being binned like all those before me.

Long Drag is the final test. It's a complete and utter bastard, a continuous day into night route. Multiple routes, but the most famous in the regiment is called 'Fan Dance', because of the central challenge Pen-y-Fan, the highest peak in south Wales. 65km, 60 lb in the Bergen, FN rifle and webbing. As I waited in the early morning light with the others, getting ready to set off, I knew I didn't ever want anything more than this. As always we only knew the first RV, although rumours of the route were widespread. They were also wrong but only because the route was changed on the day due to the heat. We would also have an extra hour added to our twenty-one hour cut of time but on the hill there was no way to know that.

As the day wore on I hit one barrier after another, exhausting my supply of Solpadine pain killers, Proplus and Lucozade. As the sun set I was using puritabs, ration-pack sugar and river water, it had been one of the hottest days of that year, and I couldn't drink enough to stay hydrated. I knew I was utterly exhausted and almost in a dream as the sun set and I faded mentally and physically. Around two in the morning I reached a lonely RV in the dark. I had for some time been worried my Bergen was under weight and had put a huge rock low down in the main compartment to make up for weight. All my water bottles were full of river water and I had nothing left physically to give. I was light headed and desperate to stop, I knew I was emotionally drained and, frankly, not fit for anything.

The DS gave me the grid for my next RV and my heart soared. It was our start RV and only 4km away from my current position. The same point we had started from and therefore likely to be the last and, even better, there were no more big ascents. I summoned all I had and went for it. Jogging and walking as the excruciating pain from my feet shouted at me to stop. I was determined to make that RV, and if they gave me another that was fine too; I could do this, I felt alive and as I finally jogged down to a waiting minibus and Land Rover, I could see others watching me beside discarded Bergens.

'I'm here staff, I came from here' I announced, pointing out the locations on my map.

'Well done, son.'

I was passed a cup of boiling-hot chicken Cup-a-Soup and immediately burnt my mouth on it. It was just over nineteen hours and forty minutes since I'd started and the cut-off had been extended to twenty-two hours due to the heat. I was utterly elated when my Bergen was weighed at over 70lb. I slightly overdid the rocks it seemed, but I didn't care. I was soon in the minibus and the lights went out in my head. I would be woken later and find out all five of us were through to continuation training, the final step before getting 'badged'.

I needed Stevie an ex-para and our tame racing snake who had stormed long drag in under seventeen hours to help me get my T-shirt off in the shower. The Bergen rubbing had worn away the skin on my back and not just the usual skin on my shoulders. As I'd slept, my T-shirt had become stuck to my back by dried puss and blood. Back at base we were given sliced bacon grill in rolls and some tins of coke. It tasted better than any Michelin five-star meal ever could.

Back in Scotland in the snow and the dark, I was loving every second. Somewhere a switch in my head was moving into an old familiar position I'd forgotten about. I pushed on up the track starting to jog faster and dodge the snow-laden branches as I felt the cold air in my lungs, the blood surging in my veins and electricity sparking through old circuits in my head, illuminating old memories. Soon I reached an open clearing and the track would end. I shouted in an update with no reply. To my right was a river in spate with icy-cold, melting water from the mountain, gushing and gurgling. All around the clearing, dense conifers indicated that crossing the river was the only way to go. I could see what appeared to be a wider bit to the river where it flowed more slowly, and was soon up to my knees feeling the water entering my boots. I didn't care at all. The other side of the river had a more open area of smaller trees and I turned and jogged parallel with the river, climbing up higher and higher. I radioed an update to JC, but couldn't hear much in reply. It sounded like he was transmitting in response but I really didn't care if aliens had invaded. I was alone again, me and the mountain.

The snow fall was starting to get lighter and if I'd been lower I'd have realised the temperature was rising, but not for long. The snow on the ground though was getting deeper as I climbed and left the river behind. I was now following a deer fence as it climbed the mountain. This gave me a reference but one that wasn't on the OS map. Dense conifer trees to my right made this the only way to go. As the cloud above me cleared and the stars came out I would get clear of the tree line and also see in the reflected starlight the ridge ahead of me. I jogged on and into a boulder-and-scree field. Suddenly I could hear snippets of JC talking through my PR. The sound was broken but it sounded like he was now through the gate and driving towards the clearing and river crossing point below me.

Even better, Bruce had shown up. I checked my map and I was now well up above 2000ft and climbing towards the ridge leading to the summit. I shouted in a grid reference but there was no reply and I started to push on, head down, jog, run, jog run, jog, run, scrambling over rocks and feeling the scree giving way under the snow blanket. I wouldn't turn on my torch, partly for fear of losing my night vision but because I was enjoying the darkness. The switch was flicked; nothing else mattered except me, the mountain, the stars and the snow. I wanted to feel the Bergen on my back again and pull my FN tight to my chest, feel the pistol grip in my right hand, left hand holding the barrel, forefinger on the groove in the gas plug below the foresight, thumb behind, ready to snap up into the aim. I had a target, a mission for the first time in years. I wanted to find our missing person but in a strange way, because I was now different to that young trooper, because I wanted to find her dead. Death was what I did and it was who I was. I could imagine her on the ridge, huddled up, and covered in white powder snow with her last few conscious thoughts of peace and tranquillity in the silent night as her life ebbed away. What a beautiful way to die. I wanted that. I felt my life turning a corner. I wasn't the person I had been, and I wasn't that impressed with who I was turning out to be.

And the switch flicked off.

Way down in the glen I could hear a distant thumping, revving and falling. I stopped and listened and I was angry that suddenly someone else was on my mountain. It belonged to me, which I can't explain, but I was in emotional free fall. Emotions and elation suddenly snapping back to reality. As I walked slowly back down in disgust at this intruder to my domain I could see light pulsing below me under the low snow clouds, then breaking out and flickering from side to side like an angry monster searching for prey. After a few more minutes the lights would turn up the hill and find me. I made my way mentally deflated back down a small distance to meet Alan Kerr the forest ranger on his quad bike, which could go no further due to the terrain.

We exchanged greetings and updated each other. JC and Bruce were indeed now in the clearing at the new RV. Alan and I jogged and walked back up towards the ridge and chatted, he was outpacing me, my legs tired from the last few hours; he'd been a soldier. As we chatted, a light from a torch came searching out the darkness in front of us.

As three of us somehow straddled on the quad bike on the way back to the RV, I pondered what had happened. It was a bit precarious sitting on one bouncy plastic wheel arch, leaning behind the hill walker to hold the other wheel arch and struggling to balance and stay on the quad bike as Alan headed back.

I was annoyed at her: firstly for climbing a mountain on New Year's Eve totally unprepared, but mainly because I suspected her and her friend had had an argument and separated for that reason. I guessed she had just waited at the top until she saw the quad bike headlight. Ironically she might have come down earlier if I hadn't been intent on staying tactically dark. What annoyed me more though was disgust at myself. I had felt alive for the first time in ages and now felt utterly despondent. As we headed back and I saw melting snow falling from branches lower down in the glen and finally met up with JC, I just wanted the me I had been back on the hill.

JC was laughing but underneath was a serious problem. The control room had heard every update and word I had said. 'Homeless' was busy calming things down but, me running up a mountain on my own rated very highly on the stupidity scale. Months later, the Divisional Chief Inspector Garnier would call me in to the office, for a chat. JC had kicked up fuck at an appraisal that I had not been thanked or acknowledged. I had repeatedly asked that Alan Kerr receive a commendation or letter of thanks, but they wouldn't send it because it showed failings in the system for recalling the police mountain-rescue team. Also she would tell me that while she might have done the same thing she couldn't commend me for going up the hill alone; it was the wrong thing to do, verging on either getting put on paper or getting a commendation, so in reality neither could happen. End of conversation. Fair enough, I had more on my mind—and I desperately wanted to be back up that mountain in the hushed, soft, falling snow, heart pounding and thoughts of death racing alongside me.

Around this time the police changed the counselling service provided for FLOs in the city from six monthly to annual to save money.

CHAPTER 16

KAISER AND POLICE CARS

Among the interesting things you came across working up on the west coast or on the islands were the characters you would meet, and the support the public had for the police. It was like a trip back in time to some idyllic wonderland. We were almost always single-crewed and free to roam our areas and make friends. It was a different style of policing, largely done by mutual respect with the people who made up the community. If you needed help there was a fair chance it was the locals who would come to your aid first. It would die away over the next nine years as cuts and re-organisation forced us to police the remote areas with the same targets and KPI's that they had in the city.

I really respected people like 'Dave the Pyjama Cop', 'The Sea Captain', The 'Griefmeister' with 'Binky', 'Marvin the Paranoid Android', 'Biscuit', 'Toot-Toot', 'The Muc' (Pronounced- Meuch Gaelic for pig) on the island, and 'Kaiser' from Lochside, who all lived and policed in remote areas where their families and even young kids were a part of it. All of them had police houses that were also police stations and in effect had no escape from work. Having the cell as an extra room was handy though and I did know one cop who had a pool table in his. Annoying if the drunk you arrested was too drunk to stand but still beat you at pool. Pyjama Cop incidentally was so called because if he was recalled to duty to move the local kids on from the war memorial late on a backshift he would sometimes grab his hat and walk down in his PJ's and slippers. Genius.

I had some experience of this style of policing too because I was well known as a cop, and it was quite usual for me to stop a car looking for insurance details or maybe just looking for some information about someone, to then find that before I had even made it home that day, they would have met my wife or gone round to my house to try and speak to me and met my kids instead. This was the reality of policing in rural, remote Scotland and something soulless idiotic gaffers in the city could never comprehend, when they demanded stop searches and intelligence reports. It meant that there was never any escape from the public, and also, for those like Bruce, Cammy and I, no escape from the realities of death.

'Kaiser' was a legend. He'd never worked anywhere else and occupied the police house at Lochside. He was friendly, professional but old-fashioned in his methods. He knew the area like the back of his hand and knew the locals even better; he was also Baytown born and bred. No one would want to cross him and, if one of the young lads did, Kaiser wouldn't need to resort to jailing him or a conditional offer ticket. A quiet word to the kid's dad, and the young miscreant would be round to apologise the next day. It was proper policing with proper local knowledge.

Kaiser had many claims to fame but the one that always made me chuckle was the time he ran over Bambi. Now, you must put this in context, because any living deer and Kaiser were natural enemies. For Kaiser a road-kill was something you shot from the car. He was a hunting, shooting, fishing type with a shed at the back of his police house where unfortunate deer could be 'graloched' or gutted, and fish could be smoked. He loved the wilds and with the exception of his desire to shoot the local high school mascot, he was generally very sporting. Admittedly he once made the papers for shooting seals in front of a tourist boat full of kids, but he wasn't actually doing anything wrong at the time and hadn't seen the tourist boat round the headland. I do have to feel sorry for the kids who saw the seal's head explode though.

But, back to Bambi. Bambi was lying dead on the road and the police car was not too badly damaged so, rather than leave it to rot and get the council out to dispose of it, Kaiser loaded it into the back of the car and turned for home and the shed. Driving west along a long straight however he looked in the mirror to see the empty road behind. Except he didn't, oh no, not at all. What he saw instead was a very miffed deer with one hell of a headache wondering why this bad man was driving back to his place without so much as a meal out or a bunch of flowers. Bambi went nuts, extensively trashing the car from the inside out. Antlers gouged seats and broke windows, before Bambi finally ran off into the hills to tell the other deer. Explain that one on a police accident report, go on I dare you.

As one of the traffic cops, I had to go to any crash with a police vehicle. Usually they were just a source of humour and ridicule for months to come, and local roads were often known by those who had crashed there, such as The Sea Captain's Bend, or Inspector Gadget's Straight, which, it turned out, was also a bend that he didn't go round. Cops have silly bumps like everyone else, and more so when the pressure is on.

One crash sticks in my head though. The cops had stopped in a layby off a tight right-bend at the end of a fast section of twisty curves. Parked at the start of the layby with its rear red strobe lights flashing the police car could protect the broken-down car and motorist they had gone to help, and both cops got out to go and see what they could do. They were well off the road and I wouldn't have given it a second thought if it had been me. However, a local boy-racer in a Vauxhall saw the strobe lights as he drove south and panicked, hitting the brakes at over 80mph. As he took the right bend he lost control, smashing sideways into the back of the parked police car. Even though the police vehicle was a heavy cell van, the impact was enough to shunt it off the road having clipped the broken down car in front. The cops themselves were lucky to get away unscathed, but the driver of the Vauxhall died at the scene, his passenger being removed to the city with serious head injuries.

I was deployed as the FLO after the first FLO had to be extracted. There had been conflicts; many of the local cops had had dealings with the family and, as a consequence, the family were very anti-police. As always except for one visit to hand over, I went on my own. Every time I went to see the family I entered an atmosphere of scepticism and dislike as I sat down to discuss things in the family living room. As always, I would leave my belt kit and CS in the car to make it feel less hostile, and, as always, I would always hold my hat under my arm, only putting it on as I walked away from the house to appear less threatening.

We would talk what happened through again and again, and every time a new slant was suggested by the uncle as to why it was the fault of the police. I really busted a gut with that family, doing anything I could think of to help them reconcile what had happened. When they asked about his key chain and house keys and suggested that their boy couldn't have been speeding because he needed fuel, I asked the fire service to help and with two of my colleagues we addressed every remaining problem. We turned up at the garage where the wrecked car was being stored. It had been a few weeks since the crash, and the car smelt of damp, petrol and dried blood. Year after year I had come to recognise the same mementos of death in cars, again and again: the half-packet of polo mints that always to seemed to be under a seat when we checked the brake pedal and servo, the crinkle-cut crisps dropped between the seat and seat runners with a few coins and clumps of dust, the coins in the centre console in congealed blood, the cracks on the windscreen and the outward curve the shape of a human head, hair and skin caught in the cracks on the shattered glass on the inside, the airbag, now deflated and lying limp over the steering wheel, human blood splattered across it as it seemed way too close to the seat, because of course it was, the flex in the roof line often deforming the top of the A pillar closing the gap. And the one I hated most: a child-seat covered in blood, One thing that always surprised me, the way the seats often were fully reclined. They hadn't been reclined of course. At impact people in the car retain the original velocity of the car as the car starts to slow. When the seat belts, pre-tensioners or the insides of the car force them to decelerate with staggering violence they are thrown back into their seats, which often recline backwards.

It was always easy to tell if someone had worn a seatbelt because the belt was pulled through the plastic-coated clasp at incredible speed and force; the plastic melts an imprint of the seat-belt material into the clasp, and the webbing of the seat belt becomes smooth and polished. As technology moved on it would increasingly be possible to simply plug the airbag control module into a computer and find out all about the crash.

Brake pedals were often flat on the floor, the mounts torn from bulkheads at impact because the driver's femur had shattered under the intense pressure. People's lives would be scattered around like memories and snippets of what they had been.

The most haunting thing, and one which I would often find in cars, was a phone, with notifications of missed calls and the first lines of unread messages still on the screen.

'Can you pick up bread on the way home.'

'Why aren't you back yet?'

'The kids want to eat, hurry up.'

'The road is closed, there's been an accident.'

'Are you stuck in traffic.'

'Are you ok?'

'Please phone me.'

And sometimes a message sent after the death message had been delivered, the saddest of all, by a parent or loved one somehow hoping it wasn't true, hoping that somehow a message sent to their phone would somehow get to them after death.

Of course we only saw what was on the lock screen, but on just one occasion I asked for the data from the phone company because I suspected someone had been on the phone when they crashed, the messages were even more haunting. Made emotionless by the print-out that the phone company produced, neatly time-stamped down to the second, then the details of the call: time, duration, then a break in the signal, then the phone re-polling the phone tower within a second and reconnecting, then, seven seconds later—the call ending.

When we reconstructed the times from the time of the first witness's 999 call, and the CCTV of the car taken forty seconds before, they matched the car at impact and rolling into the ditch, a twenty-two-year-old girl dying instantly as her neck severed.

But, back to the Vauxhall. It was nothing unusual. Just the same as always. They'd worn their seat belts and there was the usual odds and ends lying around inside the shattered skeleton of the car. We removed part of the dash, managed to reconnect the electrics and there was plenty of fuel in the tank. After removing the centre console and gear stick I found the key ring wedged into a gap that could only have existed for fractions of a second as the car deformed. We wouldn't need the fire service to cut the car to pieces after all.

Again I would return and win the family over, again I would leave and they would turn to thoughts of blame and regret, and, as always, they would blame the police. This was the only FLO deployment I would walk away from genuinely sad that I couldn't win them over and leave on good terms. They were a good family struggling to cope.

But exiting a family was rarely an option for me. In the city, in the perfect world of CID deployments or the urban sprawl, when a FLO says good bye to the family they leave usually with a hug or a hand shake and know their job is done. It's very unhealthy to see the family again; the family can't recover because every time they see the FLO the memories of what has happened will come flooding back, especially if the FLO delivered the death message. It's simply not fair, and however close they have become, there can be no contact. No favours. Just walk away.

I was offered a holiday to Disney in Florida with my kids as a thank you from one family. I couldn't afford to take the kids by myself and saying 'no, but Thank you' to that family showed how much the things I had done had meant to them. It made me feel I was helping and it would be nice to help more but ultimately the walking away had to be done.

The problem in remote areas, for myself, Cammy and other FLO's was that there was no escape; everyone knew who you were and you could never avoid the family. When I had a window replaced I knew that the builder's son had died in a road crash and I had seen him lying in a heap in the back seat of the broken car. When I called the electrician out, I'd been the FLO for his mother's death, after her car left the road in heavy rain. I'd stood and joked with Bruce, eating cakes as his mother lay under a green tarpaulin in the middle of the road. When I walked through the supermarket in the town I would meet family after family; there was no escape from the death, not for me nor any of the district cops; it was everywhere. I would have loved to have left all the memories behind, and walked off to lead a normal life again but I could rarely do that.

It's strange though how the police always cope and hide failings, it's a mentality that all police officers have because whilst every person, every member of the public, even the staff in the other two emergency services have the police to turn to, ultimately the police have no one. The flip side to this is that within the police there is very much a just-cope-and-put-up-with-it mentality.

Throughout twenty-one years I could never think of a time when I saw a police officer who was struggling to cope being treated well by the job. As Clydeside Police morphed into a new larger force under the helm of Clydeside's Chief this became truer than ever. Cops who showed any signs of stress, and in particular after the policing disaster that was the Commonwealth Games, were simply ostracised and bullied into silence or resignation.

Fundamentally, within the job there is no support for police officers other than to tick a decorative box in some upper-management form. From the very first time I went home and went to my bed off a nightshift to wake up smelling death from my pores because I'd spent the whole shift in close proximity to a rotting body, which fell apart as we tried to lift it, to the time I saw a man high on drugs cut his own throat open and die still threatening us with his bloody screaming gargles at the top of a common stairwell, I never felt that the job supported me. Even when a drug user spat in my face and boasted he was infected, no one higher than an inspector cared; only my colleagues did. You turned up for work the next day and you cracked on with it.

I was very fortunate through the bulk of my time as a FLO to have two fantastic local gaffers but, at times, I don't think they realised how close to the edge I had come. From a police senior-management point of view down in the city, it was just lip service. Other forces didn't seem to suffer from the management mafia quite as much, and I met many senior managers from the other forces whom I respected in later years.

When my eldest son was six I was deployed to the death of a six-year-old boy. He'd been killed in what I guess he considered was his own playground. Unfortunately he stayed on a farm and some of the things around him were simply lethal. It's staggering how many people are killed on building sites and farms in Britain each year. In this case he was the only son of a lovely farming couple. They hadn't believed they could conceive at all and when their son was born it had been a miracle for them. He was a happy normal six-year-old, with a fantastic caring family and a bright future. As I sat discussing post-mortem arrangements with the family I looked up at a picture of this young boy, smiling and holding his show-winning, baby Shetland Pony at a farming fair. His parents were devastated; they'd already had a close relative commit suicide and I was genuinely concerned for the father in particular. He wasn't in any way responsible, but I knew by speaking to him that he felt he could have done something.

As a kid I played on a friend's farm near my parent's house, I would climb on straw bales and when I was in my early teens I would dispatch rats in the barn with a shotgun. It was a different era, but I understood the fascination and pride this young boy would have had for his father's work and how he might have come home from school to play at being a farmer on his own, in the barn — and near the farm machine that ultimately would kill him.

I took the farmer's shotgun and a bag of cartridges and drove the three hours back to my office with them sitting next to me on the passenger seat of my police car. I couldn't leave the gun with him and keep a clear conscience, just in case he had a low moment. It didn't matter how I justified it; it was the right thing to do. The problem was, as it sat there on the car seat and I kept glancing down at it, I wasn't sure I was in a much happier place. I felt like a life-thief; I couldn't rationalise how I was able to walk away from that family's sorrow and, a few hours later, sit at home with my own son, watching cartoons, laughing out loud, and all the while, in the back of my head, the farmer and his wife were better people than me.

I made a rare choice to go to the funeral, but I wouldn't go into the church. I waited in a suit outside, discreetly in the shadows of the church, radio at the ready, just in case there were any problems with parking for the family or anything else I could fix for them. I asked for favours and got two police bikers to escort the hearse, because the son had apparently liked police bikes.

But I kept out the way and left as soon as I could. I hated those self-important FLOs who felt they had the right to feel connected to the family, and enjoyed being seen at the funeral; they were only there because of a family's misery.

As the weeks went past the memory of the kid faded a bit, but the shot gun was still in the store. I could get it any time, on the pretext of returning it to the family, and sort my own life out in a layby for good.

While I was still deployed to that family, a rather sad conclusion to the enquiry was developing: the health-and-safety executive Nazis wanted to report the father to a court. By all means make an example when no one dies, but not when a family has already lost everything. What crass cruelty. Fortunately, the court would throw it straight out in a fantastic piece of common sense, months later. But while I was helping the family with this and the clear conflict of interest between my job as a FLO supporting the family and my job as a cop supporting the investigation, I was deployed again on another case. I didn't mind the second, simultaneous FLO deployment; it was a distraction for me and it was also a straightforward two-vehicle road crash with one driver dying at the scene. That family were easy to deal with and it should have been a matter of three weeks or so from deployment to exit to get them through it all.

While all this was going on I was usually single-crewed, driving any free time I could around the roads in my area clearing my head and taking any spare calls I could. This day was different though, and the duty Sgt at Baytown, asked me to take a spare cop from his shift out for a blast in the traffic car.

Most of the time in this book I've tried to describe characters a bit but with Amber it's so easy. Have you seen the film *Madagascar*? The one with the animals escaping New York Zoo? Well, you know the tiny cute Lemur called Mort... yup, that was Amber. An easier-going, more amicable person you simply could not meet and that day she would have me and my collapsing world to contend with. We were out in the country and had been laughing and joking about the job as usual. It was a stunning sunny November day, which meant the ice-cream machine at the tourist stop up north would be turned off, but that was fine because we could go get some hot chocolate instead.

As we passed Doolally we overheard a call to a crash on the Lochord Road, outside our area, twenty miles or so away.

Now, at this time, figures and numbers were everything. Amber's Sgt would like a couple of seat-belt tickets or something for Amber's record of work and his daily report and we might well be nearer to the crash, but at that stage we wouldn't be sent because it wasn't our area. Our work would then credit another area and that was a 'Don't Do'. Only a year or two before, helping a neighbouring area was commended, but this was the new reality of working under the new Chief Constable. Numbers meant everything. So we kept heading north for hot chocolate and some tickets.

Later we were updated that it was now a serious crash and the Lochord crew were asking for a crash investigator.

Me.

Now we could cross into the other area, well, I could anyway, and Amber in the passenger seat had no choice. Loud pedal to the floor, strobes and sirens on, and we were off on the now fifty-mile blast south to the crash. When we arrived the big yellow Helimed Eurocopter helicopter was shut down in the middle of the road.

An estate car travelling south had lost control on an icy left bend, skidded, over-corrected, skidded again and exited stage left, sideways and straight into the path of a slow-moving oak tree.

Crashing 101. If you're going to hit something and have a choice, don't make it a tree. He was in a bad way although my gut instinct, looking at the way the helimed crew and ambulance paramedics were scurrying around, was that he would live. I just didn't feel death was around that day, the big guy in the cloak seemed to be elsewhere. Otherwise occupied.

As I measured up the scene and laughed and joked, the helimed helo took off for the city with the driver on board. Death was giving me a welcome day off. My mobile phone went and I recognised my wife straight away; she was struggling to speak.

My mother had been taken into hospital and had a day or two to live.

Initially I didn't say anything; I just worked away for half an hour or so, deep in thought. I was using the total station, expensive land-survey kit that measures a road crash scene in great detail and accuracy. No one else there could do it, so I just plodded on. Eventually I spoke to Davie, the traffic Sgt from Lochord, and told him about the phone call, feeling tears wanting to well up in my eyes, but somehow keeping my emotions inside. Davie offered to get someone else to take over but a crew from the crash unit in the city would be two hours away at best and I could be done by then.

I kept going but I noticed Davie and Amber leaving me alone. I worked away plotting the blood on the branches, pooling and congealing where it had dripped out the car. I immersed myself in my work and kept my head down. Play the grey man, no emotion. It was a tough day. During the hour-long drive back to the office, Amber and I talked and I struggled to hold back my emotion.

My gaffers, Davie and my Inspector, were brilliant over the next few weeks and I didn't think about work at all as I sat by my mother's death bed, the same room I had watched my father die in. I used my phone to record her telling me stories about the city after the war, and lots of things I didn't know about my family. I still keep them in my phone and listen to them occasionally. She lived longer than the doctors thought she would and died just before Christmas.

After she died, I returned from the hospital as the first light from the sun crept over the horizon and tried to sleep. I dreamt about death all round me, all the dead people were there, waiting on me quietly in the shadows, watching me.

Chapter 17

Bertha Shore

Senior managers can lead cherished and protected lives, because they are destined for great things and know the right people. I knew one cop who would blatantly hide on the back shift when the pubs spilled. She would head straight up to the old ruined castle above the town and as far away from the fighting as possible to avoid having to deal with anyone — until she'd been promoted. She would even get drunk and have to sleep it off in the medical room while others took her calls. The Wing Commander wanted to put her on paper for this but was told not to by the powers above. The rule seemed to be: keep your head down until promoted and stay out of the firing line.

One of the funniest senior managers, and the one for whom I actually had a lot of respect was Chief Inspector Garnier. It sounds strange because she was a drunk, a shagger and clearly very driven while also clearly leading a protected life, but I had a lot of time for her. She would back her troops up 100% and if you fucked up she would shout you out but then it was dealt with. Although she was never my gaffer, she was the divisional gaffer in my office and I was, in effect, a specialist guest although, in reality, I would always do as she wanted because I saw sense in a lot of her decisions.

She also reminded me of the happy days when we would get steaming drunk off the night shift. Or police social life back in the early 90s when we would go to the police club every Friday off the backshift and get too drunk to drive home – which, back then, was a major achievement. And even in the early 2000's we still had a bottle of whisky in the office for a quick nip after a particularly horrible fatal, so we could sit quietly and reflect amongst ourselves, about what we'd seen and done, before we took off our uniforms and returned to our families, smiling like nothing troublesome had happened that day at all.

Chief Inspector Garnier was however sometimes a liability and had a reputation in the town. When she came back from Codbay, an island off the west coast, she was too drunk to park the marked police car in the car deck of the ferry; the crew offered do it for her but she refused and bumped it. The crew reparked it for her, but afterwards she went upstairs on the ferry and handcuffed the barman to the ship's bar. Shame she forgot to bring a key; that was very funny for everyone for years to come. It didn't matter because Garnier was protected from above and destined for great things. She would soon head to the city and we would have a number of competent replacements—until the day Shore came.

Acting Chief Inspector Bertha Shore came to Baytown bringing a fresh atmosphere of halitosis and corruption, but this was an era of disappearing budgets under the Chief Constable. She'd come from Professional Standards and clearly had no real operational experience but a desire to do what she knew: criticise others. The problem was that the cop in the office most in need of criticism was her, she was utterly incompetent. One of her first acts was to ensure the overtime budget was cut. All recalls to duty were banned and a memo to that effect distributed. That memo seemed to disappear for some reason after what followed.

The first test of this new procedure was a fatal road crash less than a mile from a district police office at Stalker Brae. It was a good half hour for the next car to get there. The local cop 'Marvin the Paranoid Android' should have been there in minutes so he went anyway; he'd been in the traffic for years and knew pretty much all there was to know. But when the dust settled there was hell to pay and a warning to all the supervisors that recalls to duty were forbidden. It seemed the four-hour recall to duty overtime claim was more than human lives were worth under this new acting chief inspector.

Two weeks afterwards five fishermen were on the south side of Loch Errie; they were fishing, funnily enough. And drinking. Drinking it seems is a big part of fishing. Lots of people die on Loch Errie; it's a cold, deep loch with treacherous currents and poor access to many areas of the shore.

Four of the fishermen who were camping on the south side of the loch decided to take their little boat across the loch to the local boozer in the hope of refreshment and later in the evening make their way back across to the campsite. It was only a few hundred yards and the loch was calm.

But after midnight and a lengthy 'lock in' drinking session in the pub the fog had come down and they alone will know what went wrong. They had left the pub visibly drunk although the police tried to hide this CCTV footage.

Their friend at the camp on the south shore heard them screaming in the water. It was early in the night, just after 1 am. The loch is very narrow at that point and at the head of the loch a large spit of land juts out into a shallow region that the fisherman had to cross.

As a consequence of a tragic drowning in the loch some years earlier, the local cop, Bruce the 'Griefmeister', had been given flares, water-rescue throw lines and an immersion suit, etc. He also had mobile telephone numbers for many of the boat owners around the loch. This was under a scheme called 'Watch the loch' and he was at the core of it. He stayed less than five miles away.

A local special constable also stayed nearby and had a boat moored on the loch less than five minutes away, but the restriction on overtime meant he was not allowed to be called out, or even phoned. The two cops who drove for forty-five minutes to get there did their best, setting a fire, using petrol on the shore and shouting, but without a bright flare to swim towards through the fog or a boat to rescue them the four fishermen were consigned to death. Nether of the cops had the local knowledge to realise that if they had gone round and onto the spit of land that jutted out into the middle of the loch they would have been much closer to the four men trying to stay afloat in the water. It took almost three hours for the fishermen to succumb to hypothermia, and the two cops at the scene had to listen helpless to them only a hundred yards or so away as their shouts got quieter and more subdued. Two of the bodies turned up on the shore at the spit of land and toxicology reports clarified that all four had lived long enough to be sober.

Still, mistakes happen, but not publicly, not in the police. The Police fear nothing more than bad publicity. At this point though, it was just genuine errors and poor management. The local cop, Bruce, had still not been informed in the morning. When I came on duty I was asked to go to the city to give a fast escort to International Rescue.

I know! That was my reaction too.

They actually exist. Not the Thunderbird 2 and 4 from Tracy Island I had hoped for admittedly, but a real international organisation that specialises in rescuing people at natural disaster scenes and such. Damn, was I annoyed, I really wanted to meet Lady Penelope.

International Rescue were heading up with a rescue boat to search the loch. That was really bizarre news to me because I'd been in the office having tea and a cooked breakfast for well over an hour with my neighbour, and this was the first I'd heard about this incident in our area. I drove out past the loch, expecting to see a flurry of searching going on around the shore, but there was absolutely nothing. Embarrassingly, for a while most of the searching was being done by the family. The police were more concerned with cleaning up the scene and hiding the tins of beer from the camp site so that the TV crews and press didn't see them.

I soon met Thunderbird 4. It was really just a big speedboat thing being towed by Thunderbird 2 which was really just a Land Rover Defender. But when they started the run back to the loch, they went like fuck; perhaps they misunderstood 'let me give you an escort' to mean 'Honestly go as fast as you can, I really don't mind how scary it is looking in the mirror and seeing you coming round a corner sideways.'

I arrived back at the loch around lunch time when it had started to resemble a proper search scene again. Bruce finally showed up with a face like thunder. My initial thought, that he'd been away somewhere or couldn't make it were wrong—he simply didn't know about it. The one person who was in a position to make a difference hadn't been recalled for the sake of overtime. The flares might not have worked, the locals who had boats might have refused to help, and maybe the special with the boat five minutes away might not have heard the phone ring in his sleep, or maybe Bruce's local knowledge of the loch might have made no difference—but for the sake of a few hours and a phone call, to let four men with families drown was, for me, criminal.

The cost of overtime was more than the cost of the human lives. Of course this never came out at the fatal-accident inquiry because a very senior manager came up to speak to troublesome cops before they went into court. It was made clear no difficult questions would be asked anyway, the three solicitors representing each emergency service having agreed to protect each other before the hearing. The family were not represented because they didn't know they needed to be.

For anyone else, attempting to change someone's evidence is a crime called 'attempted subornation of perjury', but not for a senior officer; after all who's going to challenge them? The force solicitor tried to stop Bruce giving evidence and a subsequent witch hunt would punish him for having the audacity to be right, resulting in his leaving the job some months later.

Meanwhile, the memo instructing no recalls disappeared. The statement that Bruce gave to the force solicitor disappeared and the force solicitor tried to deny it had ever existed anyway. Even after a Freedom-of-Information-Act request with the police typist's reference number it somehow stayed hidden. A sergeant who tried to speak the truth and knew a local who worked for a newspaper was victimised and bullied by management, so much so that cops were asked to make up evidence against him to discredit him in court if he ever tried to tell the truth. Cops were threatened by supervisors and promotions depended on toeing the party line. A senior manager contacted Bruce via his personal email and they met in a layby when Bruce was at work. It was demanded that he help to protect Chief Inspector Shore, his promotion depended on what he did, and he was warned to keep quiet.

The witch hunt was astounding.

But that could be another book altogether, because, when Bruce refused to lie, the best they could do was stitch him up with phoning his partner from an office phone. I have never met a cop who at some point didn't use the office phone to make a call home. In fact, when Chief Inspector Garnier left Baytown and handed over the work mobile phone to her replacement, it was very obvious from the hilarious text messages that arrived on the official police mobile phone that she too used it for the occasional personal call.

'Bunny's coming to Baytown and looking for a warm burrow.'

Perhaps the Chief Inspector kept rabbits... .

Of course you may wonder why no one could complain further up the tree as it were. Well, some did, but complaints and discipline were simply too connected to police management for anything to happen. The Federation refused to help those involved. The reputation, and arguably a large civil case, hung on the police covering up Shore's fuck up.

HIDE-AND-SEEK

We used to play Hide-and-Seek in the office. If you got back and all the lights were off, then the game was afoot. Usually 'homeless' was hiding in the observation room or the cupboard in the muster room. No one hid in the third floor corridor above the cells because the office ghost lived there. I was scared of the office ghost. Everyone was; it was real.

CHAPTER 18

THE ONES WE LOVE LIVE ON IN OUR DREAMS.

I disliked motorcycle deaths, being a biker myself. It's a strange thing but as humans we seem to have a real problem telling someone about death. I don't know why, but I learnt that there is really no easy way to do it. It has to be factual and it has to be blunt.

<Insert name here> is dead. That sort of thing worked well, I felt.

One stunning, hot, summer day I had just arrived for back shift when a call came in for 'out country', nothing major and no need to rush. The early shift consisting of JC and Big Sam were just heading back into the office so I offered to take the call for them. They only had two hours left to work and they would take that just driving out to the scene and back. As I left the office and headed out, the world seemed a pretty good place, window down, relaxing and just enjoying a rare Scottish sunny day.

Just after Lochside the car radio came to life with another call, a road crash at Muck Bridge near to Airdsbay, less than a mile ahead of me. I turned on the blues and pressed the loud pedal to the floor, feeling the car kick down and go. Whoever phoned it in would be so impressed. Already in my head I could imagine this dishevelled biker dragging his or her pride and joy out a hedge, phoning in the crash and in a mere minute I would drop out of warp and bound out the car to help them. I came flying up the hill towards the Muck bend, flat out after the previous tight right hander. God this would look cool! I was the second car facing east. The driver of the first one already out and turning to look at me in shock as the public often did when we approached at crazy speeds.

I braked hard and came alongside, blocking the road completely and flicking on the rear, high-intensity, red strobes. Looking ahead of me, my heart sank. Lying on his back in the roadway was my biker. A red minibus was stationary on the opposing carriageway and already it was clear that the biker had crossed into the wrong carriageway and gone head to head. I grabbed a couple of accident signs and ran straight past him and round the corner. I always found the look on people's faces odd when I did that. The most important thing was to make the scene safe before dealing with it; no point doing anything else then getting wiped out by the next car to come along.

A minute later I was on my knees doing CPR and watching yet another human die. The ambulance crew soon arrived and took over and, soon after, a doctor appeared from a car that was now in the queue of traffic. Again I'd tried, and again felt ribs breaking, becoming breathless myself as I heard the rasp of someone's final breaths, felt them ebb away.

JC and Sam arrived soon after. All of us were now stuck there with the buzzing flies, the itching of Scottish midges and the heat of the day until photographers had attended and the crash investigation had been completed. We found out who the motorcyclist was, and JC requested over the radio for the family to be informed. Job well done.

Hours later, back at the office, I was typing out details for a report while JC phoned the family. We planned to go get them tomorrow; we could take them to the hospital morgue and talk to them, maybe visit the scene and close the road so they could lay flowers down. I went into my usual routine, on auto pilot as it were. This would not be any different from any other death.

Meanwhile, I overheard JC making arrangements and speaking to the man's wife, but something was clearly wrong; I heard it in JC's voice: the pause, and then the realisation of the news he was breaking. The cops who had been sent to give the death message had done their best but had been too kind, and I'd been there myself. I could imagine what they'd said, perhaps 'he's succumbed to his injuries', or maybe 'he's at rest now', maybe even 'he's passed away'; it doesn't matter and I'll never know, but when JC said to the lady that her husband was at Baytown hospital, what he didn't expect to hear back was:

'Will he be ok?'

People hear what they want desperately to hear. I know how that feels because when my own world fell apart I would cling to any tiny shred that would leave me in denial and make me think it could all work out ok. Deep down I wanted it to be ok. I think we all do.

I drove back home afterwards through the pre-dawn mist, past the scene of the crash. In my dreams I would be there, talking to him, but he couldn't say anything. I tried to tell him to wait on his family, but he couldn't.

The Scottish islands can be like going back in time to the 1950s and a slower pace of life. Things seem pretty tranquil and idyllic.

The locals always knew the police were on the islands. Barra has an airport which comprises the beach as a runway and a few 'porta cabins', (honestly — look on Youtube) but on the islands I covered, we depended on the ferry or the police helicopter.

There was simply no way to arrive without the locals knowing, and by the time I had driven off the slipway, every uninsured car was hidden off road. It didn't matter because this was community policing at its finest anyway. On one island the local police-office door didn't even lock, so usually when anyone from the mainland was sent across there would be some fresh eggs or salmon waiting on the desk as a nice gesture to say 'hello'.

The way people on the islands multi-tasked always amused me. The first time Sam and I arrived for a death I knew we would be stuck on the island for a few days so we went to get a few beers at the local supermarket. I thought I was pretty much fitting in when the checkout operator asked me if I knew when the date for the post mortem was. We mumbled our excuses and left very taken aback.

When we dropped by to see the family only an hour or so later, the checkout guy answered the door. He was the local funeral director too. A few days later the ferry was cancelled and we tried to get the scheduled British Airways flight back to civilisation — the girl who checked us in was also a receptionist at the doctor's and also the air traffic controller who told us the flight was cancelled because of sheep on the 'runway'.

The police helicopter finally came to take us home and I breathed a big sigh of relief – but I was also a bit jealous.

When the local cop who normally worked on this and one other island came back from holiday, I asked him how he managed get anyone to help him to process drink drivers. He used his teenage son. What a place…

The local cop on one of the larger islands was 'Toot-Toot', so called because he joined the pipe band after about six hours on the street. He had serious tidy issues and his house and office were immaculate. Bruce and I went to visit once when he was away on holiday and made his office even more immaculate by the medium of superglue. Everything, including the phone and handset, was stuck in place on his desk, including all his paperwork, which took ages. His gaffer was old school too, a good guy who built the most amazing, radio-controlled, model helicopters of which I was very jealous. I liked the islands a lot;

I liked the rally too. It was a fantastic event for petrol-head cops and it was looked on as a chance to have a piss-up and end the year on a high after the inevitable deaths that occupied much of the unit's time over summer, when the roads were busy.

One of the best bits of the rally was the 'closing car'. It's hard to imagine now but the procedure for closing the public roads as the rally took place involved a marked traffic car, fitted with spotlights specially fitted by the police garage so it could be driven round the circuit night stages. It was the last car to drive on the public highway and in effect also the first rally car. It was driven by a traffic cop with a rally guy alongside with pace notes and was followed by the marshal's car and the first pace car. All the cars had, in effect, rally car numbers and were timed at each stage. It was seen as a great honour to get to drive it. Usually the police garage would send up a traffic car that was due to go to auction soon anyway.

The year they sent a 4x4 Cosworth, Peter from Baytown was driving the closing car and, at the end of stage one, was officially in sixth place. He made the tour official calendar that year with a picture of the Cosworth airborne flying over a road crest. The bosses in the city got word of it and had a major tantrum. It ended not long afterwards so I didn't ever get a go.

The year we had a death on the rally changed how I felt about it. It was a clear, cool, star-lit night when we arrived at the scene. All I'd heard and smelled for hours was the loud violence of rally cars at full pelt, the speed and the smell of burnt high-octane petrol, and now I was in the peace and tranquillity of nowhere, the scene, partially illuminated by eerie lights from the road above and my ears caressed by the distant burble of a waterfall and the sound of the autumn leaves in the gentle breeze – in my nose the smell of hot oil, near the tangled deformed mess of the rally car.

The rally car had left the road on a descending, left-hand, off-camber bend, taking off and striking a tree.

Do not hit trees. Seriously do not hit trees, ever. Big car versus small car, well big car will often win. They take an amount of energy proportional to their mass to the collision and due to the physics of momentum exchange the energy is distributed unfairly against the smaller car in terms of change of speed. Hit a lamp post and it will bend; hit a brick wall it will smash; hit a tree and it will hurt. A tree's rounded cross-section is actually worse than a flat concrete surface because it focuses energy on a narrower area of the car, and that's not good.

Don't hit trees.

But this car had, and its roll cage, the rally seats and the crash helmets hadn't been enough to save the day. The co-pilot had died at the scene. What made it worse was that this was a husband and wife team. We investigated it initially as a road death and I would be the FLO. I met her husband a few times, a genuinely great guy and I wouldn't have even included this story except for one detail: the car was fitted with a video camera in the back, looking forward between the two occupants, so we could see exactly what had happened. When I first watched it I saw them in the car at the start; I saw them at the check points and having a chat with the stage marshal; I watched as they handed over a timecard at the start of the stage; I listened to the matter of fact way they spoke, the closeness and the trust, the last words they would say to each other. I saw every detail of the course, watched every turn and straight until they reached that corner. I heard her call it late. She called 'caution into left descending…', heard the panic in her voice, saw the car lights illuminating the verge, the branches — then nothing, silence, static as the camera malfunctioned for a split second due to impact, then darkness, the sound of metal being tortured, branches breaking, gravel and then nothing. For what seemed like ages, nothing, then the sound of her husband calling her name in the darkness. Again and again, each time more urgent; it was horrible to watch and listen to.

As he tried to rouse her, a strange light started to fill the screen, flickering and oscillating before slowly getting brighter. I could make out, through the shattered shape of the car windscreen, and realised what the light was — it was torch light reflecting as the sound of shouting got louder and louder. Rescue crews would soon arrive and I wouldn't watch anymore.

I saw the tape many times up until the crash, as we worked out how it happened: she had called the corner late and they had entered too fast. Every time I watched it, I wanted it to end differently and every time it didn't. Every time I hoped that she would call 'caution' sooner, but she never would.

CHAPTER 19

BITS.

I woke up with a start when the phone beside my bed rang. I knew exactly what it meant; if my phone rang when I was sleeping then someone was dead—it was my death phone. Like a lot of early-shift workers I would clock-watch on the first night. Unable to sleep properly, I would keep checking the alarm clock in fear of sleeping in, ultimately exhausted because I wouldn't sleep properly.

The phone rang way too early into the night. Even as I fumbled for it in the darkness of the room, I could imagine what the call was. It was too early to be someone asleep at the wheel, so not a morning delivery driver. Maybe a stabbing or something criminal? Maybe- but the odds were good that it was a local out on the road, pushing it too far. I listened to the office and it turned out there were two cars involved and two dead.

Time to get my favourite scythe and head to work.

I drove to the office and parked outside, walking purposefully into the front public bar and intending to walk past the usual suspects waiting on the single row of seats. There were often people there, maybe a homeless man or someone waiting on a prisoner being released, but tonight there were only three people there. An elderly man stood at the public counter looking pale and talking to Sal, one of the cops from the shift that night. A young couple were sitting listening while a young man nursed a bleeding head, presumably in reporting a pub fight. Sal saw me walking in and immediately turned to the old man and introduced me as his FLO. I was caught completely off guard and lost for words. I made excuses to leave; I would be right back, I said. I tried to slip away and at least get out of my jeans and T-shirt and into uniform.

He was clearly anxious and desperate to talk to me. I wanted to get him away from the public bar, and, as we talked, it became painfully evident he didn't yet know that both his son and daughter were dead. I was lucky not to have given that away, and I could see the tears welling up in his eyes. I was annoyed that Sal had landed me right in it, but I knew she would be run off her feet in the control room and it certainly wasn't deliberate.

I took the old man through to an interview room and left him to get a printout of the incident. As things calmed down, I was able to talk him through the details and, finally and in private, give him the news he was dreading. He already knew one of them was dead — I think that had come from the hospital, or whatever request he had received to come to the office — but the realisation that he had lost both children hit him very hard.

I ended up taking him to his house in the early morning, as the sun came up and clouds of tiny flies played in the calm morning air, only a few hundred yards from the crash scene. What he didn't see on the journey via a back road was the scene of horror on the main road. His son's car had lost control off a right-hand bend at high speed, skidded and rotated to impact sideways with a truck. The large delivery truck had mass and strength on its side and the car had, for lack of a better word, exploded. The engine and gearbox were separate from the rear half of the car and the passenger area was essentially spread over a hundred metres of roadway, along with parts of the two kids inside. Some of the larger bits of torso and limbs were easier to identify, and the cops at the scene would struggle in the morgue later that night, trying to work out which bit to put in which fridge.

When the undertaker's van arrived a problem arose because both kids were well known as drug users. The police had a contract with a local firm of undertakers who were more used to carting old people out of retirement homes than this battlefield. They refused to pick up the bits and, as a result, as always, it fell on cops, who can't say no; it's not something the police sell very well in the advertising campaigns:

'Join the police, pick up bits of infected drug user with no face masks or protective suits, and get fuck all thanks.' I really don't see that working as on a recruitment poster for some reason.

The guys were resourceful. The best tools they had to hand were a number of scissor-type accident signs in the boot of the car. They used them to scoop up body parts and get them into the body bags that we carried in each patrol car. For months after, the signs sat in our traffic garage stubbornly refusing to evaporate. I later took them to the Police College after washing them because we didn't have any there. I didn't tell anyone at the college where they came from. No one else would touch them.

When I met the old man the next day I asked him not to go to the morgue. I told him if he wanted to go I would take him, but it was only if he really wanted. I was quite brutal, no lies. None at all. I always told every family that if they wanted to not know something then don't ask the question. Lying to a family was to me unacceptable.

It didn't matter because he'd taken the walk later that morning from his house, the short distance to where his daughter and son had died. He'd found part of his daughter's jewellery and a lot more. I didn't need to explain much more to him about why I didn't want him to see his kid's bodies. He understood exactly why from what was left at the side of the road. I'm sure a gaffer somewhere would be horrified at that, but the reality is that completely sanitising the road would have taken days with the support unit and that's even assuming it could be done.

It was around this time I perfected Jelly-Baby crime scenes. I was great at them. I used to reconstruct crashes by printing out a scale plan drawing on large A0 paper and using a toy car, matching the tyre marks on the drawing to the car to see what path it had travelled. With Jelly Babies this could take on a whole new amusing and macabre realism. And you got to eat the props afterwards. Utter genius. I could get quite protective of my Jelly-Baby crime scenes if I left them set up and someone came and ate body parts. I liked to set up a few police Jelly Babies walking around the scene just to add realism on my desk.

Years later I was told by probationer students at the Police College that Professional Standards had advised them at the force training centre at Jackoff that lying to a family to hide a relative suffering as they died was an acceptable thing to do but it simply wasn't, and for them to be so simplistic and short-term was staggering—and largely because the cops in Professional Standards have usually avoided real police work to get to where they want to be.

Anyone who has dealt with death in Scotland will know that there is a report produced by the pathologist at the post-mortem examination. It goes to the Procurator Fiscal, it goes to the family doctor, but it can also be seen by the family.

I would feel awful if a family believed I had lied to them to make my job easier. I can't imagine the feeling of betrayal a family would feel if they found out the police lied about something so important, especially months later when they thought that their questions and fears had been put to rest. I emailed the Professional Standards Department and phoned to ask what exactly they told probationers about this subject during their presentation but they ignored me. No surprise there. Professional Standards are principally there to keep the plebs like me in order and protect the reputation of the police and senior managers. Never doubt it.

In the days to come of KPIs, the number counting would get worse and worse. Most of the public and the newspapers were aware of the stop searches being carried out, driven by an insatiable desire to elevate the statistics as high as possible, also the money-making tickets being issued.

Just after I left Baytown, Chief Inspector Dawson emailed all his Sgts. Included in the email was a list of every cop in the office with a list of how many stop searches, how many intelligence reports on members of the public and how many conditional-offer tickets had been written (these were for things like seat belts, bulbs out or failing to indicate at junctions). ASBO tickets became a way to criminalise members of the public who in years before would have been warned. Meanwhile the Chief Constable was on TV telling the world we had no targets.

It seemed ridiculous to me; it was very clear in the email that if figures were not met then cops would be disciplined.

No mention was made, nor allowance given, for the cop who spends the day with a grieving widow or reassuring the pensioner whose wallet's been stolen, or talking to kids outside the local school to make them realise that cops are not the bad guys. I was disgusted with the corruption and thin veneer of moral spin that covered this new way of policing.

This was a force where a young couple with kids would be detained and sent to court after two days in a police cell for sending each other an angry text message because 'domestic' was a politically-correct buzz word and the statistics would be used to record a 'detection', yet at the same time a female rape victim would be talked out of making a complaint by a male chief inspector and male Sgt because the suspect was a cop and a friend and nothing whatsoever was written down or put onto a computer system about it. I'll not expand on that because I genuinely feel that it's awful and I respect her privacy—but I also know how wrong it was.

The politically-correct statisticians had gone mad convincing the public that the new force was a success when, in reality, staff morale was as low as it could go and cops were leaving in droves.

Even Professional Standards, Complaints and Conduct, Anti-Corruption or the rubber heel squad, themselves had KPI's to meet. Now I'm all for trying to catch bad cops, but you can't catch people who haven't done anything.

When I first joined the police the Chief Constable, Les Blunt, made it well known that, as long as a police officer acted in good faith and did his or her best, he would back them up. Likewise, in the Regiment we backed each other up and our ranking officers were a part of that. We respected knowledge and a good soldier could give respected advice to a patrol commander or officer. A signaller would choose where a patrol would lie up for the night because his opinion on being able to receive messages was essential. Knowledge and experience were respected.

Just before I left a very young superintendent arrived one day and told us what great ideas he had based on his own experience on the street. He then told us lots of war stories. The problem was some of us had worked in his old division and knew exactly what a coward he'd been on the street and that the stories he told were all things he'd heard other cops had done.

The Police promotion process encourages this though. It's called 'competency-related' promotions. The idea is that an applicant fills out a form saying how great they are and then a supervisor signs it off as being correct. If it's signed, then it's accepted from then on that it's true. What happens in practice is that those cops who are full of their own self-importance sell themselves much better than others. Even worse, some applications for jobs and promotions are filled out by a supervisor on behalf of the cop. In reality many of these forms have little relevance to the cop they supposedly describe but, at the paper-sift for the job, the HR department simply have to assume the forms are correct and have no idea how many lies they contain and how many have been completed by supervisors who have personal reasons to further someone's career.

Let me give you an example.

In Baytown, when newly promoted Chief Inspector Dawson, arrived from HR, he knew exactly what to put onto an application form to get someone a job. It started with a girl on maternity leave and in the space of just a few months he created a room full of people he wanted next to his own office. All were female and good looking.

When the vacancy for a divisional intelligence officer came up, nine cops applied and the window for applications closed for a paper-sift. Then, a week after it had closed for applications, he asked one of the attractive girls in the office to apply and helped her by filling out her application, then helped some more by giving her the questions she would be asked at the interview. This behaviour was no secret and was widely discussed even by those advantaged by it, but as a supervisor he was entirely able to do this and was untouchable. It was simply outrageous and within the office his domain was known as 'the harem'. It got to the point where we had to recall police women back to duty if we got a female prisoner because there were none left on the shifts. The only plus point was that his wife ended up high in Professional Standards and he was staggeringly indiscreet, so many of us would find out who was getting into trouble for something long before it happened.

By 2012 the force was trying to pretend it was squeaky clean by showing how efficiently it dealt with corruption, but only for matters relating to cops, the cannon fodder at the expendable end of the scale, who were often trying to simply do the job.

The stats would show otherwise, 145 police officers were reported to the Procurator Fiscal that year, but underneath the statistics was a more telling story: of these 145 reports, the Procurator Fiscal would only take six to court. All the rest of the cases were red-penned as rubbish yet the new counter-corruption unit treated all the 139 other cases cops, who had done little or nothing wrong, as though they were terrorists, sometimes swooping at dawn on their houses for no reason other than to humiliate them in front the family. If any other part of the police submitted that many crap cases they would be investigated for neglect of duty. It was all over the papers as a bad thing that the general population of the police were corrupt, but no one saw the truth underneath: that Professional Standards and police management were corrupt, driven by politicians and spin to make the police look successful.

There was an answerphone hotline to report misconduct nicknamed 'shop a cop', but the only time I knew of it being used to report a chief inspector for a criminal act, the chief inspector was summoned to Coward's Castle the next day and returned having very obviously listened to the phone call—and being now well aware of who made it. Obviously the person who made the call had to leave the job not long after.

Just before I left the police a good friend of mine was working at the Police College. He'd been trained as an officer-safety instructor. I got on well with Jon from the first time we sat next to each other on a course, the same dark humour and scepticism combined with common interests. He was another grey man. Part of the training for an officer-safety qualification involves each recruit being exposed to CS gas. The Army are good at this; they put recruits in a room full of CS gas and make them work, speak and then leave the room. After all, if you have to use it on the street you need to be able, at the very least, to have an understanding of what it will do to you when you're cross-contaminated. With the police, the training involved spraying the CS into a bucket full of paper tissues. This was done outside the room and the students were then asked, one at a time, to place their heads into the bucket and then run off on a quick circuit of the grounds before handcuffing a compliant prisoner. Depending on the weather, and in particular the wind, it had little or no real effect, but there would usually be someone struggling to see or some snot and tears at worse. I loved watching it; it was very funny.

The problem was that there were, in typical bureaucratic police style, five different procedures on the college computer system for carrying this procedure out—and no clues as to which was the one to use. Some involved spraying the bucket while the student put their head in, and some would involve the student having to breathe in while their head was in the bucket.

After one particular session with over eighty students, five reacted more badly than usual. This was not unheard of and it happened every few courses, sometimes requiring a quick trip to the local accident and emergency to get the student's eyes washed out. I never felt sorry for anyone. If you didn't want to, at least, experience the effects of the gas, then you were a liability to your colleagues the first time CS was deployed for real and some blew back into your face.

On this occasion a student complained. Cops, and I use the term very loosely here, from the Professional Standards department moved into the College and interviewed every student on the course. The instructor was reported for assaulting all of them with a Section-5 firearm and when interviewed they parted with a joke: 'we won't be coming to raid your house and arrest you'. Nice. That sort of throw-away line would land a real cop in trouble.

But from a KPI point of view, Professional Standards had solved over eighty assaults with a 100% detection rate. Now, four years later Jon, has still heard nothing and his career is on hold. It all comes back to the same thing in the police: if you want to succeed, then do nothing, hide in an office, avoid the street—and the public and kiss a gaffer's ass to get promoted. Or shag one; that works even better.

I think the group most discriminated against in the police is women. Away from the politically-correct 'knitting club', the nickname given to those females in cushy day jobs promoting the role of women in the police, who seemed to publicly give themselves awards with amazing regularity, the reality was that women and young mothers in particular had it pretty shit. I lost count of the number of women I knew who would leave to have children and be reduced to tears by bullying senior managers forcing them back to work unsociable or simply impossible shifts in relation to childcare. The faceless bullies who ran operational shifts had no comprehension that childminders simply do not work at 2-am shift-finish times. Often such staff were retained simply by amazingly adaptive and supportive grandparents or relatives.

The managers didn't care and staff were there to be abused. Ironic that Chief Inspector Dawson, who years later was promoted back to the city and at one time was so keen to get pretty girls into cushy office jobs next to his office, could be horrific at terrifying others. He made one young mother drive a two-hundred-mile commute every day with a young baby in the car to do anti-social shifts, finishing in the early hours of the morning to pick her child up and drive home. The young officer was terrified to complain and did her best, but you have to sympathise about the late finishes when she could be retained on duty off a back shift finish until 3am with that journey still to do, quite apart from the effect on the child's sleep pattern.

And under the new Police machine it just got worse and worse while management hid away behind procedures and fear. Many managers didn't play the grey man; they played the invisible cowardy man, and the few good ones left were fighting against the current of those who had been promoted to their level of incompetence.

The Cardboard Car.

When Inspector Gadget asked me to get up early in the morning because of a speeding complaint I had a problem. In my book, people speeding through remote villages at 4 or 5am may well be a problem but it's one that I could do without and I knew the problem was all really just one truck driver. I'm really not sure 5am is a real time at all; maybe in the strange world of airport departure lounges it's an acceptable time, but for me it just isn't. I have a sneaking suspicion that if you drop a tennis ball it won't even fall at 5 am because even gravity doesn't work that early. It's a ridiculous time of day.

I had an idea though. And it was sheer genius. In remote Scotland we were too remote to get the Identification Branch up every time we needed them. The city was a two hour drive away after all. Instead, we had nice cameras and we would simply send off the film to the city with a request for prints. I would simply take a picture of my police car and ask for one print. A really, really big one.

Life size in fact. One that could sit at the side of the road at 5am when I was not sitting at the side of the road at 5am.

I'm a fucking god of ingenuity I thought. I took lots of lovely pictures of my Volvo T5, in a Cosmo-type way. We had a romantic day out and went to lots of nice picturesque locations together so I could leap out the car like a demented fashion photographer and snap off shots. I wanted the right angle. I wanted her to look her best. I even washed the wheels and took the newspaper and tin of coke off the dashboard. It had to look good. I sent off the film and promptly forgot all about it.

A few weeks passed and the Identification Branch got in contact; they'd printed out my picture, or, to be exact, they'd decided my picture was shit. They'd got a Merc from the traffic in the city, wheeled it into a studio and had photographed that instead. I went to get my new toy and was horrified to find out how big it was. It was *huge*. Even cut in two and rolled up it barely fitted in the Volvo which I suppose made sense. It was shiny, made from a single, huge sheet of laminated photographic film. Sadly, it was bendy and the perspective was wrong. They'd photographed the Mercedes at a jaunty three-quarter rear angle. It just looked like a flappy picture of a police car.

Shame.

It also turned out to have cost more than simply taking an old police car that was due to go to the auction and parking it at the side of the road. Whoops. I believe it's still in the visual-aid store at the Police College. I used to put it up in my classrooms. It's very cool though.

I made quite a few monumental fuck-ups in the police. Some I laughed at and some I cringe at; some went unnoticed. To be fair there were so many fuck-ups by so many people that mine were maybe hard to spot.

One fuck-up sticks in my mind as being especially cringe-worthy although I'm not really sure anyone noticed. When my trusty Volvo T5 went away to the garage in the sky, it was replaced by a BMW 5 series, one of the ones that looked like it had been congealed, rather than built. Nice and slick with that funny idrive thing. The new car had a steptronic automatic gearbox to help the resale value, and a diesel engine to make it cheaper to run. Wasn't long until someone put petrol in it of course, but that wasn't my fuck-up. But, for me, the biggest problem with it was that it had ANPR or Automatic Number Plate Recognition system. ANPR was a system of cameras mounted on the inside and roof of the car that would read a car's number plate as it passed, and quickly check it on a PNC database for MOT, road tax, insurance, and intelligence reports. Which was all great, and would mean others would use my car a lot, but the bigger problem that arose on day one was this: when the garage fitted ANPR they needed somewhere to put the on/off switch and they choose the place where the eject button was on the CD player.

This was a catastrophe because, on the first day I drove the car, I put in a CD with some very fine music indeed: Led Zeppelin, David Gilmour, Pink Floyd, Joe Cocker. It was a fantastic CD although it did become tiring around four thousand plays later; you see, every time the key went in the ignition it would start up and, despite much searching online by me, I could not find a way to get it out. To be fair, I did particularly like listening to Dave Gilmour's track 'Murder', on dark stormy nights when I was working on my own and blasting along through Glen Ord.

When a young lad from Stalkerbrae capsized in his kayak and drowned, I was deployed as the FLO. I'd recently done another one up that way after a car had lightly side-swiped a passing HGV and a tiny thin piece of aluminium trim from the truck had peeled off, gone between the wing and bonnet of the car, into a hole in the engine bulkhead, out through the air vent in the dashboard, under the driver's armpit, slicing through the edge of his seat — and straight into the heart of the rear seat passenger. I mean what the fuck? Straight out of that film final destination. When your number is up, sometimes it's just up.

But for this young chap it was a few hours floating around in the sea waiting on help that didn't come until hypothermia stopped him treading water and he drowned. It was a difficult deployment because the kid's mother and father had separated. That had happened to me a few times before and on one horrible occasion I had been deployed to a family for three days when the father had died in a motorcycle crash, before the wife decided to tell me that actually he'd been married years before and had kids from the previous marriage. That was up there as just being a horrible place to be, up there with being deployed to a family whilst they made the decision to turn a life-support machine off. I hated that. They waited until the daughter could get there to tell her comatose father that she had just got engaged before turning the machine off. Things like that had a way of making some deployments even harder than I had ever thought possible.

But anyway, as I was travelling back and forward between the mother and father, trying to remember what I'd said to each and make sure nothing was missed out or one side treated differently to another, I was also, in effect, playing marriage counsellor. It was actually a good time to work alone because I didn't need the complications of trying to remember anything a colleague said and, more importantly, the father had a bad reputation and a lot of previous convictions for police assaults. It was a good time to try and build some bridges and calm things down a bit. I knew who the father was and had never had any problem with him anyway, as long as he hadn't been drinking.

After a few days they both seemed a lot happier in each other's company, and I guess at times like these, reasons for falling out become insignificant to people who've given a fair proportion of their lives to each other. It's sort of nice to see the better side of human nature I guess.

I went to the morgue first and did my usual bit of getting the body out, having a nice chat with him about looking his best for mum and dad, cleaning him up and making it generally look as much as possible like he was having a nice sleep. I then went and collected them from the hospital café and it was nice to see the mother and father talking, surrounded by the other kids from the relationship.

As always, I left them to have as much time as they wanted to see their son for the last time. Then I popped him back in the fridge, locked up the morgue and sat and had a coffee with them before walking slowly out the hospital to say my goodbyes. I shook hands and as usual would offer to see them the next day if they wanted, but otherwise the next time would be after the post mortem.

I felt it had all gone well.

As I walked away back to my BMW, I popped the doors, jumped in and popped the key in the ignition, just in time to see the boy's father waving and walking quickly towards me. He clearly had something to say that he didn't want to say in front of his ex-wife. I quickly got back out the car, and walked towards him — just as 'Stairway to Heaven' at pretty much full volume blared out the BMW behind me. Fuck.

Strange thing was, he didn't seem to notice, and when I apologised a few days later he seemed genuinely oblivious. I guess, when we're so fixated with one thing, it's hard to see the distractions around us.

I'd like to think that whilst I seemed to have a penchant for amusing mistakes, my heart was always in the right place and I genuinely did my best. I'm sure anyone who ever reads this might disagree but inside I still felt I was a fairly moral, decent person and, while I knew my own mistakes were scrutinised and criticised, it seemed to me increasingly that the mistakes of the managers picked for greatness were swept under the carpet.

I like to think I'm a calm person, and in sixteen years of marriage I never seriously argued with my wife, although you could argue that's because like all men I was always wrong. I liked to let things wash over me, to forgive and forget. So the one occasion I felt I wanted to raise a grievance against a supervisor was a huge deal for me. Being told that I couldn't raise a grievance because he was about to get promoted was hard to take. It increasingly seemed that chosen managers were simply bullet proof, and while the chief constable was in the newspapers saying there were no targets for stop searches, down at the coal face we were harassed and bombarded with the threat of discipline and removal of specialist-post opportunities for those who couldn't bring in the required number of stop searches and ASBO tickets.

And meanwhile I couldn't be deployed to help a family whose baby had died, because of the cost of a ferry ticket. I had only dealt with two cot deaths before but it was enough to make me realise how traumatic and heart-breaking they were for a family. I ended up phoning and offering to see them in my own time, but it was more the principal of this specific death that left me angry and walking alone and sombre in the mountains, wondering how the job had turned its back on the public it was supposed to serve.

And in my mind's eye I'm back there, the stars shining high above, stunning and bright with no light pollution to spoil the splendour of the milky way. The full moon shines down making the road ahead gleam like a dark river in the moon light, winding through a barren, white wilderness. I'm surrounded by snow-capped Scottish mountains and the cold winter air is rushing past to a deafening tyre roar. I'm seeing this from low down, just above the road as cat's eyes and road markings flash by. The white snowy verge is a blur of speed and sensation as road signs and snow poles appear in the headlights and whistle past me in an instant. The tyre noise is building and the roar getting louder. The car squats down and drifts as I hurtle through the corner where the young couple died, his last words as I watched him die being to comfort his already-dead girlfriend, and I'm off down the straight and accelerating towards the hill where two German bikers died as their bike burnt in the middle of the road. Every few miles another memory of standing side by side with death. The speed builds and I'm flat out. Snow lightly drifts across the road and I hear the tyre noise disappear briefly as the car rockets through the powder, kicking up a tall spiral of red snow which quickly disappears in the tail light's glow. Faster and faster. And I know they're there waiting for me. I can feel them, waxy grey skin and dull eyes, cold morgue-stare and empty, heavy arms that won't ever hold a loved one again. I see one flash past, just a fleeting glimpse, a forgotten memory of standing at the roadside, uttering cold words of death through a soulless radio to shatter a family's lives. Faster and faster. And then he is, there right in front of me, that kid. Still in his bloody romper suit, standing holding his teddy bear, dead eyes staring straight at me as I hurtle towards him out the darkness, child seat lying in the middle of the road on its side and bloody tears streaming out his lifeless eyes. It's as though I'm off road or all the tyres have blown out, suddenly its pitch black and I feel like I'm falling. Then suddenly—nothing. It's 3am and I can hear my own son murmur in his sleep. I have to get up in three hours and face it for real. I'm awake until then, watching the minutes drift pass on the bedside alarm clock.

CHAPTER 20

'TODAY AS ALL DAYS' AND COPING

I had a lot of ways to deal with the stress of the job, but the best way was to drive; I loved it.

I would tell the control room that I was unavailable for a half an hour or so and take the car for a raz up in the mountains. In the early days of the traffic this was encouraged. It was after all important to keep skills up to date and a 'college run' as it was called was the way to do it. This involved a fast, no-speed-limits drive for twenty minutes or so with, sometimes, a commentary. This involved the driver speaking out loud and describing what they saw in detail, what they were doing and why they were doing it. If you were lucky and had a good passenger who was a police driving-instructor, they would discuss your drive at the end. Inspector Gadget encouraged what he called 'skill maintenance drives'.

Waz however was my arch nemesis. He worked from Lochord but we covered the same overall area sometimes. When he would phone to ask if I was free to neighbour-up for an evening the conversation would often go like this:

'Rob, I'll head up, see ya in forty minutes good buddy.'

'Mate, a real man would be here in thirty.'

And then the sound of the phone hanging up

About twenty-nine minutes and thirty seconds later I would stand up, put the kettle on and leisurely wonder down to watch on CCTV whilst the big BMW came howling into the town from the open road. Thirty-one minutes door to door was a very good time. Thirty-three minutes was a fast traffic drive and fifty minutes normal. The rules were: absolutely no speeding in built-up areas and no 'wrong siding' corners. Safe, smooth and controlled all the time, but no open-road speed limits. Also, no harsh braking and rough gear changes, a proper Police College advanced drive.

One summer backshift, after working with Waz the night before, I came into work just as the phone rang. Waz had headed off the night before for the return drive to his office in the T5 unmarked video car. I answered the phone and he recognised my voice, the conversation was brief.

'Rob, twenty-seven minutes, fifty-three seconds'

'Ah, indeed… it seems we have much to discuss. I shall be there directly'

Thirty-three minutes or so later I had arrived in the Lochord crew room and was watching the previous night's drive on the video. It was textbook perfect and devastatingly fast. At fastest on the long dark straights only 130 mph or so, but this was a narrow twisty road and through the bends it was amazing. The way Waz took corners always left me staggered, and if I was in the passenger seat, usually holding onto the 'Jesus' handle above the door with a slightly sweaty tight grip. Right on the edge, traction control off and the car drifting at over 100mph on uneven sweeping bends following the loch-side. I reckoned I was sharper on the overtake but he always had me in the corners. Usually with a cheerful, 'mate, never drive faster than your guardian angel can fly', followed by a manic grin as we either drifted about another high speed corner or left sparks glowing on the road way after cresting a rise.

It took me three years to better his time on the same route, after which my passenger, a young probationer, was sitting looking pale in the passenger seat of a BMW 330 which was slowly cooling and making those tinkly pinging noises in Lochord back yard. By then Waz had left the job, disillusioned and broken by a lack of senior management support: his family and children had been threatened by a local drugs dealer and the job refused to help him even although he'd been forced to move house. I always suspected the T5 was a slower car than the BMW, and Waz was the better man. I'd never ever admit that though.

As I dealt with more and more death, driving fast was a way to escape from reality. I would head up into the fast, sweeping, winter glens and clear my head as the verges and road markings flashed past, all to the dulcet tones of something good and loud: David Gilmour or Pink Floyd, maybe on a bad day, even the Smiths. It was a soul-cleansing ritual after a death or a stressful time. As the years went by I would become faster and whilst I felt I was in control. I wasn't sure everyone agreed although I never crashed at speed. When I was really down, I lived for those drives up north in winter close to midnight when I could be alone with my thoughts and the cold dark mountains, no light pollution to spoil the splendour of the milky way high above and watching the faint satellites passing over before getting back into the car and taking it as fast as it would go down long straights and drifting through sweeping bends with the dry, powdered snow lifting in huge swirls behind the car.

I never felt as alive as I did when I knew I was close to death.

Here's a strange thing though — there was really very little in the way of maintaining driver skills officially. I drove for over ten years with no official driver training or check-ups, and yet crashes are one of the most likely ways to die in the police. I knew five cops who were killed in road crashes while on duty during my service, while I didn't ever know or meet a cop who'd been shot. This is, amazingly, also the case in the USA, where road crashes are the main cause of police deaths.

Now, I don't in any way object to body armour, firearms, or officer-safety training, but in terms of real risk assessment the police were shockingly bad at looking after their staff who were drivers. The reason for this was even simpler: if a cop crashes, regardless of whom they are driving to help or what pressure they are under to go fast, the force will simply blame the cop, and hang them out to dry as a very public example to show how they punish cops who make a mess of things.

If a police officer is shot or stabbed it becomes national headline news and senior officers will be fidgeting to be on national TV, saying what an amazing cop they've lost and what a fantastic person they were and how they'd lived to uphold the law, while in reality they probably never heard the cop's name before that day. They know they'll be under scrutiny for the circumstances and decisions made, so they need to pretend to care. They'll have to justify themselves, and, God forbid, a senior officer will actually have to leave their desk and give evidence in court. That's why handcuffing and CS is an annual re-qualification and driver-training is forgotten.

Years later while working in the USA I asked my American colleague to Taser me, just so I could find out what it was like. The resultant video was very amusing, and I made noises normally reserved for pregnant whales but what really surprised me was how effective it was. I always felt it showed how little the police management and politicians really cared about cops that they would stop such a simple and effective device being issued and instead leave us to fight hostile offenders with a metal bar and CS, both of which would be far more likely to injure both them and us. Just politics going mad I guess.

Chapter 21

The body in the Tent.

In 2004 a man went missing.

This sort of thing happens all the time and very few people noticed. The usual enquiry died away and the family probably dealt with it in their own way, perhaps deciding that he'd committed suicide, which seemed realistic.

Roy Shepherd was from England, and his car was found in Glen Nelis, an hour and half's drive north of Baytown. He'd been seen in Deeside at a campsite, but it seemed reasonable as time passed that he would turn up near his car. Just one of those things. There were probably things said at the start of shifts and in briefings the length of the country but, like many other cops, it was well outside my area so I didn't pay much attention. Lots of other fun things were going on at that time anyway, including the discovery of a grave that had been dug deep in the forest a short car journey from the Bridge of Ord Hotel. It was fun, but no one out with the rural uniform cops and a few curious traffic cops was interested. It was a really impressive grave too, about 6 ft long, deep and clearly with only one purpose. I liked it and occasionally wandered into the forest to see if someone had moved in yet. Bruce checked it most weeks. Soil was piled up at one side ready to fill it in, but, given its location, it should really never have been found, had it not been for a lost dog and two walkers.

In 2009 two forestry workers were working on clearing a fire break near to the Bridge of Ord Hotel, just off an unclassified single-track road into the local shooting estate and within a few hundred metres of the West Way, a long distance footpath that runs from the city to Port Wills. They might never have seen it, but they were just far enough into the dense wood when they saw the top of a tent a short distance into the forest, only just visible from the tree line.

They found skeletal remains inside.

Good old Roy Shepherd. A long way south from Port Wills and a good two or three days' walk from his car for most fit walkers carrying a tent and a rucksack. The local cop, Bruce, attended with Binky. As usual when death was involved so was Bruce. While I had probably over a hundred-and-fifty deaths to deal with in my time in the police, Bruce was in a class of one. He was simply staggering. I've never known anyone to encounter so many bizarre deaths or strange happenings. But he was very competent, and probably one of the best and funniest cops I ever knew, although he could live up to his own hype a bit too much sometimes. But if you wanted someone who knew about death and was thorough then he was your man.

He set up a controlled route into the scene and called for a supervisor and the CID. The problem was the local CID were busy at the time with contaminated baby food and really couldn't attend. The Wing Commander attended the next day though and called for the mobile office and arranged soup at the local hotel. I decided to head up to have soup at the local hotel, and when I arrived the CID from the city were still refusing to attend because this was clearly a suicide and not in their remit.

I decided soup was in my remit and offered to help by realising bacon rolls were also in my remit, but behind the scenes things were escalating with divisional supervisors at Baytown becoming increasingly annoyed that the CID would not attend. The Wing Commander demanded that they show up but he was out-ranked by a detective inspector who insisted it wasn't suspicious so there was no need for CID. Eventually the uniform chief inspector managed to get hold of a detective chief inspector at Divisional HQ and insisted someone was sent—but I suspect by this time the CID were determined to show up the uniform resources and prove it was nothing worth their time.

Eventually a photographer attended from the city and the newest CID acting detective constable was sent up from three-and-a-half hours away, with what I assume were clear instructions to tell the 'wooden tops' to stop being a pain in the arse and deal with it themselves since this was clearly not worth the attention of any highly trained CID types.

The photographer took a look in the tent and refused to continue taking pictures; he felt he was contaminating a crime scene.

Bruce was recording the scene on the video camera and saw the two sleeping bags side by side and a large knife was clearly visible in the tent. It didn't ring true. The large knife, which was really not the sort of thing you would take hill-walking unless you were expecting to fight your way through the jungle in Borneo, was in the tent and some of the clothing worn by the dead man was clearly torn. The two sleeping bags were side by side and the general appearance of the tent suggested to the photographer that there'd been two occupants in the tent.

The CID had to now treat it as a crime scene and did so for a day, but they asked Bruce to dictate the sudden-death report and seemed to be intent on it being a suicide, which, to be fair, it still possibly was. Hard to tell, without knowing what happened to the occupant of the second sleeping bag.

As a family liaison officer I was used to watching families go through the stages of grief.

- disbelief,
- denial,
- anger,
- bargaining,
- guilt,
- depression
- acceptance

All were recognisable and could last minutes, hours or years. The difficulty with the family of Roy was that they'd long since moved to acceptance and in their own way had rationalised his disappearance, I suspect had he been found shortly after going missing, the family would have wanted to know much more and the police would never have got away with the lies they told.

After he failed to turn up, the family believed that he'd gone away to commit suicide so it was easy for the police to reinforce that belief and no investigation was needed.

Let's skip forward a month or so. The CID at divisional HQ has decided that this is a suicide and our local CID were not involved. It was one man missing and two men's clothing so the homophobes in office had no interest in investigating it anyway. I could overhear the chat in the office. One of the rucksacks had been removed from the property by HQ-CID and it was confirmed that the remains in the tent were that of Roy. Job done and enquiry complete. This meant that the local crime-scene manager was probably unaware of the presence of the second rucksack, as, I suspect, were the local CID cops who searched the remaining one.

The FLO from England contacted Bruce and asked him to search the property to look for a set of gaiters and a cuddly toy. I had until that point no dealings with the case other than to have the soup and run a cop up to the mobile office to stay at the locus on the first night—and to laugh a lot at said cop, when they were on the radio an hour later, because they were too scared to stay there alone overnight. That seemed funny to me because I now actively enjoyed being with dead people.

But I always like a good laugh and a little death before tea break, so I offered to help Bruce and away we trotted to the outdoor store that was used for larger or contaminated productions. We opened the door and there were three large body bags containing a huge amount of clothing and property, the tent itself and the clothes that Roy had been wearing. Everything smelt of damp, death and decay and the rotted sleeping bags were both full of pine needles and detritus.

It was the first time I had seen these things because I hadn't gone into the scene itself and I'd had no reason to become involved with anything to do with it until now. Straight away, there seemed to be a problem. I was aware, from a quick look at the statements, that a rucksack had been removed from the property to be searched, in order to confirm the identity of the man in the tent, and at a later date that rucksack had been returned to the Baytown, but sheer quantity of property was wrong: there were *two* rucksacks, both listed and both through the production book, also a Nike black holdall; there were two sleeping bags, but only *one* was through the production book, and two sets of hill walking boots, of different sizes; but an even bigger problem for me was the type of clothing and equipment.

One rucksack contained folded, and apparently unworn, clothes that appeared cheap and certainly, in my limited hill-walking experience, the sort chosen by someone who hasn't been outdoors much. Also, one of the sleeping bags was nylon and of poor quality.

The second rucksack and much of the clothing that was loose or worn by the deceased was expensive and good quality. The jacket was a 'Patagonia' which I knew was an expensive make.

This, for me, was the crux of the problem. I didn't know a lot about what civilian hill-walkers might carry, but I had a lot of experience in covering distances on foot from selection for the Regiment. I simply couldn't see anyway Roy could have carried this volume of stuff, plus a tent, the forty miles from his car to the place where he died.

Except, of course he could have dropped off a rucksack and the holdall and walked south to get it some days later. In the regiment we did this a lot, it was simply 'caching'. In the event those rascally Soviets deciding to invade West Germany the SAS had a simple role: get behind enemy lines and report back on what nasty things were heading to the front along the main supply routes or MSRs. We would hide up, often for weeks, within feet of a road, silently watching and transmitting everything that passed. It's what 21 and 23 SAS trained for all through the 80s and we were bloody good at it. It meant that we, potentially, needed more kit than we could carry so the solution was to 'cache' it and then go get it at a later date.

But the key to this way of working is that what you must cache are the things that you don't need straight away, the consumables, usually food, ammunition and batteries.

Here was the problem with Roy, because, if he'd cached some of his things, he either cached things he needed straight away on the first night such as sleeping bags, which made no sense at all, or he cached things he simply couldn't need at all, like a second set of boots.

He clearly didn't walk forty miles down the west way carrying two rucksacks and a hold all, certainly not down the Devil's Staircase after heading south from Port Wills. And even if he had, I struggled to imagine that someone wouldn't have noticed him.

At the original crime scene it would appear that Roy Shepherd had been lying half in and half out of the tent, and this had been explained away by the suggestion that animals had dragged him half out the tent. However, I'd never seen any wolves or mountain lions up that way so I felt this was at best unlikely. Maybe some hedgehogs had worked together.

Just as Bruce and I were discussing how uneasy we were about looking through what we both felt was potentially a crime scene, he found a used torn condom inside the sleeping bag that the dead body had been in.

The used condom was a bigger problem, clearly it had either been inside the deceased or worn by him, but again I had a big problem with this. In all the suicides I'd ever seen I knew that the people who died felt that what they last saw was the world they left behind; it never occurred to them that they might not be found for maybe weeks and that by then they would be a rotting corpse. In their heads, they would leave the world with a nice suicide note explaining all. In fact, most families I spoke to would say that their loved one was happy before he or she died and it had come as a shock to the family. Often suicide is a relief from an unhappy life and people would leave a note explaining that the suffering was over for them. The idea that anyone would want to be found wearing a used condom, or with one inside them, just didn't make sense. The idea that someone who surely didn't want to deliberately cause anguish and pain for their family, would want to die somewhere they potentially wouldn't be found for twenty or thirty years really troubled me.

We couldn't find a set of gaiters and the cuddly toy that the family wanted but we did find one other thing before we felt we had to stop looking: a 'noose' made out of what I would consider parachute chord. It was too thin to actually hang yourself with and presumably would be hugely painful and would cut rather than strangle, but also it was too long and practical to be an ornament or macabre keepsake.

See what you believe. Or believe what you see.

We were contaminating a crime scene, and we both felt that there had to have been someone else with him when he died.

We went back to the office and Bruce spoke to the duty Sgt, and he then phoned the city raising our concerns. Bruce and I discussed what we found and he had also emailed the details to a detective Sgt in the city. The used condom was lodged as a production after I'd photographed it and I assumed something had happened with what we'd found, or that what we'd found was already known about and fitted in with the bigger picture, that neither Bruce nor myself were aware of. It seemed reasonable after all.

Years later, working at the Police College, I travelled up to Baytown and asked for permission to take some of the more interesting cases away from the archives to see if there was anything interesting to teach my students. With the permission of the Chief Inspector I went to the archives and this was one of the cases that I would take away with me. It was a long time before I got round to looking through it, but there were some nice pictures that I wanted to use in relation to teaching students how to preserve a scene.

Bruce had done an outstanding job when he first arrived at the scene and it was textbook perfect. As I looked through the files I was reminded of all the things that we'd told the CID: the two sleeping bags, the two rucksacks, the black Nike holdall and the duplications of kit, including two sizes of hill-walking boots. Not everything was through the production book, but there was enough to see that there was a problem — and I couldn't see anything in the report to explain things.

In the file were the email from Bruce, and the forwarded email that had bounced through senior crime management in the city. It's funny how people forget that when they forward an email the previous conversation thread is still there. The reply from the city was that everything was to be disposed of. A quick look and a photocopy of the production book confirmed that this had happened.

Everything had been removed and incinerated.

I felt uneasy. It had been too easy to make this a non-crime in a 1984 Orwellian type way, because in the police there is no one to report something like this who isn't also connected to police management, who are probably behind the desire to fiddle figures and save money anyway. Roy Shepherd had died at the start of the time when senior management were financially rewarded for their divisional crime figures and not for public satisfaction.

If a single female had been found in a tent dead with a condom inside them and with a man's rucksack and clothing nearby there would have been a huge enquiry with senior gaffers on TV and with pleas for the public to come forward, but this was a man and no one cared. The evidence could be made to disappear so as not to upset the spreadsheet or overtime budget. I could understand the rationale, because it would have been very expensive to investigate what was potentially a homophobic hate crime nearly three years old and with little evidence and no suspects.

It certainly isn't the worst thing I've seen by any means, and, deep down, I wondered if maybe Roy Shepherd had committed suicide, but, either way, it deserved to be investigated and his family deserved to know the truth- because I didn't believe he was alone. Perhaps whoever he met had left to go to the hotel and then returned to find him dead, or maybe he died during some asphyxiation sex game with the noose. No one will ever know, but the apparent rationale for senior management hiding it seemed entirely driven by a desire to meet a financial-performance statistic. The people making this decision had never seen the scene, the productions nor probably even read the report, which demonstrated how the management failings in the police and a lack of any accountability to anyone other than themselves made the management unfit for purpose. It was obvious to me that police management and the operational management of investigations should be completely separate; the police is not a business and the only statistic that matters is serving the public.

When things like this happen, there is no one to approach who are not themselves linked with senior management – and *they* are unfit for purpose.

Chapter 22

Nightmares and the College

I would dream that there was a dead body and I needed to get rid of it. But usually the dead body was someone I cared a lot about and they were still walking around and talking to me. In my dreams no one else noticed the dead body; it was just me, and I was with death. It troubled me most when the dead were in my house or my garden and I was trying to hide them from my kids. Maybe I should have turned to drink, which would have been what you might expect, but I've never been much of a drinker. I'm not violent, and I guess I worry too much; I bottle things up. Trouble was, I was starting to fail and be human and in the politically-correct world of the police we're not allowed to be human. I would lie awake for hours, upset and angry at the way the job seemed to bully everyone. When the dreams of death woke me, my mind would usually become stuck on something, like a scratched record, and for hours I would lie in the darkness, replaying the same thoughts and frustrations again and again until I was exhausted.

I didn't have a line manager as such, the department I was in had been disbanded, leaving me a refugee of cost-cutting in an office where, operationally, I was part of a divisional shift but in terms of management I was part of a support division with a manager in the city whom I never saw. I hadn't had an appraisal for years nor even spoken to my line management in the city for well over a year.

The constant death was a strange thing. I knew of only one other crash investigator who was also a FLO. Generally, doing both jobs was rare and frowned upon because each on its own would heavily immerse someone in death. I found ways of dealing with myself and coped with what, by now, was the inevitable vomit first thing every morning. Driving the traffic car alone and fast was my way out, but it was also when I had the most time to brood and worry. Driving fast in the snow-capped mountains was amazing, watching the side of the road flash past as road markings and snow poles turned to a blur. I loved seeing the deer running across the mountain ridges in the moonlight and the rainbows forming low in the glen as the morning sun broke through the rain clouds. Sometimes in a full moon I would turn the headlights down to sidelights and push my knowledge of the road to the limit. I knew every undulation and off camber twist for a hundred miles.

Deep down though, I just wanted it all to end.

In terms of sheer volume of death due to FLO deployments, myself and Cammy at Lochord seemed to be well ahead of most others. I'm not by any means certain that no one else in the country was getting hammered as much because one of the things about policing is that usually no one complains or does anything about something until it's too late. I suspect for me it was still fine at this stage because I'd convinced myself that I was cold to it all and I actively wanted death around me. I could refuse a deployment, that was one of the rules of being an FLO, but I never did because I was too keen to help. I can't imagine many FLO's turning down a deployment because of the desire to help others when they really need you. I was given a dedicated mobile phone for use during deployments that was supposed to be turned off when I was off duty. I always kept mine on and told my families to phone me even if it was the middle of the night. If it troubled them then it troubled me, and that was why I wanted to be a FLO. Even the dreams didn't put me off, and anyway, I shook them off easily when I was awake. It would take something more than dreams to take me to the edge. I relished being responsible for other's happiness and caring for them and it's ironic that, when the end came, it was from someone who I thought did the same for me.

For my own morbid enjoyment, the more horrible and numerous the deaths the better, and that was strange because I genuinely care about people. I think, bizarrely, I enjoyed being immersed in any new enquiry because it took my mind off all the previous ones. And while I cared hugely about the families, I seemed, with the exception of a cot death, to be entirely able to blot out all thoughts about the victim, apart from the dreams. Even losing someone's brain was just funny — it was jet-washed away incidentally by accident when the road was cleaned up. And yet at the same time I really cared.

One particular crash showed the paradox. An HGV straddling the main carriageway while reversing into a side road, had been struck by a small hatchback at speed. The truck was carrying sheep, and the hatchback carrying two young girls and cannabis, probably partly why they didn't see the HGV in front of them. The car caught fire and the driver burnt alive, and so did the sheepdog in its kennel under the truck. I had no idea that the drivers even kept them there.

I was sad. Poor doggie. I spent a while walking around with my crash investigator's head on although I wasn't doing this one. I knew the crash investigator who was doing the report well and had a lot of respect for him; it was just professional to learn and watch someone else. But I was genuinely sad about the dog; I could smell the burnt fur and see where it had been. I had a look at the dead human too, but just in passing; that was just an annoyance. Human death was fine; it was good; even a whole family in a light aircraft was fine. Another biker, another cyclist, another driver, another drowning, another pedestrian, another day—in my head it was all fine.

And I loved looking after the family, taking them to the morgue, being there to offer advice. I was doing at least ten FLO deployments a year, all single-crewed, and sometimes fourteen in a year, and, in the last few years, between four and six crash investigations for fatal road crashes each year. That's up to twenty dead people a year. I was starting to struggle to remember names although I didn't mind. It was only a problem if I was actually speaking to a family and started to get confused.

Despite all the death and even after a cot death, the only time I was ever offered a critical incident debrief was after an incident where nobody died. A critical incident debrief is really just an official cuddle from management so that they can all congratulate themselves on being good people managers. That'll be why they were so rare. I'd heard of one before, when two kids had drowned in Loch Errie, but this was the first time I'd actually been offered one myself. I'd become a non-cop, a shiny-arsed office dweller for the first time in eighteen years. I felt bad about that and missed being on the street, but I was tired and had come to see police work as too routine. I always said to myself that if the day ever came where I didn't enjoy being a cop on the street, then it was time to find another job. I genuinely can't understand a cop not wanting to be out doing the job.

I think by this stage it was becoming impossible for me to continue in the police. I loved my job but the police machine had eaten away at my morals, my self-respect and my sense of what the police were actually there to do. I thought about death a lot but not too often suicide, although I suspect a big part of that is that I still hadn't found a good way to do it, at least not one I was entirely happy would be painless and that would meet my criteria for being found. More importantly, I was still very driven by an inner sense of outrage at the corruption and the blatancy of what went on. My own doctor referred me to the police recuperation home for two weeks so I could finally talk to someone and have a bit of time away from work. I don't think anyone in work even noticed, certainly no one from management wanted to talk to me about it.

Watching Bertha Shore arrive smugly as a freshly promoted superintendent when I was at the College one day filled me with horror. I firmly believed she had indirectly killed four members of the public through sheer utter incompetence, after a career criticizing others trying to do their job to the best of their ability. And yet there she was, bullet-proof and destined for promotion, because that was how the police machine worked. I watched time and time again as incompetent office dwellers, some of whom had never even given evidence in court or completed a sudden-death report, would be selected for stardom. It almost seemed the last thing the police wanted was actual police officers interacting with the public.

The Counselling service had fallen by the wayside because the unit I was in had been disbanded to save money. In theory I should have been going to the city to speak to a counsellor once a year or so, but now I never went and no one cared or checked. There was a FLO mentor who I bumped into at the occasional FLO conference, but no one in the city contacted me or seemed to notice. I didn't want to discuss what was in my head anyway. I was lucky to sleep for four hours a night and I always woke feeling exhausted. As the time ticked towards dawn on my alarm clock, I would be wide awake, brain racing between death and frustration at the corruption and incompetence before finally surrendering to sleep for an hour or so when it was time to get up anyway. The only time I was truly happy was when being deployed to a family or trying to reconstruct a fatal, or being in the mountains alone, wishing I could understand what was wrong with me.

It was going to take a big change in my life to set things right, so I applied to transfer to the College as an instructor. The timing was good and I moved to the College almost as soon as I returned from the nice long chats and cups of tea that my doctor had arranged. It had been a big deal for me to talk to a counsellor and a difficult thing to do. I didn't like opening up about my emotions but, to some extent, I did.

And then while I was at the College something wonderful happened.

I was sitting at my desk, playing with a toy Lego motorbike that a class had bought me as a present after a course and contemplating how much I hated the job and how much I would like to see some people I knew die horribly. The class had also bought me a nice bottle of gin but, tempting though it was, I probably should save that for when I was away from my desk. Fiona, one of my fellow instructors, took a phone call from reception who were looking for a first-aider because one of the security staff had complained of feeling faint and had now collapsed. A Baywatch moment! Myself, all Hoff-like, and Fiona, all Pamela-like, running down the corridor shouting 'ooot they way!', in her Falkirk accent, which admittedly doesn't really feature on Baywatch. Well, that's certainly how I choose to remember it, but it was maybe more dumb and dumber.

Fiona grabbed that nice heart-defibrillator thing from the wall that I'd kept wanting to try experiments with and we were off. When we arrived at reception, the security man was sitting hunched over a table with his tongue out and a deep dark red colour all over his face; he was turning grey as I watched. I tried to get him to respond but all we got in response was gasping, so we lowered him to the floor and as Fiona went to dial 999 for an ambulance while I tried to open an airway and get a pulse. One of the things that pops through my head is saying out loud 'ah, here we go again' and getting a strange look from Fiona, who by now was asking the operator for an ambulance.

I like speaking out loud to people who are dead or about to be dead, I think it might be comforting for them to hear something. I told the security man it was all going to be ok and if he saw any bright lights or dead relatives beckoning, for fuck's sake not to walk towards them, and with that I started CPR.

As I did compressions and felt his ribs break under my hands, I knew he was dead. I could hear the death rattle in his breathing that I had heard so many times before. Pretty sure the big guy with the scythe was just walking into the lobby as the defibrillator was connected up. John, one of the first-aid instructors, and our inspector had also come down and John was plugging in the defibrillator pads as I kept doing compressions. Fiona was constantly updating the ambulance controller, which, bizarrely, I found very reassuring because we had an idea someone would be there soon. I'd never had that before. The inspector took over rescue breaths when I tired.

And, much to my amazement, the defibrillator actually did its stuff and worked. What the fuck? He was shocked twice and within a minute or so was awake and desperate to get up, repeatedly being told by the inspector and myself to lie down. All of us were grinning and I was utterly gobsmacked at how quickly he recovered. The ambulance crew were there in what seemed a few minutes and I wandered away, my 100% killing streak at CPR finally broken. It was a lovely day and whilst no one from management would come to say 'thanks' or 'well done', it made me grin for ages.

Seeing him back at work a few months later and speaking to him was fantastic.

Sometimes the Police IS the best job in the world, and while it doesn't happen often, when it does happen it's suddenly worth all the bad days. I was very glad we saved him.

Plus, I'm sure he owed the tea fund a couple of quid and he wasn't getting away that easily.

Maybe things were on the up; maybe I just needed a break from the death after eighteen years at the sharp end; perhaps my first time as a cowardly office dweller was just what I needed. The strange thing was that I never saved him; he saved me. He saved me from the bad place I was in. He gave me a tiny bit of faith back, that the job could be a good place.

Chapter 23

Sweet Dreams and a Happy Ending.

I've generally kept away from my personal life in this account and that's more to protect others than to hide my own failings. I'm not a good person, and I'm fairly sure anyone reading this will realise I've done a lot of things I'm not proud of.

I spoke to a psychologist about the dreams and he told me there is often a trigger, something that just can't be dealt with, but it acts like a dam, stopping you dealing with the past. The strange thing was that my trigger wasn't a death but a loss. It was odd that until now Post Traumatic Stress Disorder or PTSD hadn't really been mentioned, and, when it was, that I wouldn't recognise it as relating to me anyway.

When I returned to be an instructor at the Police College, I found it had become a mass production-line. The senior management at the college were very good and, I suspect, very aware of the failings in the system. They did what they could while being strangled financially and having to cope with the high turn-around of cops which would have been unthinkable many years before. My immediate line managers were good too, and when my sister phoned me one day immediately before I went into class to teach, and to my horror I found she was trying to do CPR alone in her house, having found her husband unresponsive, they immediately let me leave and drive to her. By the time I got there the police and ambulance crews had arrived and my brother-in-law had died. Time off for the funeral was given and for the first time in ages there seemed to be good senior managers and kindness and support.

It didn't survive the change as the forces merged.

Two years later, once the Clydeside machine had fully taken over the College, one of my students asked for the day off after her wedding weekend and was turned down. I was so disheartened by the way decent cops were being treated and it seemed that hardly a day went past without hearing another horror story. At the College I would see the enthusiasm in new students and wonder how many would still be working for the police five or ten years later.

Many of the basic skills had disappeared from the curriculum and even the final written exam had been simplified down to multiple choices, with trick answers to catch people out. Students were keener and a higher-quality than ever, but the emphasis was on recruiting people with degree qualifications, who would often leave quickly disillusioned with the reality of something that was not really a graduate job.

When I left the College, the senior management had been replaced by Clydeside yes-men, all afraid of the Chief. It had been 'Clydeside'ed', by the Chief Constable and all that mattered was money and numbers.

Of all the changes to the College the most notable improvement was in the number of permanent civilian instructors, who provided a consistent approach as opposed to the constant rotation of police officers. For years in the police, civilians had been treated as second-class but at the College they provided the organisation and stability behind probationer training, while cops came and went with varying ideas of how to do things. I came to trust Jen, Roger and John a lot more than many cops I knew. I did sometimes wonder how they all coped with the constant 'change for change's sake' that was a hallmark of management in the police.

Other improvements were the addition of a modular practical training area, with a mock shop, bank, court, house, police office etc., all located in the mythical town of Brookbank, so that students could attend a call and follow it though right up to going to court. In reality it was hardly used as intended; with 150 students on each course and only eight weeks in total to take them through basic training, they would be lucky to get a couple of goes at a mock call each, and no related report, statements or court to attend. Brookbank had been conceived in a time when courses consisted of about forty to sixty recruits and at a time and they would spend a total of sixteen to eighteen weeks at the college. Now it was eight weeks, followed by three weeks of, largely, exams, and 150 recruits on a course.

The fitness test had hugely changed from the standard Royal Marine test of 105 press ups, 85 sit ups, 40 squat thrusts, and 14 pull ups, with two minutes allowed for each and a similar recovery time between exercises, a one mile run and 6 sprints. It turned into just a beep test, although a mile and half run was also part of the course in later years, the mile route no longer existing due to the construction of the new staff accommodation block, Tanatallon.

Student accommodation would also change hugely; students were forced to occupy tiny rooms in twos and threes, with little ventilation and, more importantly, little hot water. Over my last few months as an instructor at the College we would frequently have to advise students to go to the gym block in order to use the toilets and showers, because the old College buildings had not been designed for more than one person per room. My last courses were only moved to another block after a student threatened to go home after five weeks with no hot shower and a toilet that couldn't be flushed in the morning.

And the food had become even worse and I hadn't thought that possible. The rumour is it costs less per day to feed a student at the Police College than a police dog. This seems entirely credible.

But a change was as good as a rest and when I first went to the College I was keen to be a good role-model and instructor. It was fun to see lots of keen cops following the career I had taken.

Also I needed escape from the death and the despair of my own life. I relished the moment I walked through the door and met a class of enthusiasm and bubbling vitality, desperate to do the job I had once loved. And I put on a great act, telling only the good stories and teaching the legislation as well as I could. I knew many of my students over the years began to refer to my classes as the Michael McIntyre show, which I would like to think was reference to my light-hearted way of covering the tedious and often dull legislation, rather than a reference to me being slightly short or slightly overweight. Sometimes being happy and making people laugh is the easiest way to hide the memories and what's really underneath. Sometimes the people who look calm are the ones kicking hardest to stay afloat.

On arrival at the Police College I was ushered into the Superintendent's office for a nice chat. He was a nice, genuine and clearly very moral man, and clearly felt awkward about discussing issues of personal relationships at the college, which was odd because the police in general and the College in particular was a huge hotbed (if you pardon the pun) of illicit sexual liaisons.

I suppose in the police this is unavoidable. Cops in close stressful situations, with other cops for company, will become attracted and end up playing horizontal games with each other. I guess it's just human attraction, and the archaic way that the College forces students to stay during the initial training courses inevitably means that students get to know each other a little too well. In Clydeside it had been well known that when a female cop had sex in a police car they got to keep the vehicle-fleet number-tag from the key ring. I bet the garages got seriously fed up replacing them. Cops get divorced a lot.

Despite nineteen years of this, it had never happened to me because, despite my marriage failing, I didn't stand out. I'd only had two girlfriends before and no one, especially no ladies, noticed me; I was unremarkable and I played the grey man very well. The College was something special though. Every female student I knew from Clydeside on my basic course left their original partner during the ten-week course and hitched up with some cop—and that was back in the days of separate dormitories. There is danger in being an instructor as well, new cops regardless of age look to you as being experienced and a good cop. They never ask themselves the question- if my instructor is that good a cop why are they here and not out on the street?

At the College, the scandal seemed never-ending but most of it was kept within the police. In later years, newspapers would expose things like 'rookie nookie', the story of three students in a shower, but, by then, I was in the traffic, and had eaten quite a lot of fried food and I couldn't really understand how the shower could accommodate a single adult officer let alone three naked probationers. The logistics of it was of more fascination to me than what they actually got up to—if they got up to anything. I mean, the showers are seriously tiny.

At my welcome meeting at the college the Superintendant was rather vague.

'Please keep your relationships at the College personal'

He seemed very uncomfortable so I agreed wholeheartedly and thought nothing more of it. It didn't matter anyway because, regardless what the company line was or how frustrated I was with lack of attention at home, nothing would distract me. When someone in my area had needed a Family Liaison Officer for the last few years they asked me. I had gone home smiling to my kids after recovering the body of a man who had set fire to himself listening to his Sony Walkman on a remote hillside, the stench of petrol and burnt flesh in my nostrils for the rest of the day, but I had laughed it off as we broke his rigid arms to get him into the body bag, his melted headphones stuck to his head. I had seen an entire family wiped out in a plane crash, foxes taking much of the remains away, and happily laughed and joked. Left a cot death and gone home to play with my kids. I wasn't unsympathetic; I cared but I felt that I had never been affected.

Now I was contented and the College was a nice break from all the death — and I wouldn't be led astray by a pretty face, no way.

Many years before I had been on a crash investigation course where we all introduced ourselves and described our police careers. One cop from New Zealand told us:

'Oh just beat cop, specialist, promoted, shagged a police woman and got divorced, then she left me for another cop, the normal police career path'.

I laughed and thought that would never ever happen to me.

I did my best to make classes at the College fun, and I did genuinely care about my students; they were embarking on a journey I had started many years before and had no idea what was in front of them. It was fun to see them bond and work together as a class. Overplaying my enthusiasm for car chases and dealing with death kept me happy, that and making the class hot chocolates at the end of the course as a reward for putting up with me. It sometimes surprised me how many strange stories and tales of death I knew and I became the 'go-to guy' for anything to do with the subject. I remembered being a student at the College myself and how I had thought that many of the instructors' stories and anecdotes were made up, entertaining but sometimes so corny as to clearly be space-fillers in a boring lesson. I had a few tales I took from working with Bruce, or things I'd seen others do rather than actually done myself, but in general I told things that had happened to me pretty much as they were, casting a good light on the job and hopefully leaving my students happy.

I tried anyway, even though my own life was far from happy. In fact, deep down, there weren't many times in life I'd been this unhappy.

Don't be noticed; disappear into the shadows and have everyone forget about you. Play the grey man.

I feel I should apologise, or buy you a drink, because this is such a crap ending to my story. It should be a horrific crime scene that tipped me over the edge, or maybe some twist but it wasn't like that.

Kate:

She told me she loved me.

She said she would always be there for me.

The first time I really noticed Kate I really don't know quite what happened. I just looked and saw her looking right at me in a doe-eye type way that I'd never seen in a pretty woman before. She had natural brown long hair in a tight bun, because that's how uniform police ladies have to be at the college, and a pretty face, with deep brown eyes. An inch or so shorter than me and slim but I had never seen her out of uniform which was probably a good thing. Instructors drank in a different bar. Also probably a good thing.

I guess I tried not to care about anyone much back then.

Lynn was a cop I knew from Clydeside who was very much used to working in the city and had an attitude to match. In the words of a cop I'd heard many years before, you wouldn't want to go home to her with a busted pay packet. I had a lot of time for her; she genuinely knew her stuff and called things as she saw them. She cared a lot too and had a heart of gold.

She spoke to me one day as I discussed taking a day off:

'Awww, Kate will be sad'

'Why?'

'Because she likes you, everyone else knows'.

As was normal for every course, there would be a night out at the end. The 'Copper lounge' is a bar within the Police College situated within the 'recreational' gym-and-pool building. It's been there since I was at College and is well known to every police officer in Scotland. It's been changed and redesigned over the years, but it's always been a good money maker for the College, especially on a Thursday night.

I went to the final night for the course that Kate was on and generally mingled quietly before aiming to leave and head back to my room. At the end of the night, at the final dance and without any warning, we were pushed together by her drunk friends as the last dance started. I held her closer than I should and it felt great. She looked amazing in a black dress with her long soft hair touching my face as we danced, and every so often I would look into her stunning eyes and feel quite sad. I'd never really looked at her like this before and she looked amazing as she grinned back at me and pulled my body tight against hers. On Friday she would be gone and for those precious moments dancing together I wanted to treasure every second. It was clearly nothing more than a crush that she had though, and I was sad because I felt a spark was there, mainly physical because we simply didn't know each other that well.

The next day before she left I spoke to her. She came to see me in the modular practical area, and entered the room sheepishly, looking ashamed as she apologised, telling me how embarrassed she was by what had happened, and that I shouldn't have known how she felt about me. I was so proud that someone so thoughtful and pretty would feel this about me. I told her it was a huge compliment.

And it was.

Inside though, I was in freefall. It was as if I'd seen the light go green inside the Hercules, looked out the aircraft door into the cold night sky, as I'd done years before then taken that step over the edge. I was out there falling and nothing could stop me and, just as surely as before, the ground was coming up to meet me.

After the course was over Kate sent me a friend request on Facebook. I would occasionally see her updates, her boyfriend John, and her cute little black pug, Dug. She seemed to be a really lovely person. I guess my feeling for her faded away a bit although I kept thinking about her.

Half a year later, Lynn walked grinning up to me and elbowed me in the ribs before saying 'Kate's back next week'. I acted very surprised and unconcerned but I was very acutely aware that Kate was coming back to the College. It was normal to see people again and again at the College, sometimes bumping into people from way back when I joined. Kate was very special to me. I was still desperately trying to be my professional self and nothing more, but deep inside I really wanted to see her.

Monday the next week, Jon and I were walking to breakfast down the central corridor towards the parade square when I saw her standing side-on to me laughing and talking with her friend Amy. Amy had highlighted curly hair and was very chirpy and bubbly; she'd been a laugh, but she might as well have not been there. When Kate turned and looked at me I don't know what happened. The next three of four minutes were an awkward blur of conversation and emotion for me. I wanted to hug Kate, but that would have been unprofessional.

Over the next three weeks I didn't want to see her, and I did my best to avoid her because I didn't want to care. When I spoke to her occasionally she was so easy to get on with, and I was determined not to fall for someone whom I knew I couldn't be with. Too many people fall foul of the police trap; it has a magic that's hard to describe, and the College has made and broken way too many relationships over the years.

But I made sure I went to her final course night-out to say goodbye forever. I drove a hundred miles to get there but she would never know that. She looked stunning and we tried to speak above the music for a while. It was awkward for me because I was very conscious of the number of people there, both students and staff, who were clearly watching us and I don't like being watched. When I left I felt sad but relieved because I had got through it unscathed. I went back to my room and tried not to think about what had happened or what could have happened.

I didn't know how she felt; I didn't know, until she told me months later, that she'd come into the staff block and had been outside my room during her course, terrified of being caught and unable to raise the courage to knock on my door. I didn't know she used to look at my picture on the staff information board. I couldn't have guessed how she felt but I knew I cared a lot about her.

A few more weeks passed and the world was a good place. I was booking a ski holiday and sitting on the sofa watching TV, my Facebook update-page open.

Kate was engaged.

Missed chances, and what could have been. But that was ok, because I was emotionless; I'd been here before with things that should have changed me but it didn't, disappear into the shadows and have everyone forget about you, that's what the grey man would do, that was the right thing to do.

But I'd spent my whole life being unremarkable, underachieving and hiding and now I had one chance to punch above my weight, and be with the most amazing woman I'd ever met.

Do you remember those books they used to do years ago where you decide the storyline and outcome by going to different pages? They were usually of the 'Dungeons and Dragons' or 'Famous Five' type.

If you would like Rob Moon to do nothing and carry on with life, then turn to page 284.

If you would like Rob Moon to contact Kate, then move to the next page…

Good choice! That's exactly what I did too. After all she wasn't my student anymore and hadn't been for a long time. We were just cops and colleagues now and she wouldn't be back at the college.

So, I sent her a message

'Congratulations Kate. He's a very lucky guy. I'm gutted, that's one less beautiful single girl in the world. All the best, Rob'

I got a reply straight away and my fingers were quickly and nervously typing away as we chatted,

I was falling again, the stars above me, the darkness all round me, the clouds below me. Inexorably tumbling and rushing groundward as the silent C130 Hercules faded in the distance. But there was no wind noise, just silence; I was blanking out everything else as I typed to Kate, my world collapsing around me. By the time we'd finished chatting, I'd forgotten everything around me. Her last message was bouncing around in my head.

'I'll always be there for you'

And we'd arranged to meet.

I picked Kate up in Juliet Alpha, in the area where I'd worked my very first day in the job. I was late because I'd misjudged rush hour and I arrived to see her waiting at the side of the road.

She looked simply stunning, her long beautiful hair falling over her shoulders and her pretty face pale in the cold February air.

For the first time in years, I felt completely out of control. I'd been the guy who turned up at a scene of carnage and I was the man in control. I was the one families turned to in their hour of need because I knew how to reassure them and give them the answers they needed. I was the crash investigator who turned up at a scene of carnage and made it calm and took possession of it. And now, one pretty girl had me dizzy and stunned like a rabbit in car headlights. Kate jumped into the car and I drove away from the city. I really didn't know where we were going; my head was a complete nervous mess. I hoped I came across as confident and calm as we discussed the job and how she was doing. It was all very awkward.

We drove to the Forth Road Bridge before turning north and heading finally to a hotel near Glen Devon. I'd not been there for a few years but, as it turned out, I couldn't have chosen better. Although it was quite busy we managed to get a small table in the corner of the restaurant. It was warm with a log burning fire crackling in the lobby but, as we sat opposite each other and chatted away, I noticed she wasn't eating much. Maybe she didn't want to be here; maybe she didn't like me, but, as we kept talking, the conversation became much less strained and more fun.

I found out months later she was so nervous she couldn't eat. We talked about everything from turn-ons to dogs and movies. We laughed awkwardly about *Fifty Shades of Grey* and when we left for the drive back to the city I suggested we have another drink. I wanted to spend as much time with her as I could, even if she didn't want to see me again. Tonight I was the luckiest guy in the world sitting with the prettiest girl I'd ever met. We went to an old haunt of mine and had a few drinks before I finally took her back to Alpha.

The more time I spent with her, the more I realised how amazing she was and, in a strange sort of way, she was grey too; she didn't boast or try to be something she wasn't. She didn't try to stand out or make fools of those she helped in life, and she didn't play games with emotions. Underneath she was courageous and strong to have taken the chance and told me how she felt.

She had taken another chance too; she had told her fiancée that she was out with Amy and he would be in the flat. I parked the car around the corner and looked into her eyes in the dim street light, and saw her looking anxiously back at me. I told her I'd had an amazing night and would love to see her again. She smiled back. Then I tried to be the perfect gentleman and I asked if it would be ok to kiss her goodnight, and before I knew it her lips were on mine and her arm holding me tight. It was the most nervous sloppy, wet and terrifying kiss of my life. I smelt her perfume and felt her soft hair falling across my cheek as her mouth gently sucked my lip and teased me. I'd never ever been kissed like that in my life. It went on and I loved it.

The clouds were there below me again, and I was falling in silence, totally out of control, stars above me twinkling in the clear warm night, no parachute, but now two of us hurtling towards the ground.

By the time I was back in my room at the College I was elated and excited. It turned out Kate returned just as her fiancée had left the flat to walk their dog. If he'd left a minute earlier he would have caught us in the car. I felt guilty but so alive, terrified and happy for the first time in ages. I had been so calm and in control my whole life, nothing fazed me, and yet now her love was scaring me senseless. We were soon spending as much time as possible with each other. I would sneak away from the College to be with her, and she would drive up to see me until, finally, I booked a night for us at a remote hotel in Glen Coe, a place where I'd always been so lonely and thoughtful.

It was wonderful being with her, waking in the same bed and holding her close. This was what I'd wanted my whole life.

A few months later Kate left her fiancée and wanted to be alone for a few days. She moved back to her parent's house, with Dug, her little black pug. Over the next few months we would meet to go to the cinema, go out for meals, walk and search for Dug in the woods near the college after the little pug had decided that it was possible to catch a wild deer, or we would just hang out and, at every opportunity we could, spent time together.

I was faithful to her from the very first day we kissed if that means anything and I cared for her way too much — so it hurt when she dated with someone else. She didn't hide it from me and, as always, she was very honest. She said she had to start dating someone she could make plans with, so while I was going to the USA to work for four months I think we both knew that it would be hard; I was also still hugely supportive to my wife, my kids and the family ideal that I wanted for them.

Kate started seeing a cop from the CID and, deep down, I knew it was the best thing for her but inside I was hurting so badly. I loved her and wanted the very best for her, but our circumstances could not have made things more difficult. We still messaged twenty or thirty times every day and I was genuinely happy for her. I've never lost contact with an ex before and I thought about her all the time, but I could not change the situation or who we both were. After all, she'd been engaged when we first met and neither of us had had any qualms about what had happened between us. She'd left her fiancée for me, and I cared hugely; but if she was happier with her new CID friend then I understood.

Three weeks later I was sitting in a diner in Chicago when she sent the message that changed everything for me. Something really bad had happened in her life, and she was scared, angry and in trouble. The job had betrayed her more than anyone I'd ever known before, I found I cared so much that it was all I could think about. And that was the trigger. I didn't care that she might want someone else, and if all I could be was her friend then I would settle for that; I would be anything for her and risk everything. I felt helpless and despondent, but I knew then exactly how much I loved her. I wanted to hold her in my arms and to protect her. I offered to fly home, but it was hard for me to get back for at least two weeks. I wanted to come home so badly it was all I could think about and the cop I was working with became my sounding-board and confidant.

If I couldn't get to her I could bring her to me.

I sent flowers to her, phoned her as much as I could and found the money to buy her tickets to the USA and some internal flights. I wanted to be there for her, to see her and look deeply into her eyes and hold her. I needed to know she was safe and with me, and I suspect already I knew I wanted to spend the rest of my life with her. I look back sometimes at the text messages we exchanged over those next few weeks, as I sat alone in my cold Chicago apartment, sometimes a hundred messages a day each, and I soak in again the feelings I had when she told me how much she loved me and we chatted about the future.

When she walked out of the airport arrivals area and into my arms I knew exactly how I felt. Her flight had been delayed six hours and she had been travelling almost twenty hours but she looked amazing, long hair falling round her shoulders and beaming with a smile and her whole face lighting up as soon as she saw me. That next day, walking around an icy Chicago with her, crunching hand in hand through the deep snow and seeing her smile and laugh that meant everything to me. She was clearly stressed and upset by what had happened to her, and a job that had let her down, but she was amazingly strong too, and I loved her for that.

I had two weeks, in which I could try and be there for her as a good man. I was becoming a better person because of her and the love she showed me.

As we swam in the moonlight in a deserted swimming pool on top of our skyscraper, with deep cold snow lying on the balcony outside the window, I tried to work out how I could be what she needed, and it didn't matter what I sacrificed to be her man.

I'd arranged a holiday for us, a romantic evening meal looking out over Lake Michigan, then off to LA and a convertible car for a road trip up the west coast from LA to Vegas, Death Valley and San Francisco. I wanted her to come back to me but if she wouldn't then I wanted her to be happy.

We stayed in Vegas and hardly left the hotel room; we drank cocktails on the strip and she told me she loved me. I tried to woo her and surprise her with champagne at the Grand Canyon, and as the sun set and the moon rose over the canyon edge, we kissed and as we kissed she held me tight against her and she looked simply amazing in the evening light. I promised I'd always be there for her as we watched the stars light up the desert, and then the next night I drove north through Death Valley as she slept with her head resting on my shoulder.

I'd promised her exactly what she'd promised me nearly a year before. And I really meant it. For two weeks I couldn't have been happier, and everything I did was intended to make her smile and laugh. But in reality she was saving me from what I'd become.

She made me laugh and she made me proud. Being with her made everything ok and, for probably the first time in ten years, I forgot all about the job, the death and the dreams. All I thought about was her. We talked about the future and I told her I belonged to her. She just needed to let me sort things out at home in a dignified and decent way and I would be there for her. When I watched her walk away and into airport security after our two weeks together I desperately wanted to chase after her and tell her everything that was going through my head, and explain how happy being with her made me.

Over the next few weeks when I phoned her at work and asked how her day was, I knew I really cared and it wasn't just a question; and when she'd had a bad day or was upset by what had happened to her, I realised it upset me more than her. Just the thought of her could make me smile and every time something good happened she was the first person I wanted to tell.

But when I returned to Scotland and for the months that followed I was also increasingly angry about the police, because watching the job bullying staff and becoming more and more corrupt was soul destroying. While she didn't know it, she was the one keeping me afloat in some very emotional rough seas.

I think any of the other seven forces always looked at the largest, Clydeside, as being the least professional force but, as they merged, Clydeside ways were forced on everyone. What was ironic was that they were genuinely not the best in many respects. In particular Clydeside managed personnel by bullying and by having a Police Federation that would defend the job before it defended the cops. I had seen this first hand when the Federation's solution to some very serious allegations of corruption and harassment was to simply refuse to answer the phone or respond to help the police officer involved. I think cops sometimes forget the first loyalty the Federation have is to the 'efficiency of the police'.

For me, the crunch point came when a supervisor from the counter-corruption unit got drunk in the bar at the Police College and started talking too loudly about a pending case. I'd always respected the 'rubber heelers' to some extent because they did a job that needed done, but the idea that they would deliberately intimidate a witness and make up evidence to protect a senior manager was morally repugnant to me — and it was personal because I knew the cop involved; I'd worked with them years before.

So I handed back my medals in disgust and refused my long-service medal and I was simply told the CCU were untouchable. They played to a different set of rules, the Gestapo of the police who could make and break the rules with impunity.

When I'd sat as a probationer years before I'd been told that taking away someone's liberty was the most powerful weapon the police had and it should never be abused. And here it was abused by the very people who were supposed to uphold the rules, and they didn't even have the decency to discuss confidential information in private. I suspect I should have been off work by now with stress but Kate kept me going. I loved doing silly things for her. Silly stupid little things, taking her to the zoo or buying her flowers, but I always felt she most appreciated the things that cost nothing, like walking the dog in the rain, massaging her hands or making her breakfast. And I knew she was still stressed and dealing with her own problems too. It wasn't fair to expect her to deal with me as well. Except she did.

She was struggling to sleep and was stressed about her job, and the most I could do was be there when she needed to talk and take her nice places to relax. She was the kindest, most honest person I've ever met. She also put up with me as I struggled through the pain and the journey through divorce and the worst time of my life. She was my rock, my happy place, and the one I needed more than anything. But I have always dealt with things in my own way, slowly and by contemplating them, so I rarely told her what was going on. At the time I believed she simply saw me as more distant or quiet, the reality was that she thought I was lying to her—and to a small extent that was true. It wasn't the real me though and I suspect I was a very different person during our last few months together. In addition, she told me once that she didn't like men who cry which I took to mean I should hide the pain from her. In retrospect, I know I let her down.

As the summer passed into autumn we planned our future and my divorce slowly progressed, until one evening she made me realise what I'd given everything up for and how proud I was of her. We'd driven to spend the weekend with Bruce, his wife Carole and their new baby Maisie, and while Bruce and I chatted in the kitchen, Kate and Carole sat on the sofa, playing with the new baby, laughing and drinking. When I left the kitchen I caught the end of their conversation in the lounge. Carole had told Kate that the next year would be hell for me because she'd been through it herself, and Kate just needed to be there for me- to get me through it. Kate said she would, just as I walked into the room and saw her cradling Maisie in her arms. Maisie was giggling and smiling and Kate looked up at me and beamed a smile that melted my heart; she would get me through this, however tough it was.

I didn't want to make my time with her to be anything less than perfect so, in my head, she didn't need to know the times I spent sitting in the car desperately trying to arrange to see my kids, or sitting in a lay-by, tears welling up in my eyes at messages on my phone from my youngest son. I visited my kids on Christmas Day then left to spend it with her family after only seeing my own kids for an hour, because nothing was more important to me than her happiness, and that's an almost impossibly painful thing for any father to do. I realise that for most people reading this that makes me a bit of a bastard. I put my own happiness and my love for Kate before my kids and I suppose karma has a bit of a wicked twist there.

I was a wreck but also the happiest I'd ever been in my life. Then things looked up. Out the blue and for the first time in years, Lady Luck smiled upon me and I landed a fantastic job away from the corruption and bullying of the police, earning more money than I ever had before. I needed time to sort my life out. We had our first holiday away together and Kate found a house for us to live in, and her father wanted to help us get it ready. It was big enough for my kids to come and visit and perfect for a family. Her parents supported her although God knows what they thought of me, but I would be there for their daughter come hell or high water and I guess that's what any parent wants.

CHAPTER 24

OF DEAD MEN AND GREY MEN

'There is nothing to writing, all you do is sit down at a typewriter and bleed'

Ernest Hemingway.

Contentment is a dangerous thing, and just when you least suspect it you can forget the ones who really matter. I tried to be strong and I tried to play the grey man, but for the first time in my life I couldn't manage it.

So this is possibly the most self-serving and brutally honest part of my story. It's not a pity trip because I deserve exactly what I got. Karma is a cruel bastard. I'm not a good person and I'd hate anyone to think I've painted a picture that I am but what happened next tortures me every day.

She taught me a lot, taught me the value of the truth.

Less than a year after I'd left the police in disgust to start a new life I would lie to the most amazing and important person in my life and betray her trust in me. I think the fact that we had both lied to others when we met made it very important that we would never lie to each other but then I did. And I knew so much better: for years I'd told families the truth regardless of how brutal it was.

Apparently the three most stressful things you can do in life are to change job, move house or get a divorce, and I was struggling to do all three at once. Every chance I got I would drive the three hours to see her and hold her in my arms again, knowing that soon we would be together every day. In a year I put 30,000 miles on a car just to see her face and hold her close and I dreamed of our life and future together and it was amazing.

And so, I arranged a spa hotel near Inverness for the weekend, to thank her for staying with me through the tough time that was Christmas and New Year, when I was missing my kids. I'd really struggled and let Kate down more than anyone else in my life. I don't want to seem pathetic here, but I need to be honest. I broke down at New Year. I thought my ex-wife was suicidal and my youngest had pleaded with me by text message. I was mentally exhausted, manipulated and I didn't put the one I loved first. I had left Kate to sort things out and let her down and I knew I really needed to make up for it.

That was our last weekend together. I had arranged champagne in the room and we walked hand in hand along the beach before a candle-lit dinner. Every tiny thing she did made me happy, and looking into her eyes as we held hands in the candle light over dinner and sipped fizzy wine, I knew life couldn't get any better. I suspect she knew I was saving up a month's wages for an engagement ring, and we talked a lot about kids and the future. I loved seeing her smile when she saw me, and the way she pounced on me and held me close, kissing me passionately in the hotel lift, then giggling and pretending nothing had happened when the door opened and other guests got in.

I loved the mornings staying in bed for hours, the late nights staring at the stars and the funny noise she made when we saw a cute animal. I loved the way she squeezed my hand

and told me Dug and I were her favourite stupid creatures. I loved that she could swear like a sailor and seconds later be the most beautiful classy lady in the room when she walked into a five-star restaurant. I was hopelessly in love and she repaid that with her love for me and a kindness that I'd never known in my life before. She put so much thought and kindness into the things she did and the things she bought for me.

The next week I flew off to work in Paris for a few days. I was only away three nights, but it was the anniversary of my break-up from my wife exactly a year before, who emailed me. It was a tough time and a tougher email and I struggled to read it. I needed Kate more than ever and couldn't wait to get home and see her. She made me ambitious. She made me want to be a great man for her.

When I returned home Kate asked me if my wife had been in touch when I had been away.

I said no.

I just couldn't cope with the pain and discussion that would follow; it was all too raw and it hurt too much. I'd brought her home a treat from Paris and stopped to get her flowers on the way to her house. We ordered a Chinese meal, drank Prosecco, talked and enjoyed our evening; it was all I wanted, just time to relax with the lady I loved and forget about the email. It was easier, cleaner and simpler to lie and I wouldn't have to dig into the hurt and discuss anything. I remember with crystal clarity that last evening, lying on the couch eating Macaroons from Paris, rubbing her feet before walking Dug.

Later, lying in bed as she dozed off, I stroked her soft long hair. She looked beautiful as she slept, her head resting on my chest. I can still smell her perfume, I can hear the cars outside and feel her against me. And it was heaven. I loved her. I worshiped her.

But underneath that perfect moment was an imperfect lie.

The next day I was caught out when I told her about the email—and it was over.

It was my fault but the timing was awful; I had committed to buying the house that she'd found for us both. I had left my career, kids, wife and life and given up everything I could to be with her. As I drove away from her house I was devastated, she had seemed so calm, no tears, texting on her phone and just sitting calmly on the sofa telling me to go. I had let her down and I knew I had.

In my head she could have shouted at me and maybe I could have had a chance to say sorry, but she said it was over and she was right. She was a very honest person and couldn't cope with me lying to her. I wish I had a better reason to tell you for us splitting up; maybe if I'd fucked about, or treated her badly it wouldn't torture me so much, if she simply couldn't wait for my divorce or found someone else, but I genuinely hurt her. I let her down, and I destroyed her faith in me.

We stayed good friends from that spring until late autumn, hill-walking, kayaking and going out for meals. She helped me move house and sent me messages or phoned me every day almost as if nothing had happened. She said she still loved me, and even though I offered to move back to the city to be near her and change job, she wouldn't give me another chance.

I took her out for her birthday and bought her flowers; we cuddled and we laughed but there was no going back. We went to Gleneagles Hotel for my birthday in July and I always hoped I could win her back somehow. I couldn't win her over with presents or expensive gifts because I knew she was too genuine for that. I'd bought plenty of things for her in the past and I knew that the days I made her a nice steak or walked her dog in the driving rain counted for so much more.

So I told her how I felt. For all I lied about the email, I never lied about my emotions. I laid them out for her as I'd never for anyone else in my life.

A month and a half later Kate told me that she'd been seeing someone for a while, but she didn't want to tell me until she was certain it would work out between them. I guess I respected that, because it meant she still cared and didn't want to hurt me. I knew she kept a silver 'Tiffany' bean on her charm bracelet, that I'd bought her to let her know how much being at 'The Bean' in Chicago had meant to me, and in my head that meant she still cared and would always be there for me as a friend. She told me her friends thought her new man was a replacement me, he liked the same things — motorbikes, hillwalking and shooting — and that hurt me a lot. And for a while she did try to stay friends while I struggled to cope with my life falling to bits, but I don't think Kate realised how much I was hurting from giving up my kids and life for her, and then losing it all.

When I realised she'd sent me pictures of her menu on a romantic date with her new man I was genuinely devastated, and even sending me funny pictures of his puppy wearing a cute neck scarf and his parents little dog in a huge dog bed to cheer me up just left me feeling more and more lost. My friends thought she was deliberately trying to hurt me by rubbing my nose in it, but I was never sure, and every time she sent me a 'cheer-up' picture I knew the man just out of the picture was once me, and if I hadn't been a dick I still would be.

We'd arranged months before to go to a Kevin Bridges concert together and I offered her and her new boyfriend the tickets but she told me she was working. A few weeks later we arranged to meet and after we had a meal together, Kate wanted to go for a drive with me. I drove up Loch Lomond side in the evening sun and I already knew that it would be the last time we would ever see each other. It was odd how we'd swapped places since our first meal together, and now I was the one too nervous to eat and she was the sceptic, balancing her options. I could see it in her face and hear it in her voice. Many of my friends were sceptical about why she broke up with me but when I held her hand, and told her how I felt and apologised again for lying she stared for a second and I saw her eyes getting teary.

'You're not the only one who's heartbroken', she whispered back, before looking away to hide her tears, and I knew how much I'd really hurt her.

We drove in silence for a few minutes before she smiled, touched my hand and chatted away about her mum and dad. It was amazing how she knew just how to lift my soul again.

It was a long drive on a beautiful evening and she looked amazing. We stopped overlooking the Loch and talked and laughed as though nothing had happened, I'd asked her not to talk about her new boyfriend because I wanted to know nothing about him but she told me things anyway, and she told me enough to know she was proud of him; he was a good guy and she would be happy. That mattered to me.

In the back of my mind though, I knew that day was the day she'd told me she couldn't take the tickets to the concert because she was working. I knew she'd lied. Sometimes there are good lies and it was odd that when I was on the end of those lies. I appreciated it for what it was, but when I lost her because of my own lie it left me feeling disgusted at myself because I'd let her down.

I never saw her again.

Every time I thought about how much I'd hurt her and what I'd lost, it hit me like an express train. Even though I knew it was coming, like the man waiting with his back to death on the tracks years before, but for me it happened again and again and again. I dreaded sleep because I knew I would wake up. I was travelling the world and that suited me because I dreaded being alone in the house that she'd found for us.

Eventually, on a business trip abroad I asked her to unfriend me and block me, because if she did it I couldn't undo it; it hurt too much. Some days I look at that last message asking her to do that and I hugely regret it; other days I don't. Please don't feel sorry for me, because I only have myself to blame and, as I said earlier, I'm not a good man. And it's all just my perspective, she would probably tell you other things that upset her but she didn't tell me what they were. And please don't forget, that for all that my marriage was failing for years before all this, I let my kids, my ex and even Kate's fiancé down badly too; none of them deserved what we did to them.

The nightmares came back. I now dreaded that moment in the grey dawn light between realising I'd dreamt that I'd lost her and the reality of waking up and realising I actually had. And this time the dreams were different, and not just about losing her but mingled with loss and death. It was like waking up in free fall as the clouds cleared and with the ground rushing up.

'Ground rush' is when you get hypnotised by the ground coming up. It's especially dangerous at night during military parachute jumps, because trying to concentrate on other things suddenly becomes difficult. The ground rush draws you towards it literally and metaphorically. Into a fascinated hypnotic dream, watching, waiting, stunned, like a rabbit in the headlights.

Then it's there, suddenly, and it's way too late, surging out of the black night, dull shapes on the ground becoming recognisable as way too close. For me it was a feeling of dread, of overwhelming loss, of despair, death and emptiness.

The ground hit me. Reality hit me. The death and loss caught up, it was all I could think about.

It was everywhere around me mixed with loneliness and longing for someone who had given up on me because of my failings.

I'd never felt this low before, but I'd been close.

I started this book with the Regiment, and that's how it finishes. Because, with the exception of one perfect day with Kate in Chicago, there is one other perfect high in my life that I can't miss out. I've not written about the regiment much on purpose in this book. I am very loyal to them and haven't put anything to paper that wasn't public knowledge anyway.

TQ, or RTI, or Interrogation, it's the end of selection for many, and nearly was for me. After I'd left it became the norm to put recruits through it straight after 'long drag' but, although physically and mentally shattered, most recruits are on an adrenaline high at that point. Then it was carried out after Escape and Evasion training, but the problem with that was that it made an artificial end the E&E, and people were sometimes physically broken rather than mentally. When I did selection TQ, it followed off the back of an exercise.

We were taken one evening into a classroom off the parade square, and the rules were explained. We would go out that night for a final exercise, a test of all we'd been taught. The last few months had been exhausting, live firing contact drills, river crossings, constant physical training, and now the culmination of it all. We'd been up since dawn for an eight-mile run in full kit and bergens and everything that day had seemed to be designed to exhaust us. We watched a video, explaining how an enemy would try to trick us if we were captured and how little things we did could give away a lot and compromise everyone else. A signed chitty for food became a confession, a few words said to a camera could be misinterpreted and edited, a tattoo with a female name could become a weakness during questioning. It went on and on. Eventually the Staff would speak to us all in serious hushed tones. They knew us all well by then and I think to a man wanted us all to pass.

There were four things we could answer: name, rank, number, date of birth. Anything else got an 'I can't answer that question, sir'.

We couldn't talk to our captors or ask for anything. The rule was: don't fail to comply with a legitimate order but volunteer nothing. If they offer food take it and eat it as soon as you can, if you need to go, just piss or shit where you stand.

And one last rule.

'Gents, you are going out on exercise, at some point you WILL be captured and handed over by the hunter force to JSIW (Joint Services Interrogation Wing). If anyone tries to resist you will be binned, this rule will only ever apply this one time. After this on exercise you will always have the option of escape, but not this time. Is that understood?'

I spent the evening getting ready; ration packs were opened up and I took what I needed for a few days. I took six hundred rounds of ammo; I had no idea what I would need. I test-fired my weapon, and oiled it again. I cammed up — my weapon was wrapped in shreds of scrim netting and Hessian. Bergen rucksack now indistinguishable from the one I started selection with, covered in knotted strands of vegetation and an old sack to break up any outline. I put my faithful black woollen Tammy hat in my pocket and stood next to two of the guys I'd known since the start of selection, and smiled as a picture was taken by another lad. I still look at the black-and-white print of that picture and see the hope and enthusiasm in those eyes. When it was time to go, we left, shaking hands and nodding quietly in unspoken admiration for each other.

My patrol was dropped off in the mist and cold of the mountains above a quarry and we had a fair distance to cover before dawn to our LUP (daytime hidey place), where we would meet other patrols. In each patrol were DS who were all 'Sabre' (active, fully trained) squadron members, watching us and assessing our every move. It started raining hard as we moved through tough terrain. This was no selection route though, this was tactical, moving slowly, scanning around all the time, the 'tail-end Charlie' turning and walking backwards every fifteen seconds or so. Every few minutes we would melt into the shadows, waiting and listening for any sign of the hunter force, everyone alert, our weapons tight in our shoulders and up in the aim, slowly sweeping from side to side. As the night wore on we crossed barbed-wire fences and country roads, waded through rivers, silently stalked through trees and finally, soaking through, arrived at the RV point to meet our contact for the LUP. The patrol was led into a dense conifer wood, the sound of rain on the trees above as we doubled back on ourselves and deep into the wood. That way anyone following our tracks would be forced to walk in front of us through a killing zone as we lay up.

As point man on the way in I put a few feet of thread on the end of my weapon, one end tied to the flash eliminator and the other tied to a tiny bit of fungus. I learnt to find the right fungus at the base of trees; it has a slight luminescent glow. As we slowly made our way in I swept from side to side watching the glow for any sign of a trip wire. More to let the DS see I was alert than from any real fear of being ambushed this early on in the exercise.

We lay awake most of the day, each man getting sleep or time to eat for one hour in every three.

One hour sleeping, one hour awake, watching the route into the hide, and one hour out at an OP watching and waiting. The long day was cold and the rain kept pouring down. I lay shivering and waiting for my turn to sleep. When it came I was too wet and cold. We'd been given old roll-up, goose-down, army sleeping-bags on purpose, our newer Gortex ones forbidden for this one exercise. They were now heavy and soaked in cold water.

When the night came we moved to our offensive role for a target attack. We cached our Bergen rucksacks and wore our fighting webbing. Again the patrol moved silently through the black night, rain now pouring down heavier than before, rain running down my back and my boots full of cold water. Our patrol commander made the move slow, painfully so; we were covering less than a kilometre an hour, sometimes stopping and waiting while lying in shallow muddy pools of rain water, or standing in the shadows, frozen, staring through night-sights at a target that wasn't there.

Just before dawn we were back in a hide with our bergens again. Exhausted, soaking and having found no target. It was simply never there — and the DS knew; they were watching us, looking for weakness or frustration.

There was none.

Again the day passed as had the previous, and as did the next, but on the third day the rain let off in the afternoon and I could get my hour's sleep when my turn came. I kept awake by resting my weapon on the pine-needle ground and putting my chin on the upper-part, rear battle-sight on top of the optical sight. If my head started to go it would dig in and wake me.

When the evening came, we were off again into the night, but this time we would watch a track to ambush a target, a target that never came. We hadn't been there long when my patrol DS received a message on his radio, less tactical now, we were up and moving quickly through the woods then down and waiting. He was clearly aiming to have us in a particular place at a particular time.

As we waited, a hunter force patrol from the 'Royal Green Jackets' rounded the corner in the track just down from us; they walked to within ten metres of us. I was lying in a rut in the pine forest between rows of trees and. I saw one of them looking around but I was facing the wrong way, looking under my armpit, to see him in the shadows. I was terrified he would see the soles of my boots shining wet in the low light, but he turned and walked away. Strangely, my other fear was that he would piss on me although at least that would warm me up. With hindsight I don't know why I didn't want captured at that point as it would have meant getting out the exercise sooner, but no one thinks like that.

Soon we were up and moving through the darkness again, eventually reaching a muddy farm-track junction. The weather was dry at last but cold and getting slightly windy with the stars above occasionally blotted out by the clouds. I'd managed to eat a few biscuits-fruit (Garibaldis if you've no idea what I'm on about; they're a ration-pack delicacy). I was still soaking and was only staying warm thanks to our movement.

At least it was almost over. We approached the final RV crawling through a small clump of dense gorse bushes towards the point where we were to meet an agent for extraction — and I waited for the patrol to get ambushed. As is normal at an RV there's a designated time during which it is 'open', and outside those times anyone approaching is considered hostile. Caution is everything. We lay in wait for half an hour in the sharp, wet gorse watching the RV point and yet still I could see no sign of the hunter force. Sitting in the dark only twenty yards away in the lee of a stone wall, almost invisible until a tiny movement gave him away, was our contact, an M16 rifle low and just visible. We watched and waited for the RV to open, and then continued to watch as our twenty-minute window to enter the RV ticked past. In the far distance I could make out the sodium glow of streetlights from a distant town and, as I listened in the dark, the occasional sound of wildlife or the breeze through the bushes. No sign of the inevitable ambush.

With a few minutes to go until the RV closed, our DS, tapped me on the shoulder and the two of us slowly stood and hesitantly made our way out of the cover. We covered the ground slowly, sweeping left and right arcs with our weapons in our shoulders, until we heard a whispered challenge. I slowly lowered to one knee and watched for the first sign of ambush as passwords were exchanged in low whispers and the DS alone moved forward into the RV. Any moment now.

As the seconds ticked by my forefinger started to take up the pressure on the trigger. I was determined to let a magazine go before I was captured. Clearly I was right in the hunter force killing zone and out there in the darkness I was being watched. The DS slowly came back and dropped to one knee behind me whispering in my ear.

'RV clear'.

Really?

I made my way back and whispered to the other two. 'RV clear'. I got the same surprised look I was no doubt giving them.

Maybe as we all moved into the RV it would all be over. Except it wasn't.

Surely something had gone wrong with the exercise? I couldn't believe my luck. They'd got it wrong. The 'Royal Green Jackets' were obviously meant to catch us and had failed. We would be too late for capture and would need to do the exercise again, but that was ok because I would be rested and better prepared. A four-tonne truck rounded the corner and we scrambled into the back. I shed my Bergen with the others and huddled up trying to stay warm; it was bliss. If I'd had anything dry I would have stripped and put it on, but everything was soaking. I couldn't quite understand why the stuff in my Bergen was soaking too because it had been dry when we'd cached it for the attack the night before, but I wasn't thinking straight. I felt giddy and sick, exhausted. As the truck twisted and turned through narrow lanes, I hunched up watching the DS sitting at the back of the truck and started to doze.

I was woken by a huge bang and the truck screaming to a halt, and all at once the world went mad. It felt like the sun was shining into the back of the truck, huge searchlights burning out the darkness and dazzling us all, a dog barking and the sound of screaming as I heard the truck door open. I went for my weapon and started to lift in into the aim, as yelling filled my ears and my memory flooded back.

'You WILL be captured.'

No choices.

Gunfire now behind me and more screaming, the driver shouting for help, then another burst of gun fire and then silence and feet landing on the flatbed of the truck and shapes moving quickly against the blinding lights. I could just make out our DS having a hood thrown over his head and being dragged out the truck. There was more shouting and gunfire as I was knocked forward and screamed at:

'Turn the fuck round you little shit bag!'

'Face the fucking front!'

I didn't recognise any voices; it wasn't any of the DS staff. My weapon was taken from me and my belt kit and the truck was off again. Driving at speed and twisting and turning, as we drove. My hands were bound together and a hood was placed over my head, the stench of burnt diesel filling my nostrils as the truck shook and shuddered over rough ground and gravel. Any attempt to move or turn round resulted in instant shouting and a soft kick, just enough that you knew someone was really there.

Holy fuck this was real. All sorts of thoughts flashing through my mind: what if this was real? what if the IRA were attacking the exercise? These thoughts faded though as we kept driving, and in my head I counted the bends and turns. What became apparent was that we were going round a circular route, hitting the same cattle grid at speed with a loud crash again and again. Then there was a change and the truck stopped in the darkness. Unlike the previous chaos, this was calm and controlled. No light was visible under the edge of my hood, just the sound of us, one at a time, being grabbed, forced upright and walked, crouching, out the truck. I was last and I felt the end of the flatbed disappear under my feet as I was manhandled and stumbled to the ground. Then with no time to recover, grabbed by both thumbs held together and off running. This was nice because I was warming up, but unnerving. I was worried they would run me into a wall or trip me and I felt the ground under my feet. It was not rough nor grass, but not roadway either.

THE WALL. WILLOW FARM.

I was untied and placed leaning forward, legs spread, and hands out stretched, leaning forward on a cold, hard wall. There were no words or instructions, but if I adjusted my position at all I was immediately grabbed and kicked in the back of the legs, before being repositioned again. After time this stress position became agony, my muscles aching as I shivered again with cold. I started to quietly sob in pain, and felt hands grab me and kick the legs out from under me, then I was forced to sit squatting, hands on my head. Again any attempt to move was immediately met with calm but forceful hands, forcing me back in position, never words.

I started to try and make sense of where I was. A loud, diesel generator or engine was running at a high idle nearby and there was no breeze, although I recalled it getting windy as we got into the truck. Despite this I didn't think I was inside. I occasionally heard a cough. I didn't realise until afterwards that it was one of the others in my patrol trying to communicate. I was obviously being watched very closely as every time I showed any sign of collapsing I was immediately moved back to the alternate stress position, and any small movement got an immediate rebuke. Suddenly we were up and moving again. Thumbs grabbed and running round in circles. Then nothing.

I stood waiting.

The hood was whipped of and in front of me two men sat calmly at a wooden table. We were in a large army tent, electric lights hanging from above and behind me and I could sense men behind ready to grab me. The two at the table were very different types. A smaller fair-haired man smiled and looked me over curiously; a larger-built, tall bearded man just looked angry. Both had huge steaming mugs of something in front of them and it looked amazing; I was shivering cold.

The little guy started first: friendly questions. The big four then lots of minor ones, and each time my reply of 'I can't answer that question' met by a friendly smile sometimes a joke or a 'oh come on, Rob, we know who you are'.

The bearded man said nothing.

Then they told me to remove my clothes, one at a time. Until I was naked. Each item was given a cursory search, then thrown on the ground beside the table. I do wish they'd searched my Bergen. I'd been shitting in poly bags as was the normal for an SAS patrol and keeping them in my side pocket. I'd have laughed my head off if they had tried to search them. Finally, I was told to choose two items of clothing to wear. I took my SAS smock jacket and my lightweight combat trousers, both of which were muddy and soaking, but were the best I had. They took them off me and started searching them again, more thoroughly. I had a razor, snare, fishing wire and an escape kit hidden in both. As they searched, the little guy suddenly turned on me and became aggressive. It's strange that I was so low that even although I knew what to expect, having someone suddenly behave like they hated me so intensely, knocked my morale and self-confidence so low. Maybe it was partial exhaustion, or because I had expected beardy to be the bad guy. As he felt along the seams of my jacket and found my escape kit, beardy got up and started walking slowly round me, fair-haired man now shouting at the top of his voice.

'If I cut myself, I'll fucking break your nose, you little shit' And it got worse and worse as I stood naked waiting for them to find the razor or fishing hooks. They repeatedly demanded if there was anything sharp and as always I replied:

'I can't answer that question, sir.'

Finally, everything found, they handed over my two items of clothing. They demanded I sign for them but I did nothing, staring straight ahead. They ordered me to sign and I did nothing. They shouted and I ignored them. I was allowed to put my two items of clothing on and they cut the laces in my boots and threw them back at me to put on too.

Then it was beardie's turn for a solo performance. He kept walking slowly round me before stopping just out of sight behind my right shoulder then started quietly asking questions, inches from my ear. He became annoyed with me as I became confused and couldn't keep up with his questions. Little guy just stared at me from his seat, shaking his head slowly and occasionally smiling in contempt before seeming to make notes. Then beardie started shouting, with questions yelled at full volume, the same questions again and again: name, rank, number, date of birth, age. I replied as fast as I could, struggling not to reply to the trick age question with 'I can't answer that question'. I became more and more confused and lagging behind his questions and he became more and more angry, changing questions to unexpected easy-to-answer ones after a run of the big 4, again and again.

And finally silence.

'Get this fucking piece of shit out of here.'

It went black as the sack went over my head, and it was back to the wall. The next time they came and took me the hood came off in a small warm room. In front of me, a man in a clean combat jacket sat at a table. He wore an armband saying 'Umpire'.

'Listen to me Rob; I'm the doctor, do you understand?'

'I can't answer that question sir.'

'Ok Rob. I'm going to take your temperature. Don't bite the fucking thermometer.'

After a short while he took it back and examined it, glancing at whoever was behind me, then hood on and I was off running round in circles again and again, boots flapping on my feet with no laces.

Then back to the nice doctor man. He gave me a dry jacket to put on and took my wet one away. Then back to the wall.

This routine went on for what seemed like a few hours, although my perception of time was seriously fucked. The tent, the shouting, the threats, the wall, the running, the doctor, the wall, the cold. I was broken and as low as I thought I could go. Each time I was in a stress position I was in pain. I tried to roll my head back to ease my neck and gritted my teeth counting the fractions of a second before I was grabbed and forced back into position. I felt like it was around 0400hrs, maybe, at best, dawn. I'd started singing, in my head: Genesis, the Lyrics from 'Supper's ready'. Which was odd because I've always been more of a Pink Floyd fan, but the lyrics from 'Supper's ready' are long and needed a bit of thought, enough to keep me awake and distracted.

Over and over again, and again and again. Trying to keep my brain working.

'… If you go down to Willow Farm,
to look for butterflies, flutterbyes, gutterflies
Open your eyes, it's full of surprise, everyone lies,
Like the fox on the rocks,
And the musical box.'

'If you go down to Willow farm'—that's the bit I always seem to start at now if I say them in my head, but back then I knew the whole song pretty well. They're long lyrics and it kept me from breaking and thinking about the pain.

And the pain went on. It must be 5am surely? I was on the verge of sleeping standing, every time my head started to dip I would wake and snap back but I'd noticed that the guards were not as rough now, even gentle, taking pity on me. They would move me between stress positions before I was in agony, almost at the first sign of pain. Then I was grabbed again, and off running, this time round in circles for a few laps and finally back in the tiny room but this time no doctor. I'd seen the doctor two or three times, but genuinely I can't be certain exactly how many. My mind was seriously fucked.

If you go down to willow farm…

A man I hadn't seen before looked up at me. Not the doctor and no sign of impending interrogation. I was surprised. Something different, but I was woozy and confused.

To look for butterflies… flutterbyes… gutterflies…

'See my armband, I am umpire staff and this is END EX. Well done.'

END EX, the words tumbled through my mind, falling out of control.

Open your eyes, it's full of surprise…

'Are you ok?' he asked staring straight at me.

Everyone lies…

'I can't answer that question sir,' I replied, but he was clearly used to this.

Like the fox on the rocks and the musical box…

'You've been in here before. You had hypothermia, by the way. Now grab your stuff and get on the minibus. Do not speak to anyone until you're on that vehicle.'

All my kit minus my Bergen and rifle was in a large clear plastic bag beside the table. A number was written on the bag in permanent marker. My number. My kit. I wanted it back, they'd taken everything from me and mainly my dignity and I needed something back in my muddled mind.

Without another word I left the office carrying the big clear bag of clothes, and shuffled, mentally exhausted and physically broken with my flapping untied boots, making silly clumping noises on a cobbled courtyard, as I strained to see into the bright daylight outside, the sun clearly high in the clear blue sky. One of the hunter force guards walked with me silently, appearing hesitant to look me in the face.

It was late the next day. Twelve hours of being interrogated had felt like three and my concept of time had been destroyed.

We were being held on the firing range we'd been using a week before for live-firing contact drills. Behind me an old building normally used as the range control and target storage area, with a courtyard surrounded by a high wall, had been our holding area. Not everyone was out yet. The diesel generator that had been running all night was still chattering away in the courtyard, apparently not connected to anything. Just white noise. On the minibus I was welcomed by a couple of friendly faces and I found out that the ambush had been back in the camp on the parade square itself. Within minutes my lights went out and sleep hit me in a wave of nausea and exhaustion.

When I got back to camp and some left over cold pizza from lunch, our bergens were piled up and our rifles back in the armoury. Lots of admin to do but the half-an-hour sleep and the adrenaline had kicked in now. I'd passed TQ and felt great.

It didn't last.

A few hours later I was summoned to the CO's office and the door closed. Beside him stood one of the DS looking serious.

'Well, Mr Moon I'm afraid you made a fatal mistake in TQ; you signed the form.'

I denied it, my world collapsing around me. He looked back at me, staring for what felt like ages, like he was trying to size me up, to see if I understood what was happening. I could hardly speak, words chocking up inside me, my mind desperately searching my hazy memories of the tent.

I was absolutely clear I hadn't signed anything. I remembered that bit pretty distinctly.

'If I find out you're lying you will never do selection again, do you understand?'

I nodded and was told to go back to my bunk. I ran through the camp and was quickly back there, eyes red, and met by the others as I walked in. Half an hour earlier we'd been joking and cleaning our weapons and now I was in pieces. One of them pointed into the one of the rooms but said nothing, and as soon as I walked in my patrol DS saw me and smiled, patting me on the shoulder and quietly told me: 'well done, we know you didn't sign anything'. And he walked off.

Years after I would see this done again, when they were worried someone was not that aware of themselves, on autopilot, maybe too cold or tired, so they had to know for sure if they were really switched on.

A few months' continuation training later, all of us from that selection cadre would finish a live-firing contact-drill exercise in the snow to be met by the RSM and an officer or 'Rupert'. The RSM tried to get us into some sort of parade, and make us march but it just ended in piss-taking. As usual, we were scruffy in our personalised kit, couldn't march for fuck all and after a few days in the field looked like shit: rough, unshaven and dishevelled. The RSM jokingly apologised on our behalf with a grin, saying he'd never actually seen any two of us scruffy fuckers wearing any matching items of uniform at the same time anyway, let alone marching in time. Then, without ceremony, the 'Rupert' quietly walked down the line and, smiling, shook our hands and handed us each a light sand-coloured beret with that cap badge I wanted so badly.

We had been badged.

'Who Dares Wins.'

There was no pompous ceremony, no tinned music playing over loudspeakers, no pish, no senior managers with twelve years' service making a crappy written in five-minutes speech, no team-building posters, no certificates or rounds of applause, just a quiet atmosphere of being one amongst those who had been there too. No need to say anything. It felt amazing, and later that week as I met my new squadron and people shook hands and smiled at the new guys, I no longer looked at 'them' with quiet respect, because I was one too. I was a grey man.

I would never feel high like that again until I woke up next to her, held her hand as we walked through the snow in Chicago and I knew she was safe, and I would never feel that low again until I lied and lost her. And it was entirely my fault because, she was the one keeping me together but she didn't know it. I felt responsible for her happiness as I'd felt responsible for the happiness of countless relatives of all the dead and the destruction that went with the deaths that I'd witnessed for years, and yet she didn't feel responsible for mine. And when I lost her it wasn't like a relationship failing, which would have been tough, because she was an amazing, kind and thoughtful person; but a relationship failing is just that, and she was not the reason I was in this state. Lots of people break up, and it's not a huge deal; millions survive it every year, and move on, as she did with me.

In my head I deserved a second chance, because when she had needed me an ocean couldn't stop me from being there for her. But when I desperately needed her beside me she walked away. For her I'd given up my family, my career, my house, my soul and more than anything else, as I walked alone in the mountains on Christmas Day I realised I'd lost my sons for her.

As I lie in the pre-dawn light my memories of death, of fun times and sad times are all I have left now, and in my head I'm back against the wall, back on Willow Farm, in pain, ashamed and all my emotions naked. When I'm alone in the mountains I'm happier. In the deep snow under the stars, or walking through the dark evening mist, rain trickling down my back and cold against my face. I pull the straps on my Bergen tight, put my head down and imagine pulling the FN into my shoulder before making for the next RV in the distance. I need to get to life's final RV, and until then, I'll be better than I was, the best I can be. I will get up again and I'll be the one no one notices in the shadows, playing the grey man and nothing more until I can say those words again:

'Staff, I'm here, I came from here.'

'Well done soldier, that's the end, the final RV. You got through it, so take that weight off your shoulders and go get a brew. You're one of us now mate.'

The End.

Seriously? Well OK then, Rob stays in the Police and maybe gets promoted and retires and dies a week later. Life sucks. You happy now? Are you though?

Really?

Piss off back to page 247.

20108904R00161

Printed in Great Britain
by Amazon